Crosscurrents / MODERN CRITIQUES

Harry T. Moore, *General Editor*

DOS PASSOS, the Critics, and the Writer's Intention

EDITED BY Allen Belkind

WITH A PREFACE BY
Harry T. Moore

SOUTHERN ILLINOIS UNIVERSITY PRESS
Carbondale and Edwardsville

FEFFER & SIMONS, INC.
London and Amsterdam

In Memory of
Professor Bruce R. McElderry, Jr.

Contents

v

Preface

To those of us who were keeping up with contemporary novels in high school in the 1920s, John Dos Passos seemed to be an important writer. Some of us didn't read Three Soldiers (1921) until several years after it came out, but when we did discover the book, it was a shock, for as small children we had been told that the Allied cause in the First World War was a holy one. Our fathers had been on the Western Front, and at home the incessant anti-German propaganda reached all of us. Then, a few years later, Three Soldiers seemed to be saying that the American army had been a little less than glorious in the war and in its aftermath. The book apparently didn't make a full impression on American readers; it was not until 1929 that war novels became popular, with Remarque's All Quiet on the Western Front, Aldington's Death of a Hero, and Hemingway's A Farewell to Arms. But Three Soldiers deserves better than Hemingway's curt dismissal of it in the introduction to his 1942 anthology, Men at War. He asserted that he had reread Three Soldiers and rather sneeringly said it didn't hold up across the years. Of course Hemingway was often mean minded, and in the recent Spanish war he had quarreled with Dos Passos. In 1951, Dos Passos' portrait of him in a rather poor novel, Chosen Country, infuriated Hemingway. But Dos Passos was a magnanimous man, and shortly before Hemingway's death he received a friendly little note from Dos Passos.

Back to our high-school readers: Manhattan Transfer

(1925) was an exciting discovery for us, the orchestration on the mammoth city, so full of American life. Then, a few years later, The 42nd Parallel (first volume of the U.S.A. trilogy) appeared, and we were really swept away, as we were by the two succeeding books in the series.

U.S.A. remains Dos Passos' most emphatically important achievement. It has some weaknesses, such as more bulk than depth, but it is still an impressive series of novels. The avant-garde techniques didn't startle us, for by the time of the trilogy we knew Joyce's Ulysses, from which Dos Passos had obviously borrowed, even to the extent of running words together (engineroom), not a common practice in those days. Of course we saw Joyce as a giant, out of the range of Dos Passos, whom we tended to measure against his contemporaries, such as Fitzgerald, Hemingway, Dreiser, and Faulkner, who still come through to us; Fitzgerald's reputation has soared—amazingly and quite justly—though Dos Passos has been in a condition of semi-oblivion, if not disgrace, largely because most critics are seasoned liberals (survivors of the battles of the 1930s and remaining somewhat left of center) who cannot forgive him for the District of Columbia trilogy whose first volume was published in 1939, its third in 1949.

In these books Dos Passos seemed highly critical of American liberalism, not only as it manifests itself in theory but also in its pragmatic applications such as the New Deal. He also made various attempts at rewriting American history. It was not until 1961, with Midcentury, that he produced another novel which might be thought of as at the very least a good one. (As Time's critic reasonably remarked, Midcentury was "the best novel from Dos Passos since his U.S.A. trilogy.") But the idea that he had abandoned his talent when he moved somewhat to the right was an idea that persisted, and (in general) the book was not friendlily received.

My discussion of it on the front page of the New

York Times Book Review was, however, a vote for the affirmative, though I regard myself as a seasoned liberal in terms of the definition provided earlier. The book, in my allowance, recovered much of the old Dos Passos verve, particularly in the interchapters which presented biographies, documentation, and observations. Among other things, the story showed businessmen of our time as what the sociologist David Riesman and his associates called "other directed."

If Midcentury offered some rather unfavorable views of the labor movement, it came at a time when unions weren't (except for those led by Walter Reuther) for the most part working in the national interest. In speaking of the miniature biographies of labor leaders, including James Hoffa, the review pointed out that "under the circumstances a few of them seem to escape rather lightly."

In his never-failing advocacy of individualism, Dos Passos has two of the principal characters in the story, a business executive and his son-in-law, "take part in exciting battles at the management level where the villainy of unions is only incidental. In adding this dimension, Dos Passos proves again that he can write about business—which doesn't have to be a dull subject —better than anyone since Theodore Dreiser. The sequences concerned with it in Midcentury are worth a dozen grey-flannel-suit and executive-suite novels." And so on—anyone interested enough can find this discussion in the files of the Times or in my book of essays which is just being published as this Preface is being written: Age of the Modern. There is still plenty of antagonism to Dos Passos in the critical world, and the last word on Midcentury hasn't been said, on either or whatever side; but to dismiss the book in a casual sentence in any survey of Dos Passos is critical irresponsibility.

There is a somewhat ironic and at least mildly amusing sequel to the foregoing. A few years ago I conducted a telephone course in "American Life as Seen by Contemporary Writers," for the Fund for the Advancement of Education, and Dos Passos was one of the authors (novelists, poets, critics) who took part in the conversations. (On Mondays I lectured, on Wednesdays the students discussed the work under consideration, on Fridays the writers took over.) Professor Charles F. Madden, then of Stephens College, directed the course and, with the help of his invariable amiability and tact, we were able to line up a number of such authors.

The course (February to May 1964) was wired into Stephens and several other colleges, most of them attended predominately by black students—since such schools rarely had the money to attract big-name writers as lecturers, the Ford Foundation decided to supply them on a telephone-into-the-classroom basis, with the participating authors presenting some comments and then answering questions from the students.

The writers taking part included Horace Gregory, Arthur Mizener, Carvel Collins, Warren Beck, and Carlos Baker (all as critics, respectively discussing Sherwood Anderson, F. Scott Fitzgerald, William Faulkner, John Steinbeck, and Ernest Hemingway), as well as James T. Farrell, Karl Shapiro, Murial Rukeyser, Anne Sexton, Richard Wilbur, Vance Bourjaily, Saul Bellow, Kay Boyle, and John Updike (all commenting on their own work.) We had also invited John Malcolm Brinnin to discuss his poetry, but unfortunately he was undergoing an operation and couldn't join us. The only black author we enlisted was Ralph Ellison; we tried to obtain the services of James Baldwin, but he was in Europe; we didn't know much about LeRoi Jones then, and we regrettably didn't think of Gwendolyn Brooks. The discussions have been printed in a book, Talks With Authors (1968), which unhappily omits three of the men who either didn't want to stand by what they said or got a negative from their agents.

Fortunately, John Dos Passos wasn't one of the participants who refused to appear in the book, which includes his discussion of Midcentury. But ("and thereby hangs a tale") why not one of his really top works, part of the U.S.A. trilogy, say? We couldn't take up the entire trilogy because we were having the students read only one book a week; we then considered the last of the U.S.A. volumes, The Big Money; those who deeply responded to it would have an incentive to read the first two books. We had arranged with John Dos Passos to deal with The Big Money, and then I reread it to make sure of it. Toward the end, an episode I hadn't remembered leaned out of the book and punched me in the eye: Dick Savage and a girl he has met named Pat Doolittle go to a Harlem black-and-tan speakeasy that is referred to as a "dump." Dick and Pat are the only whites there. Soon, "Pat was dancing with a pale pretty mulatto girl in a yellow dress. Dick was dancing with a softhanded brown boy in a tightfitting suit the color of his skin. The boy was whispering in Dick's ear that his name was Gloria Swanson." Dick abruptly removes Pat, who scolds him as they go downtown in a taxi: "You spoil everything. . . . You'll never go through with anything."

This was certainly not the proper novel for our program, and I wrote to Dos Passos to tell him, giving the reasons, why I felt that Midcentury would be better for the black students. He replied with a vigorous denial that he was anti-Negro, which I knew and hadn't even attempted to suggest; it was just a matter of appropriateness. He accepted this explanation friendlily enough, and he and the students had a lively discussion of Midcentury, as Talks With Authors shows. Some of the young people tried to nail him down on liberal-against-conservative grounds, but he said that all his life he had tried to avoid such labels. He made some interesting statements, explaining that he was a satirist, and that he found satirists "always basically optimistic. The satirist's complaint about society is always that it doesn't measure up to a fairly high ideal he has. I think that even the bitterest satirist, even a man like Swift, was probably rather an optimist at heart."

Dos Passos further said that his work had been influenced by Defoe, Fielding, Smollett, and Joyce, as well as the film director Eisenstein. On being asked whether he felt that the style of Midcentury should be used by social-commentary American novelists, he said he didn't think so because he believed that "every writer has to work up his own style. . . . Anybody who is going to do anything great is always going to work up his own particular way of expressing it."

Words such as these, coming from a craftsman, are always of particular interest to those engaged in studying such material. The life and career of John Dos Passos (1896–1970) provide a fascinating picture of an American in our time, however much some of us may regret the direction that life sometimes took; a few years after I had found Midcentury to be a book one could praise for its artistry, if not to some extent its treatment of the newer type of business executive, I was disappointed to learn that Dos Passos had voted (in 1964) for Barry Goldwater!

But certainly all of us who have read very much of Dos Passos—particularly Manhattan Transfer, U.S.A., and Midcentury—will have an increased awareness of our own lives and of those about us. Dos Passos today may not stand with some of the authors I mentioned earlier (Fitzgerald, Faulkner, Dreiser, Hemingway), but surely his good points as a novelist will be recognized, and his best work will not just fade away, for he did something for our time which no one else has quite done. Fictionally—and in the U.S.A. biographical passages, factually—he has provided a relevant panorama of twentieth-century Americans.

HARRY T. MOORE

Southern Illinois University
March 4, 1971

Notes on Contributors

JOSEPH WARREN BEACH, late Professor of English Literature at the University of Minnesota and one of the pioneer critics of the modern novel, was the author of *The Method of Henry James, The Outlook for American Prose, The Twentieth Century Novel, American Fiction 1920–1940, The Concept of Nature in English Poetry, The Comic Spirit in George Meredith, The Technique of Thomas Hardy, The Romantic View of Poetry,* as well as a novel and two volumes of poetry.

ALLEN BELKIND has taught at the Universities of Southern California and Nevada and is currently Associate Professor of English at California State College, Bakersfield. During 1969–70 he was a Fulbright lecturer on American Studies in Helsinki, Finland. A former professional musician, his other main interests are in comparative literature, ethnic studies, and such interdisciplinary areas as literature and psychology. Kent State University Press recently published his book *Sartre (and existentialism) in English: A Bibliographical Guide.* He currently reviews books for *Journal of Modern Literature* and *Books Abroad* and is working on both a checklist and critical study of Dos Passos.

MALCOLM COWLEY is recognized as an influential critic of American fiction of the twenties and thirties. A former literary editor of the *New Republic,* poet, literary historian, and translator, he is the author of *Exile's Return, After the Genteel Tradition: American Writers Since 1910, The Literary Situation,* and two volumes of verse. He has edited numerous volumes, among them *The Portable Hemingway*, *The Portable Faulkner*, *The Complete Walt Whitman*, and *The Portable Hawthorne*. Currently a literary adviser to the Viking Press, his latest works have been *The Faulkner-Cowley File: Letters and Memories 1944–1962*, *Think Back on Us*, a collection of his earlier articles, and *A Many-Windowed House: Collected essays on American Writers and Writing*.

CHESTER E. EISINGER is Professor of English and Chairman of the Committee on American Studies at Purdue University. A critic and literary historian, he is the author of *Fiction of the Forties* and of articles on American agrarianism, and is the editor of a new edition of Norman Mailer's *The Naked and the Dead* and of *The 1940's: Profile of a Nation in Crisis*.

BLANCHE H. GELFANT is Associate Professor of English at the New York State University, Syracuse. Her main interests have been in the techniques and sociological backgrounds of modern American and British fiction. She is the author of an important book on American fiction, *The American City Novel*, and has contributed numerous essays to scholarly periodicals including *PMLA* and *Criticism*.

GRANVILLE HICKS was an influential Marxist critic during the thirties who resigned from the Communist Party in 1939. Among his many books are *The Great Tradition*, *John Reed—The Making of a Revolutionary*, and *Where We Came Out*. He is a coeditor (with Joseph Freeman) of *Proletarian Literature in the U.S.* and (with Ella Winter) of *The Letters of Lincoln Steffens*. He has also been a teacher and, for many years, a reviewer of fiction for the *Saturday Review*.

MARTIN KALLICH is Professor of English at Northern Illinois University. His main interests have been in eighteenth-century criticism and in modern American Literature. Besides several articles on Dos Passos, he has published a book, *Heav'n's First Law: Rhetoric and Order in Pope's Essay on Man*, and numerous articles on Pope, Swift, Johnson, Collins, and Gray in such periodicals as *Criticism*, *Ten-*

nessee Studies in Literature, English Language Notes, Journal of Aesthetics and Art Criticism, and *The Explicator.*

ALFRED KAZIN is Professor of English at the New York State University at Stony Brook. A well-known critic, teacher, editor, reviewer, and memoirist, he is the author of *On Native Grounds, The Inmost Leaf, Starting Out in the Thirties, A Walker in the City,* and *Contemporaries,* the co-editor (with Daniel Aaron) of *Emerson: A Modern Anthology,* and the editor of *The Portable William Blake* and *F. Scott Fitzgerald: The Man and his Work.*

GEORGE KNOX, Professor and Chairman of the English Department at the University of California, Riverside, is the author of *Critical Moments,* the coauthor (with Herbert Stahl) of *Dos Passos and "the Revolting Playwrights,"* and the coeditor (with Donald Greene) of *Treaty Trip.* He has held two Fulbright lectureships at the Universities of Vienna and Erlangen and has written numerous articles on modern British and American fiction and poetry. He holds a special interest in the relationships between literature and painting, and is currently at work on a book about Hart Crane.

RICHARD LEHAN is Professor of English at the University of California, Los Angeles. A specialist in both American studies and in American-French literary relations, he has published numerous articles on modern fiction and is the author of the critical study, *F. Scott Fitzgerald and the Craft of Fiction.* He is presently associate editor of *Nineteenth Century Fiction,* a member of the bibliography committee of *American Literature,* and has just completed *Theodore Dreiser: His World and His Novels.*

JOHN LYDENBERG is Professor of English at Hobart and Smith College. A Fulbright lecturer at the University of Strasbourg (1960–61) and at Aix-Marseille (1968–69), his main interests have been in American civilization, American social literature, and American intellectual history. He has contributed articles on John Dos Passos, Henry Adams, William Faulkner, Theodore Dreiser, and other American writers to such periodicals as *Pacific Spectator, American Literature,* and the *South Atlantic Quarterly.*

MARSHALL MCLUHAN is Director of the Center for Culture and Technology at the University of Toronto, and a frequent speaker and panelist both on television and in lecture halls. Formerly a professor of English literature at Toronto, he has taught at universities in the United States and Canada, and has become widely known for such books on the mass media as *Understanding Media, The Mechanical Bride,* and *The Gutenberg Galaxy.*

ARTHUR MIZENER is Professor of English at Cornell University, having taught formerly at Carleton College and Yale University. He is the author of a biography of F. Scott Fitzgerald, *The Far Side of Paradise,* and has edited other works on Fitzgerald. As a critic and reviewer, he has written many articles on American and modern British fiction and is the author of *The Sense of Life in the Modern Novel,* and *Twelve Great American Novels.* He recently completed *The Saddest Story,* a biography of Ford Madox Ford.

DAVID SANDERS, Professor of English at Harvey Mudd College and at the Claremont Graduate School, has published several articles on Dos Passos during the last few years in such periodicals as *South Atlantic Quarterly, Shenandoah,* and *Wisconsin Studies in Contemporary Literature.* He was Fulbright Lecturer at the University of Salamanca, Spain (1966–67), and is now completing a book-length critical study of Dos Passos.

JEAN-PAUL SARTRE, French philosopher, critic, playwright, and novelist, has been recognized as one of the most versatile men of letters of our time, as well as the leading contemporary figure of the Existentialist movement. He was awarded, but refused, the Nobel Prize for Literature in 1964. Some of his important philosophical and critical works that have been translated into English are *Being and Nothingness, Anti-Semite and Jew, Saint Genet,* and *Situations*; his novels include *Nausea* and *The Roads to Freedom*; and his better known plays include *No Exit, Dirty Hands,* and *The Condemned of Altona.*

BEN STOLTZFUS is Professor of French and French Literature at the University of California, Riverside. He taught previously at Smith College and has been the recipient of two Fulbright research grants. He has published three books of criticism: *Alain Robbe-Grillet and the New French Novel, Georges Chenneviere et l'unanimisme,* and *Gide's Eagles,* and a novel, *The Eye of the Needle.* He is currently doing research on Albert Camus' Anglo-French literary affinities and writing another novel.

LIONEL TRILLING is Professor of English at Columbia University. A recognized teacher, critic, and writer, he is the author of such critical studies as *Matthew Arnold* and *E. M. Forster* and of collections of criticism and social commentary such as *The Liberal Imagination, The Opposing Self, A Gathering of Fugitives,* and *Beyond Culture.* He is also the author of a novel, *The Middle of the Journey,* and of several short stories, and has edited *The Portable Matthew Arnold, The Letters of John Keats* and a collection of literary masterpieces, *The Experience of Literature.*

CHARLES C. WALCUTT, Professor of English at Queens College, is the author of *American Literary Naturalism: A Divided Stream, Man's Changing Mask: Modes and Methods of Characterization in Fiction,* and *Jack London.* He has written numerous articles on British and American literature and is the coeditor of *The Explicator Cyclopedia,* collected essays from *The Explicator* on English and American poets.

Introduction

The violent decade of the 1960s with its political as-
sassinations, the Vietnam War, and the growing militancy of student and black movements has produced a
hybrid blend of novelistic journalism and historical or
journalistic fiction that reminds one of the reportage fiction fashionable in the 1920s and '30s. Among such
works belonging to this mixed genre of journalism or fiction—depending upon the writer's intention to emphasize either the documentary or imaginative treatment of
his subject—Truman Capote's *In Cold Blood,* William
Styron's *The Confessions of Nat Turner,* Tom Wolfe's
Radical Chic and Mau-Mauing the Flak Catchers, and
Norman Mailer's *Miami Beach and the Siege of
Chicago* and *The Armies of the Night* represent a variety
of styles and approaches.

In this hybrid type of fiction or journalism, the writer
has drawn his subject matter from historical documents and/or his personal experience of contemporary
history, but has taken the kind of imaginative liberties
in his treatment of actual people and events that a
novelist does with his fictional materials. By doing so
he is able to transcend the historian's strictly factual
account and freely recreate the living human drama of
history. In his effort to transform historical documentation into human experience, he does not hesitate to
intrude into the private area of his characters' inner
thoughts and feelings or to interpret the collective
mentality of a particular group or class of people. By

selectively recording individual dialects, public statements, details of dress, mannerism, and background, he
brings into sharp focus the life-styles of famous or
notorious public figures and the colorful atmospheric
presence of the event.

But because the writer who blends fiction with nonfiction subjects the controversial materials of history to
his personal impressions, attitudes, and intentions, he
becomes vulnerable to the historian's judgments about
the accuracy of his "history as a novel" and the critic's
pronouncements about the literary merits of his "novel
as history." As a result, he often becomes as controversial as his material. Since his work, if widely read,
can influence public opinion and shape contemporary
history, the writer quickly attracts the admiration of
those who agree with his interpretation and the hostility
of others who accuse him of personal bias or political
distortion. Criticism of the writer becomes partisan;
political and literary judgments become confused; and
his popularity or literary reputation sometimes hangs
precariously in the balance.

From its inception the writing of John Dos Passos
(1896–1970) has been notable for its unique blend of
fiction and documentary. In the 1920s and '30s the technique of vividly recording historical events and shaping
them into an esthetic form that usually conveyed a
radical and critical viewpoint was called "reportage";
and Dos Passos became known as the master of the
reportage novel. Just as the violent sixties has produced,
in the work of Mailer, some first-rate political reportage,
the shock of World War I, its aftermath of social injustice, the stock market crash of 1929, and the crisis of
the depression thirties precipitated Dos Passos' kind of
documentary novel which both recreated and mordantly
commented upon these events. His *Three Soldiers*
(1921) so carefully documented his humiliating experiences as a common soldier that his novel was considered either a slanderous attack on or an indictment
of the Army. Its ironic treatment and panoramic tech-

nique set the pattern for subsequent antiwar fiction in America and established him as a foremost spokesman of America's "Lost Generation." The brilliant "collective" technique of *Manhattan Transfer* (1925) with its shifting cinematic scenes interspersed with prose poems, news headlines, and bits of historical gossip, added up to an impressionistic history of the commercial growth and moral stagnation of America's largest city. In the *U.S.A.* trilogy (1930–36; collected edition, 1938), the finest example of the "collective novel," Dos Passos extended his coverage to all America. Creating original narrative devices for this purpose, he simultaneously recorded the private histories of his many fictional characters, the personal history of the author, the public record of events contained in the newspapers, and the biographies of famous American personalities who were instrumental in shaping American history.

At the time he completed *U.S.A.*, Dos Passos was one of the most important and influential American writers. Indeed, one cannot overestimate his influence as a culture hero and literary innovator upon a whole school of budding writers, like Mailer, reaching maturity during the thirties and early forties. *The Naked and the Dead*, Mailer's collective novel about an army battalion in the Pacific, with its episodic scenes and its "Time Machine" biographies of each soldier, is indebted to Dos Passos' fiction. This indebtedness extends also to Mailer's most successful reportage work, *The Armies of the Night*, with its long shots of the epical march on the Pentagon, its close-up biographies of leading personalities connected with it, its newspaper accounts, and a kind of camera-eye continuously trained upon the leading star, Norman Mailer, who describes this work, perhaps somewhat ineptly, as a "condensation of a collective novel" (Penguin, p. 268). But by the end of World War II, Dos Passos' career had suffered a dramatic decline in popularity and in literary reputation, the fate of the journalistic novelist, whose work is susceptible to the perils of time and the attacks of both political and literary critics with differing ideologies and changing esthetic tastes. Although a brief flurry of interest in his last novel, *Midcentury* (1961), reawakened public attention to Dos Passos for a time, now, shortly after his death, his work again seems to have fallen into neglect.

The topic of Dos Passos' literary decline is interesting from the standpoint of both personal and literary history. About ten years ago, the novelist James T. Farrell, one of Dos Passos' most loyal supporters, regretfully summed up the prevailing critical opinion of the fiction that Dos Passos had produced since his great trilogy: Dos Passos, it was generally believed, had been writing in a state of mental rigor mortis.[1] What had caused the sudden drastic decline in his imaginative powers? According to his critics, Dos Passos, along with Hemingway and others, had gone to Spain during the Spanish Civil War to make a film about the Spanish people. There he not only witnessed the Communists' domination of the various Loyalist factions, but was shocked to discover their execution of a good friend as a supposed Fascist spy. The passionate radicalism that had fired his fiction up to that time had suddenly cooled and bitter disillusionment had set in. His later fiction seemed obsessively hostile to the "progressive" ideals to which he had once committed himself. And with his apparent shift to political conservatism and vehement anti-communism, his fiction, said the critics, had lost its former conviction, vividness, and technical originality.

A counterview expressed by Farrell, Arthur Mizener,[2] and a few others is that the critics hostile to Dos Passos' writing after his political divorce from the Left had all along misunderstood the basic mode and intention of his work; thus unprepared for his change in politics, they could not objectively evaluate the literary merits of his later work. They insist that Dos Passos' critics have been more concerned with the presumed disastrous effect of his disillusionment—his psychic wound—than with a close and unbiased reading of his later novels. Actually, say Farrell and Mizener, the real causes of Dos Passos'

decline in reputation have been, first of all, his critics'
continuing resentment of the different ideological cast
of his fiction and, second, the postwar shift of fashion
away from the broad canvas of Dos Passos's kind of
historical fiction to a fiction of less scope and more
depth, with little political and more personal and psychological concern.

At this date the question of the degree of Dos Passos'
presumed artistic deterioration still appears to be open
to discussion. Only two critical books in English on
his work as a whole have appeared,[3] and there has been
almost no extended critical discussion of his seven
novels which followed *U.S.A.* Thus, before an adequate
assessment of Dos Passos' later fiction can be made, one
must first await further studies and, second, attempt to
disentangle the various critical disagreements and con-
fusions in important existing criticism with the idea of
positing a satisfactory critical theory of his work. To
fulfill the latter task I have collected a representative
sampling of such criticism (there had to be limitations
set upon the length of this book). In the introduction I
have reviewed this and other important criticism on Dos
Passos with the idea of sketching out a critical theory of
his work that transcends the categories and clichés of the
thirties, because I believe that there is much in his best
work that transcends any historical period into the universality of literary art. Finally, I have included a
selective bibliography of some significant books, articles,
and reviews for those who wish to extend their interest
in Dos Passos.

The wide variety of approaches to Dos Passos and his
work—formalist, historical, sociological, political, psychological, biographical, existential, interdisciplinary,
and a combination of these—attests to both the versatil-
ity of his critics and the complexity of their subject. But
besides contributing valuable insights about Dos Passos
from these different points of view, these studies reveal

existing areas of disagreement about the intention, mode, method, and style of Dos Passos' fiction, the political and social ideas it reflects, and its sources and influences. Many of his critics seem to have approached his work either by attempting, without complete success, to resolve these existing complexities, divisions, and ambiguities, or to substitute labels which tend to neglect or hide them.

The first questions posed about Dos Passos were those concerning apparent divisions in his political, social, and moral views, and their relation to the intention of his fiction. Was Dos Passos a "proletarian" writer committed to Marxism and "the class struggle," or was he skeptical about political ideologies? Was he a Romantic and an esthete, compelled to flee from modern industrial America or a social critic dedicated to reforming it? Was he primarily a determinist who portrayed his characters as being helplessly caught in the grip of hostile environmental forces, or a moralist who held his characters responsible for their own tragic predicaments? Was he a "realist" or "naturalist," whose treatment of his subject matter was mainly impersonal and objective; or was his so-called impersonal method a stylistic disguise for embittered idealism, for satire, or for political propaganda? Was he a collectivist, interested in portraying the behavior of the social group, or an individualist who sided with the underdog who resisted dominant group pressures?

The first critics to notice apparent divisions of intention in Dos Passos' fiction were those, like himself, who were sympathetic to the aims of the political Left during the twenties and thirties. Their judgments of his fiction were conditioned by their belief that literature, in order to be considered important, had to be relevant to the times, and that the word "relevant" implied an adherence to a Marxist theory of history and a loyalty to the workers in "the class struggle." Granville Hicks and Malcolm Cowley, among the most perceptive of these critics associated with Marxist politics during the thirties, both viewed Dos Passos as a former escapist-esthete turned revolutionary, with the consequent change from confusion to conviction in his novels. Although Dos Passos began his literary career as one of the Harvard poets, says Hicks, he was "less completely drugged than his companions by Baudelaire, Petronius, and the old Howard." [4] Hicks notices that Dos Passos had been critical of industrialism from the beginning of his career, but it was not until *Manhattan Transfer* (1925) that Dos Passos decided to "take a long look at the world that he had hated and sometimes fled from." Although an important criticism of urban society, *Manhattan Transfer* is weakened by "the author's bewilderment," not unlike that of his hero, Jimmy Herf, whose "departure [from the city] is no real solution to his own problems and can have no bearing upon the problems of the other characters still struggling in the metropolitan wilderness." But, says Hicks, in *The 42nd Parallel* and *1919*, (the first two novels of *U.S.A.*), an understanding of the class struggle, "deeply realized in the emotions and translated into action has given Dos Passos a sensitiveness to the world about him. . . . and enabled him to see the fundamental unity beneath the seemingly chaotic complexity of American life."

Like Hicks, but less certain about Dos Passos' Marxist commitment, Malcolm Cowley also found a divided purpose in Dos Passos' fiction. To Cowley, Dos Passos is "in reality two novelists. One of them is a late-Romantic, an individualist, an esthete moving about the world in a portable ivory tower; the other is a collectivist, a radical historian of the class struggle." [5] Cowley, too, finds that Dos Passos, the esthete-individualist, had written most of *Three Soldiers* and *Manhattan Transfer*, while Dos Passos, the radical, had written most of the later and more "convincing" *U.S.A.* novels. *Three Soldiers* and *Manhattan Transfer*, says Cowley, are imperfect examples of the "art novel"—a genre popular during Dos Passos' Harvard years—whose dominant theme was the defeat of the sensitive young poet by a crude, hostile world. Attempting to reconcile the earlier esthete-individualist with the later radical-collectivist, Cowley points out that the "art novel" and the "collective novel" as conceived by Dos Passos are not in fundamental opposition. Whereas the narratives of *U.S.A.* focus outwardly upon the whole social group, the Camera Eye sections resemble the art novel in depicting the impressions of a sensitive individual, and thus provide the necessary "inwardness" of experience lacking in the other sections. Cowley also maintains that Dos Passos' collective novels, like his earlier art novels, portray society as being stupid, omnipotent, and fundamentally evil, bringing either doom to those who oppose it or damnation to those who sell out to its corruption. Linking the pessimistic determinism in *U.S.A.* to the defeatist theme of the art novel still remaining in the trilogy—a pessimism inimical to Marxian optimism about historical and social change—Cowley is disappointed because these novels have failed "to express one side of contemporary life, the will to struggle ahead, the comradeship in the struggle, the consciousness of new men and new forces continually rising."

The views of Cowley and Hicks were influential in establishing the image of Dos Passos as the "radical historian of the class struggle." Yet, Cowley's interpretation of Dos Passos as both revolutionary and pessimist posed another ambiguity that Lionel Trilling questioned in a later (1938) article for *Partisan Review*.[6] Although Trilling was also in sympathy with the aims of the intellectual Left during the thirties, he was more discriminating and less absolutist than the Marxists in his views about the necessary political function of literature. Taking issue with Cowley, Trilling declares that Dos Passos is basically neither a radical historian, nor collectivist, nor determinist. Dos Passos, he says does not write of a class struggle since his characters are mainly middle-class types (although Trilling neglects the biographies) rather than factory workers or moneyed capitalists; nor is he much concerned with the idea of class in the political sense. Although Trilling agrees with Cowley that Dos Passos hates the values of industrial capitalism, he argues that Dos Passos' pessimism is the result of his mature perception "that the creeds and idealisms of the Left may bring corruption quite as well as the greeds and cynicism of the established order. . . ."

Trilling is also unable to accept Cowley's view of Dos Passos' pessimistic determinism as being connected with his apparent adherence to the defeatist theme of the art novel. The "historical apparatus" of *U.S.A.*, says Trilling, serves primarily as a background for individual decisions rather than simply as a determining force over his characters' fates; and if Dos Passos is a social historian, "he is that in order to be a more complete moralist" who holds his characters just as responsible for their own tragic ends as the hostile society that surrounds them. Following Cowley's suggestion that Dos Passos' morality is "Romantic," he compares Dos Passos' American types with the characters in the poetic narratives of Browning and Burns, who, after sinning against themselves, suffer a spiritual death evidenced in their "petrification of feeling." Thus, Trilling observes, the social breakdown depicted in *U.S.A.* is mainly the result of "moral degeneration through moral choice."

Most subsequent speculations about the intention of Dos Passos' fiction seem to have been interesting variations upon Cowley and Trilling, viewing his work as having divided aims that fall between the individualist-collectivist, moralist-determinist, esthete-radical critic, romantic-realist categories. For example, Alfred Kazin, in one of the best general treatments of Dos Passos' career up to 1941, agrees essentially with Cowley's thesis about Dos Passos' esthete-radical historian dichotomy and about the defeatism and determinism in Dos Passos' fiction up to *U.S.A.*[7] But, at the same time, he seems to agree with Trilling's interpretation of the individualistic morality implied in *U.S.A.* Kazin first characterizes Dos Passos' fiction as being a "direct link between the post-war decade and the crisis novel of the depression period" in which "the defeatism of the lost generation has been slowly and subtly transferred by him from [individual] persons to society itself." But Kazin stresses that *U.S.A.* is collectivistic only in form, and that Dos Passos is not as concerned with mass behavior as with the fate of individual and outsider—e.g., Thorstein Veblen, John Reed, or Randolph Bourne —who remains faithful to his ideals to the bitter end. As Kazin says:

> It is in this concern with the primacy of the individual, with his need to save the individual from society rather than to establish him in or over it, that one can trace the conflict that runs all through Dos Passos' work— between his estheticism and strong social interests, his profound absorption in the total operations of modern society and his overscrupulous withdrawal from all of them; the iron, satirical prose he hammered out in *U.S.A.* (a machine prose for a machine world) and the youthful stammering lyricism that pulses under it.

Trilling and Cowley were among the first to pose the question as to whether Dos Passos was or was not a pessimistic determinist who viewed modern society as an inexorable destructive force upon the individual. Because the lives of most of Dos Passos' characters usually end either in a dimly recognized moral defeat or in violent catastrophe, and because his documentary method follows in the tradition of Dreiser, many literary critics and historians, with some justification, have labeled him a determinist or naturalist.

"Naturalism" has been a useful—though slippery and variously used—term to historically identify the group of writers (Hamlin Garland, Stephen Crane, Frank Norris, Theodore Dreiser, Jack London, Upton Sinclair, among them) influenced by the deterministic ideas contained in nineteenth-century biological and social science and the literature-science analogies in the pronouncements of

Émile Zola; writers who wished to expose—in the name of scientific objectivity—the amoral, starkly brutal side of American life previously suppressed in fiction. But, although valid and useful in describing similar philosophical aims among these so-called naturalists and later-generation writers, such as Dos Passos, seemingly influenced by them, the term is inadequate in pointing out differences of intention, structure and style between individual authors of this school (compare the novels of Crane, Norris, and Dreiser, for example). And as two theorists of naturalism (who have linked Dos Passos to the earlier naturalists), Malcolm Cowley [8] and Philip Rahv,[9] have noted, the term can be confusing as a descriptive tool because the personal styles and aims of many so-called naturalists diverge from their authors' theories about scientific objectivity into such religious and political philosophies as mysticism and socialism. Actually, according to Cowley, the most interesting so-called naturalistic novels are not those that are "scientific or objective," in accordance with naturalist theory, but those that are "most personal and lyrical." One also might cite Henry Steele Commager's perceptive observations of the different treatment of their characters given by Dreiser and Dos Passos, two so-called naturalists, to illustrate the critical imprecision of this term in describing a novelist's intention:

> it is no less than startling to contrast Van Harrington, Hugh Paret, and Frank Cowperwood with Dos Passos' representatives of Big Business, J. Ward Moorehouse and Charley Anderson. For those earlier titans of finance and of industry are amoral and ruthless, but they are never contemptible or obscene . . . and as for the fabulous Cowperwood, Dreiser can scarcely conceal his admiration for the man who was, after all, merely obeying those laws of nature which Darwin and Nietzsche had deciphered. But Anderson and Moorehouse have no redeeming qualities, nor is their creator troubled for a moment by any twinges of

sympathy for them. They inspire disgust and justify it.[10]

Charles C. Walcutt and John Lydenberg have managed to fit Dos Passos's fiction into the naturalist category only by characterizing his work—like Cowley, Trilling, and Kazin—as having divided, rather than unified, aims. Walcutt places Dos Passos within the confines of his particular definition of naturalism that includes not only pessimistic determinism, but apparent non-naturalistic characteristics such as moral idealism and optimistic faith in reform.[11] According to Walcutt, American literary naturalists inherited a "divided stream" of materialistic determinism and moral idealism from post-Darwinian science and the transcendental tradition in American thought. Therefore, "all naturalistic novels exist in a tension between determinism and its antithesis." The early naturalists, he says, believed not only in the powerful determining conditions of heredity and environment upon man, but also in the beneficial results of changing these conditions. Hence, they wrote pessimistic novels with an implied optimistic purpose: social reform.

But Walcutt interprets Dos Passos as an embittered pessimist who has little or no hope for reform. Dos Passos' place in the naturalist group, says Walcutt, is at the extreme "end point in the evolution of naturalistic forms" because his fiction illustrates the attitude that environmental forces have grown too complex and destructive to cope with. Thus, the earlier naturalists' optimistic faith in science as a remedy for human ills appears in Dos Passos' novels as both dark pessimism and uncontrolled indignation at the helplessness of the individual at the mercy of these environmental forces. Walcutt finds *Manhattan Transfer* divided, on one hand, by the determinism of its "kaleidoscopic form" and "clinically detached" method which records America's moral chaos; and, on the other, by its "grim and sensational tone" which suggests Dos Passos' despairing idealism about the possibilities of change. He finds *U.S.A.* also split by the impersonal tone of its narratives and the Camera Eye's outcries of "uncontrolled protest" and "unreliable indignation" about modern America "being corrupted, debauched, and enslaved by the forces of commercial rapacity." [12]

Walcutt's approach to American literary naturalism is probably the most thoughtful to date, but his attempt to link Dos Passos with other so-called determinists causes him to minimize Dos Passos' moral concern with his characters [13] and to assume that Dos Passos' apparently impersonal method of narration reflects an objective and impartial attitude. For instance, Walcutt disregards the moral overtones in Dos Passos' imagistic descriptions of his characters' psychological conflicts as they sin against themselves for power and success. He calls this passage concerning Ellen Thatcher's decision to marry the politician, George Baldwin—a man whom she detests but weds for security and status—just an example of Dos Passos' "sentimental awareness" of his people's agonies and defeats:

> She had made up her mind. . . . Ellen felt herself sitting with her ankles crossed, rigid as a porcelain figure under her clothes, everything about her seemed to be growing hard and enameled, the air bluestreaked with cigarettesmoke, was turning to glass.

But in this passage Ellen has made a conscious moral decision and Dos Passos has commented on it by means of imagery that suggests the type of spiritual death that Trilling has mentioned. A closer examination of this kind of so-called "impersonal" comment seems to reveal not mere determinism, but Dos Passos' implicit criticism of his characters' moral weaknesses. Marshall McLuhan, I believe, is more accurate about the tone and implicit intention in this kind of characterization when he says: "Even satire is managed by Dos Passos in a direct, lyric mode, though the technique seems to be impersonal." [14]

John Lydenberg's thesis, that *U.S.A.* is "strongly

naturalistic and deterministic," also emphasizes Dos Passos' divided attitude towards his subject matter.[15] Says Lydenberg, "None of its [*U.S.A.*'s] characters has free will, none determines his fate, all move like automatons." Dos Passos makes us feel that his characters' actions are determined "by showing their choices to be non-choices. . . . we do not feel their choices to be decisions." Yet, according to Lydenberg, "a large part of the book's success comes precisely from the author's failure to be as deterministic as he thinks he wants to be." Despite their apparent lack of free choice, the reader tends to morally judge these typical and unexceptional characters "just as though they were in fact responsible human beings making free choices."

Thus Lydenberg changes his emphasis from Dos Passos' apparent determinism and explores a more important line of thought similar to the one that Trilling had introduced earlier: that Dos Passos *is* concerned with the personal moral decisions of his characters, especially those of such exploiters as J. Ward Moorehouse and Dick Savage. Dos Passos, he says, has always been concerned about "problems of social values" to the point of obsession about the words his characters use— the lies, the tired slogans, the banal speech—that reflect the deviation of the "new America" away from the honorable ideals, "the clean words" of the American forefathers. Although Dos Passos' later work despairingly continues his obsession with these ruined words that have become symbolic of America's moral decay, the honest words of Mac, Ben Compton, and Mary French in *U.S.A.* carry the optimistic hope that "the ruined words might be rebuilt." Dos Passos' "dual vision of the words," he says, created a tension between idealism and cynicism, hope and despair, that gave *U.S.A.* a vitality and creative energy he would never be able to muster again.

Most critics of Dos Passos' fiction have recognized that his portrait of American society is one-sided or slanted in its criticism, that Dos Passos stresses the ruthless, amoral, and selfish aspects of those characters who do not reject "the system" and conspicuously leaves out any positive or redeeming qualities they might have. Thus, since his novels tend to sacrifice balance and impartiality to the ends of criticism, and since many of his characters tend to remain caricatures, terms such as "realistic" or "naturalistic" are useful only in describing the quality of social Darwinism in Dos Passos' interpretation of the American experience and the technical departure of his novels from more conventionally narrated romantic novels. Nevertheless, some critics using these terms include even Dos Passos' distortions as one aspect of his particular brand of realism or naturalism. For example, Charles C. Walcutt, as previously mentioned, makes Dos Passos' "unreliable" depiction of America's total "moral deterioration" compatible with naturalism by linking naturalism with frustrated idealism and pessimism. The late Professor Joseph Warren Beach and Professor Blanche Gelfant also have recognized that Dos Passos presents a predominantly repulsive view of urban America, but have defended his depiction as credible and as an intrinsic part of Dos Passos' realistic method of ironic social criticism.

In his important book on the techniques of the modern American novel, Beach [16] associates Dos Passos' realism with the avoidance of conventional romantic tricks of characterization and with his criticism of American society implied in his collectivist technique. In the creation of his characters, says Beach, Dos Passos refrains from adopting such devices as Faulkner's "appeal to terror, to mystery and suspense," Dickens' and Caldwell's picturesque character sketching, Steinbeck's sentimentality, or Wolfe's use of gargantuan heroes. Instead, Dos Passos has adopted a "behaviorist method" of portraying American types motivated not by high ideals but by a pattern of stimulus and response, pleasure and pain, toward common goals of money, love, or diversion. Dos Passos' "destructive criticism" of these types is so systematically applied, says Beach, that the "ordinary reader is left with a dreary sense of human nature as a mean and shallow lot."

Combining a subject matter "naturally repellent to him" with a series of brilliant technical devices, Dos Passos created *Manhattan Transfer*, the first collective novel in American fiction and an original contribution to the modern novel. In this new type of novel, the city, rather than any single character, became the main protagonist. Its cinematic method of narrative discontinuity, says Beach, reflects the moral and psychic discontinuity of its many urban dwellers, and its cumulative collectivist effect produces an impression of a lonely crowd of individuals simultaneously living and working together in a city dominated by individualistic self-interest, and lacking human qualities of "affection, gratitude, obligation, cooperation that bind people together in an orderly society."

Indebted to Beach's analysis, but providing many brilliant critical insights of her own, Blanche Gelfant admits that Dos Passos' portrait of Manhattan is distorted, but justifies the distortion as essential to the novel's "impressionistic realism" and its "abstract" design.[17] The harsh sounds and putrid odors, the unpleasant mechanistic connotations of such recurring urban symbols as "revolving doors" and "skyscrapers," the futile "squirrelcage" existence of the characters, she says, become the means by which Dos Passos, in his "synoptic novel," objectifies his social commentary about the state of American society: "the trend towards a mechanized kind of life that is expressed, in economic terms, in monopoly capitalism and, in human terms, in the loss of man's capacities for love and self-realization." Comparing the realistic methods of Dreiser and Dos Passos, she finds that "whereas Dreiser accumulates details in order to reproduce actuality as closely as possible, Dos Passos selects a few evocative details that are to suggest the essential impression of the whole." Dos Passos' impressionistic method and critical intentions, she says, "committed him to exclusion as much as to inclusion." Thus, his realism involves a considerable distortion of actuality, but it is "a realism to which the imagination can give assent."

But Mrs. Gelfant's theory of Dos Passos as a realist is burdened by having to account for a portrait of the city which, she says, "is not a faithful reproduction of complementary and balancing details" and for characters who "are only representatives of a human state of mind intrinsic to the city—they are not fully realized flesh and blood people, but abstract states of being." Mrs. Gelfant is herself aware that many of Dos Passos' critics have not given their imaginative "assent" to his portrayal, but have seriously questioned the credibility of his interpretation of life in New York City. For example, Edmund Wilson has attacked the novel on the grounds that Dos Passos' political "disapproval of capitalist society seems to imply a distaste for all the beings who go to compose it," and that "no human life under any conditions can ever have been so unattractive." [18] Alfred Kazin has suggested that Dos Passos "had become fascinated with a kind of mass and pictorial ugliness" and that "what one saw in *Manhattan Transfer* was not the broad city pattern at all, but a wistful absorption in monstrousness." [19] To Marshall McLuhan, Manhattan is "not envisaged as providing anything more than a phantasmagoric backdrop for [the characters'] frustrations and defeats. The city is felt as alien, meaningless." [20] Henry Longan Stuart has declared that Dos Passos "has an exasperated sense of the unpleasant" and that his study of New York "too often freezes into a set piece of horror." [21] And George Snell has called *Manhattan Transfer* "a depressing spectacle. . . . a civilization set in a mold . . . the mechanism of modern life which makes city-dwellers hardly more than robots going through automatic motions." [22]

Perhaps Jean-Paul Sartre, the French philosopher and novelist, has perceived Dos Passos' fictional intentions more accurately than many American critics. To Sartre, whose fictional technique has been influenced by the works of Dos Passos and who once regarded Dos Passos "as the greatest writer of our time," Dos Passos is a determinist in method but not in philosophy.[23] Interpreting Dos Passos' work as reflecting an existentialist rather than determinist philosophy, Sartre says that Dos Passos deliberately created his frozen, determined world of past history filled with futile, empty lives in order to arouse the reader's indignation and to impel him toward a revolt against his own self-deception and moral complacency. Mentioning Dos Passos' trick of "distorting mirrors," Sartre says that Dos Passos has "done everything possible to make his novel [1919] seem a mere reflection" of reality, but that "his art is not gratuitous; he wants to prove something." Through his "behaviorist style" and his "statistical determinism," Dos Passos forces the reader to compare his own freedom and the existing moral choices still available to him with the petrified destinies of the fictional characters on the other side of the mirror:

> With the opening lines of his book, Dos Passos settles down into death. The lives he tells about are all closed in on themselves. . . . We constantly have the feeling that these vague, human lives are destinies. Our own past is not at all like this. There is not one of our acts whose meaning and value we cannot still transform even now.

Sartre's view, that because "Dos Passos' hate, despair, and lofty contempt are real. . . . that is precisely why his world is not real: it is a created object," adds further support to the idea that terms such as "realist" or "naturalist" are inadequate in determining the main intention of his work. Because Dos Passos distorts reality to magnify and expose social evils and because his fiction is primarily ironic in tone, the term "satire" seems to better characterize both its main intention and stylistic effect, and to provide a more unified, rather than divided, theory about his work. Importantly, the term satire also allows for the device of distortion as a legitimate technique that need not be critized or justified, and provides the motivation for this distortion: the anger of the frustrated idealist about the supposed low level of morality in contemporary society.

Because of the politically controversial nature of Dos Passos' fiction and its close attention to contemporary history, there have been relatively few objective appraisals of its literary merits as satire. Understandably, his hostile critics have been unable to remain impartial to its slant, its exaggeration and oversimplification, and other rhetorical devices that have been traditionally associated with satiric writing through the centuries from Juvenal to Orwell. They have also not made necessary distinctions when judging his work between realism as a "means" and realism as an "end." In this connection, it should be kept in mind that a satirist's personal animus towards his subject matter usually overrides any allegiance he may have toward criteria of realistic objectivity and fairness of treatment. Wayne Booth has said in *The Rhetoric of Fiction*:

> There is a radical difference between those who seek some sort of realism as an end in itself . . . and those for whom realism is a means to other ends. Satirists like Swift and Voltaire . . . will clearly sacrifice realism whenever their satirical ends require the sacrifice.[24]

And theoreticians of satire such as Gilbert Highet have pointed out that realistically based satire traditionally distorts reality in order to show its ridiculous or repellent qualities. Highet says in *The Anatomy of Satire*:

> A satirical picture of our world, which shows only human beings as its inhabitants must pretend to be a photograph, and in fact be a caricature. It must display their more ridiculous and repellent qualities in full flower, minimize their ability for healthy

normal living, mock their virtues and exaggerate their vices. . . . And it must do all this while protesting that it is a truthful, unbiased, as nearly as possible dispassionate witness.[25]

Although no extended analysis of Dos Passos' fiction as satire exists in print, both hostile and friendly critics since the twenties and thirties have either alluded to the "objectionable" qualities in his novels that one associates with the satirical method or have labeled his work as satire. When *Three Soldiers*, a scathing attack on both war and army bureaucracy, appeared in 1921, some reviewers attacked Dos Passos for his supposed slanted, unfair, and propagandistic attack upon the AEF and overlooked his literary skills.[26] In 1930, John Chamberlain, a perceptive reviewer of Dos Passos' work over the years, called *The 42nd Parallel* "a satire on the tremendous haphazardness of life in expansionist America we all have known, the America which came into birth with the defeat of Jefferson's dream of an agricultural democracy."[27] In 1936, Horace Gregory, in his highly favorable review of *The Big Money*, declared that Dos Passos "more than any other living American writer, has exposed to public satire those peculiar contradictions of our poverty in the midst of plenty."[28] And in the same year, Max Lerner praised Dos Passos as a writer with "an acid intelligence" who had attempted "to apply a novelist's scalpel to murder on an organized scale in *Three Soldiers* and to the entire anatomy of a diseased social system" in *U.S.A.* Dos Passos, he said, bestows upon his portrait of America "that desperate tenderness that can only flow from love and solicitude turned into satire. . . . he is the Veblen of American fiction."[29]

During the Depression Thirties when literature and politics in the United States were more closely related than in our own time, many of Dos Passos' critics viewed him as an important cultural critic in his own right and agreed with his portrait of American society as a diseased organism hopelessly crippled by monopoly capitalism. Sociologically rather than rhetorically oriented, they did not, in this period of social crisis, consider methodological distinctions between realism and satire in his fiction to be important. They simply admired the satirical edge of his novels because they considered them radical and meliorative and judged them to be credible as fiction and truthful as history— that is, "realistic." Later, however, in *Adventures of a Young Man* (1939), when the target of his satire shifted more dramatically from corrupt capitalism to pragmatic communism, leftist critics who were shocked by his apparently sudden change in politics began attacking his fiction for various reasons, including its supposed distortion of contemporary history. Since his exposure of abuses within the radical movement represented an attack on many of his critics' cherished beliefs, their retaliation was based, in large part, on the fact that they considered Dos Passos' fiction to be politically irresponsible and reactionary.[30] From a partisan standpoint, undoubtedly it was; but actually, Dos Passos had only continued to apply the tools of the satirist to expose abuses committed by any institution or group that valued power and expediency above the lives of dissenting individuals.

Again in the forties, Dos Passos received similar hostile treatment from literary critics who were Rooseveltian liberals, when his novel *The Grand Design* (1949) attacked the supposed bureaucratic sluggishness of the New Deal administration. Since there were also political implications in this novel, although the characters were fictitious, these critics believed that Dos Passos' views needed correction and the book needed to be judged on political and historical grounds. Though justified in attempting to restore the political balance, they condemned the literary value of the book as well. Maxwell Geismar's change of attitude toward Dos Passos' post-*U.S.A.* novels is a good case in point here. Geismar, who has admired *U.S.A.* since the thirties, declared on one occasion that in the trilogy Dos Passos "showed his early gift as a satirist of the upper classes" and that *The Big Money* was "the most acerbic novel in twentieth-century American prose fiction." [31] But in his negative review of *The Grand Design*, Geismar condemns Dos Passos' treatment of the Roosevelt administration as being "both distorted as history and lacking in essential literary and human values." Geismar says nothing in this review about Dos Passos' portrait of the New Deal as satire. Instead, he compares Dos Passos unfavorably with Dreiser, using his own criterion of realism as the standard of comparison. Dos Passos, unlike Dreiser, says Geismar, lacks "an interest in people as such . . . a curiosity about life simply as life." [32]

In various articles, speeches, and interviews over the span of his career, Dos Passos repeatedly mentioned his satirical intentions and, one one occasion, even admitted his fictional distortions.[33] In the thirties he discussed his indebtedness to the satirical method of the artist George Grosz, whose mordant drawings he had discovered in Europe during World War I. He described Grosz's intentions in a manner that aptly applies to his own:

> A Satirist is a man whose flesh creeps so at the ugly and the savage and the incongruous aspects of society that he has to express them as brutally and nakedly as possible to get relief.[34]

When speaking about his literary intentions in an address to the American Academy of Arts and Letters in 1957, he implied that he was a satirist who criticized men as he observed them in particular moments because they did not measure up to his idealistic expectations of human nature in general.[35] Several times during the sixties he described himself as a satirical chronicler of contemporary society who was moved to write his "chronicles of protest" by the social injustices he had observed during his lifetime, and who had become "more and more satirical as the years went by." [36] And in Charles F. Madden's recent *Talks With Authors*,

Dos Passos, when interviewed by Harry T. Moore, reiterated that he was a satirist whose supposedly pessimistic fiction was motivated by the optimistic hopes he still held about the possibilities of moral and social change.[37]

Up to the present time it seems that only one American critic, Arthur Mizener, has made relevant distinctions between Dos Passos, the satirist, and Dos Passos, the realist and/or naturalist, "social novelist," or "collectivist." [38] Mizener says that few have recognized that Dos Passos has been writing a kind of fiction "almost unique in our time" that is best approached "by way of the tradition of serious comedy exemplified by . . . Ben Jonson and Swift." Like these two great satirists who exposed to ridicule the discrepancies between the professed ideals and the actual conduct of their own societies, Dos Passos takes seriously "the anarchistic individualism and the egalitarianism of the American democratic tradition and attacks with satire the institutionalized corruption and the disintegrated lives produced by the two mighty opposites of our society—industry and politics."

Mizener's approach, I believe, not only clarifies the problem of Dos Passos' main intention, but persuasively resolves (although some ambiguities remain) the problem of Dos Passos' distortions, his continuing use of two-dimensional character types, the recurrent pattern of defeat in his work, and his deterministic method. The characteristic fictional form for this mode of dark satiric comedy, Mizener says, is the picaresque tale which elucidates the manners and customs of a society through the various adventures of its hero or heroes. Like Ben Jonson, Dos Passos deliberately creates "two-dimensional" characters, "representative cases," each of whom spouts the clichés of his class or social group and, in so doing, "contributes to our understanding of the drift of the community's life." All "innocents" at the beginning, these characters soon become identified as either idealists who uphold the traditions of the "old"

America, or rascals and exploiters who compromise themselves to "corrupting forces" of the "new" America. The pattern of defeat and the determinism in Dos Passos' novels—the inner moral degeneration of the exploiters and society's forceful destruction of the idealists—stresses the relentless evil influence of our social institutions and becomes a mordant satire of them.[39]

Though he stresses the traditional rather than the modern aspects of Dos Passos' satire, Mizener convincingly associates the strong deterministic bent in Dos Passos with his particular satirical intentions rather than, as many critics have supposed, with a more general naturalistic style of writing. However, Mizener, like other critics, seems divided in his views about the degree of social determinism exerted upon Dos Passos' characters: that is, whether Dos Passos holds the characters themselves or society primarily responsible for their ensuing corruption or catastrophe. For Mizener, like Trilling, also insists that Dos Passos is mainly concerned with the individual's moral choice:

> But always, from the day Fainy McCreary had to decide between his feelings for Maisie and his loyalty to the IWW, the core of Dos Passos's work has been an isolating, individual struggle between stubborn idealism and the corrupting forces of an organized society which demands conformity.

The cost of a character's decision to either conform to or resist this corruption, says Mizener, "is always not less than everything." His conformity either costs him his individuality, and he dies inside, or his resistance defeats or dooms him. Thus the grim humor of the satire. However, it is not clear if Mizener views these individual choices to be, in fact, illusory, since they are only of the extreme "either-or" variety and since the fates of these characters seem to have been determined beforehand.

Perhaps one can resolve the free-will-determinism dilemma in Dos Passos' fiction by showing that Dos

Passos endows his characters with varying degrees of moral awareness and obtuseness, and with varying degrees of freedom from or entrapment by social and economic circumstances. Dos Passos' "generic heroes," as Blanche Gelfant calls them,[40] are all morally perceptive individuals in conflict with a corrupt "system" —the Army, the city, capitalism, communism, big government and big unionism—and choose to resist it. The main exception seems to be Dick Savage, at first a sympathetic character, who compromises his standards for "the big money" and is heavily damned for it.

At the other extreme, opportunists of *U.S.A.* such as J. Ward Moorehouse and Eleanor Stoddard seem to have no particular conflict about their materialistic conniving, although the reader feels that they live empty lives. Both inevitably choose the easiest road to fame and fortune. They are morally shallow and seem the more comic for being so. Charley Anderson and Eveline Hutchins, however, are more interesting characters because they eventually recognize their wasted lives. Eveline, from an upper-middle class background, has drifted through life not knowing what she wants. She finally commits suicide because she feels bored, unhappy, and purposeless. Anderson sacrifices a promising career as an aviation inventor for the big money and a socialite wife. Alienated from that time on because his wealth alone does not bring him satisfaction, he finally destroys himself in an auto accident resulting from an absurd race with a train.

The lives of other less-fortunate characters at or near the bottom of the economic scale seem to be completely determined by their social and economic circumstances. All are defeated by an oppressive system; hence, the indictment against this system. Joe Williams, the lowly merchant seaman of *1919* is buffeted about by a series of misfortunes and indignities until he loses his life in a barroom brawl in France. Dutch Robertson, the ex-soldier of *Manhattan Transfer* is forced by unemployment into robbery for which he receives an overly severe twenty-year jail sentence. And Anna Cohen brought up in the ghetto with little education becomes an exploited garment worker who dies in a fire in Madame Soubrine's dress shop. Typically, in the contrast between Anna's social victimization and Ellen Thatcher's willful bad-faith, Dos Passos stresses the idea of moral responsibility for another human being which Ellen, involved in her selfish opportunism, lacks.

Although Mizener's interpretation of Dos Passos' main intention is convincing, the various disagreements among other important critics of Dos Passos' fiction suggest the possibility that Dos Passos did not satisfactorily resolve all problems of method and intention. If Dos Passos had wished to write in a more purely realistic vein, that is, had wished to be the social historian or Balzacian chronicler of twentieth-century America, his impatience with human corruption and his alienation from modern industrial society prevented this. Perhaps, as the psychological critics of Dos Passos have suggested, he became too ego-involved with his characters—and the social forces they represent—to remain impartial or to allow them more complexity of existence. But if to some critics, Dos Passos' lack of balance and objectivity has diminished his status as a realistic novelist, to others it has enhanced his achievement as a satirist.

But for whatever reasons, Dos Passos has continued to be relentlessly critical of modern industrial America and, by implication, of modern industrial society in general for its destructiveness upon the individual. James T. Farrell once pointed out quite importantly that Dos Passos' work as a whole was "concerned with unfolding patterns of American life, the course of American destinies, showing by such an unfoldment, the character of American society, and the manner in which this society either destroys integrity, or ruins those who struggle to maintain it." [41] This has been a continuing theme perhaps unpleasant to contemplate, but serious criticism that sustains the general relevance and importance of his fiction to date.

His continuing negative slant in his treatment of current historical trends distasteful to him, his tendency to reduce to caricatures those prominent historical figures and average American types representative of these trends, and his accurate ear for the clichés and institutionalized jargon of influential government bureaucrats (*The Grand Design*), Communist Party affiliates (*Most Likely to Succeed*), and labor bosses (*Midcentury*) demonstrates a consistency of satirical intention, and provides, I believe, a useful approach to his total fictional achievement. Recognizing this, further questions should be posed about the comparative literary value of particular novels in which Dos Passos has succeeded or failed in his intention, about his imaginative or unimaginative use of historical materials, about his degree of skill in adapting rhetorical devices associated with traditional satiric methods, about how his type of mordant modern satire might compare with that of, say Mark Twain (the adventures of Mac remind us of Huck Finn), or Orwell, whose dominant metaphor is also the odious machinery of organized power, and so on.

Those unable to dissociate Dos Passos' literary merits from his current social or political beliefs might well remember Orwell's comments about Swift.[42] Although politically and morally aligned against Swift's supposed antiutopian and misanthropic ideas, Orwell declares that he admires the Dean "with least reserve" and could never tire of *Gulliver's Travels*. The best books of any one age, says Orwell, have always been written from several viewpoints representing progressive and reactionary ideas, "some of them palpably more false than others." The political expression of Swift's ideas must, thinks Orwell, be either reactionary or nihilistic. Yet, he says admiringly, that Swift possessed

a terrible intensity of vision, capable of picking out a single hidden truth and then magnifying it and distorting it. The durability of *Gulliver's Travels* goes to show that, if the force of belief is behind it, a world-view which only just passes the test of sanity is sufficient to produce a great work of art.

As confused about his political and social philosophy as his literary aims, Dos Passos' reading audience during the span of his career has labelled him almost everything on the political spectrum from a Marxist radical to a reactionary. A fellow-traveler of the political Left for over twenty years because he considered the movement a force against injustice, he openly criticized the Communists on specific issues during the twenties and thirties, suddenly broke his ties with radicalism after a trip to Spain during the Spanish Civil War, and has become identified as an outspoken anti-Communist and libertarian conservative from that time on. His subsequent depiction of the Communist Party, the New Deal administration, and labor unions in this country as oppressive forces just as threatening to the individual as monopoly capitalism had been in his earlier work has alienated many of his earlier readers, who now refer to Dos Passos as a traitor and turncoat to his former "progressive" ideals. Yet a careful examination of Dos Passos' early and later political views reveals that he has remained faithful to the brand of liberalism that has stressed decentralization and self-government; that his consistent rugged individualism has been sustained by his continuing fear that corporate power groups within the United States have been harmful to the human spirit; and that his appraisal—correct or incorrect—of the shift in power structures within this country has conditioned his own shift in his contemporary political alliances from Left to Right.

In the three essays on Dos Passos' politics reprinted in this collection, Granville Hicks documents his unchanging individualist philosophy; David Sanders points out that Dos Passos' belated conservatism is an outgrowth of his basic philosophical anarchism; and Chester E. Eisinger illustrates how the subtle shifts in liberal politics during the thirties affected the political position of men such as Dos Passos who were skeptical of ideologies and upheld traditional concepts of self-government.

Tracing Dos Passos' political involvements from his rebellious student days at Harvard to his later conservative and anti-Communist position, Hicks surmises that Dos Passos has not become "a weary, cynical defender of the vested interests" that many have thought him to be, but has remained a humane idealist on the side of "the people who get pushed around by big government and big business." [43] An idealist who was traumatized first by America's entrance into World War I and later by the Sacco-Vanzetti executions, Dos Passos became a militant radical and "campfollower" of the Communist Party. His alliance with the Communists, says Hicks, nevertheless remained an uneasy compromise between his own liberal and humanitarian beliefs and the Party's pragmatic aims. Yet, because Dos Passos' prestige and sincerity went unchallenged by his liberal audience, his writing rendered the Party a more valuable service than most of its members. No one "had more influence on the leftward swing of the intellectuals in the early '30s" than Dos Passos. But a third trauma, the Communists' execution of his close friend, José Robles Pazos, in Spain, finally convinced him that the Party was dedicated to increasing its own power at the expense of the individual, and precipitated his disaffiliation with radicalism. Since the Roosevelt administration, says Hicks, Dos Passos perceives that big government has become a greater threat to freedom than big business. Retaining his belief that "power corrupts" and finding no suitable "alternative to both bignesses. . . . his growing fear of government has been accompanied by a growing toleration of business."

David Sanders' thesis is that Dos Passos "has been driven to his present conservative alignment by an anarchistic philosophy which . . . now identifies [contemporary] liberalism with big government and the submergence of the individual." [44] Sanders goes back as far as *Rosinante to the Road Again* (1922), Dos

Passos' impressionistic travelogue and cultural study of Spain and its artists and intellectuals, to point out the recurrent anarchist theme in his writings. In Spain, Dos Passos, in the role of Telemachus, discovered that his own anarchistic idealism was an ingrained character trait of his Iberian ancestors. He found in the Spanish character an extreme individualism, fostered by a culture that evolved out of isolated village communities, and which had extended from the classical Spanish painters down to contemporary Spanish writers. His revolutionary sensibilities were greatly influenced by Unamuno's lesson of the artist's lonely "cry in the wilderness" and Baroja's mission as a writer "to put the acid test to existing institutions."

Sanders neglects to include in this article some of the earlier anarchist themes in Dos Passos' *One Man's Initiation*—1917 and *Three Soldiers*. But he correctly mentions that Dos Passos' anarchist sympathies did not find purposeful political direction until he committed himself to the defense of Sacco and Vanzetti, whom he believed were executed not for their alleged crime but for their anarchism. After this, the theme of anarchism became important in the organization of *U.S.A.* (1930–36) and *District of Columbia* (1939–49). In both trilogies, argues Sanders, one finds the recurrent pattern of one isolated figure representing "the anarchist pattern" and "individual self-government" (e.g., Mac, Ben Compton, Mary French, Glenn Spotswood, Millard Carroll, Paul Graves) standing up to, but being defeated by, an entire lineup of corrupt institutions.

Chester E. Eisinger's interpretation of Dos Passos' relationship to the "new liberalism" movement supports the views of Hicks and Sanders by also emphasizing Dos Passos' basic distrust of centralized power.[45] Eisinger's view is that during the critical thirties, Dos Passos, like Orwell, Silone, Hicks, Schlesinger, McCarthy, and Trilling, rejected such utopian ideologies as communism and fascism for a more skeptical and self-critical view of man and society. In place of total solutions, he "returned to the American tradition of improvisation and experimentalism" in order to preserve and improve the working of democratic government in this country.

However, says Eisinger, Dos Passos' new liberalism "lies more in what he has rejected than in what he has embraced." Once an old-fashioned liberal who nearly embraced socialism, Dos Passos turned away from the political Left, the "social-service state," and "the planned society" toward the traditional Jeffersonian conception of liberalism which stressed individualism and self-government. Says Eisinger: "Dos Passos found he could not savor the historical irony that had made Jefferson the patron saint of the liberals who, in the thirties, sanctioned the growth of the corporate state." There was further irony in the fact that Dos Passos' attack on New-Deal liberalism brought him into an apparently sympathetic relationship with the segment of the political Right that had, paradoxically, also founded its conservatism on Jeffersonian liberalism. Dos Passos' quest for individual political fulfillment, says Eisinger, identifies him with "the new liberalism"; but his nostalgic longing to return to the age of Jeffersonian agrarianism and his Whitman-like "mystical transcendental faith in the people" separate him from its empirical and self-critical attitudes.

One might, at this point, further suggest that the theory of Dos Passos as satirist is also quite relevant to his essentially conservative vision—his longing for the "good old days"—and his hostile attitude towards existing realities of the industrial society. Alvin B. Kernan, for example, has pointed out that the satiric narrator, usually present in many works of formal satire and satiric fiction from Juvenal to Philip Wylie, presents himself to his reading public in the pose of a simple, honest man whose moral code is "traditional" and "straightforward" in that he upholds the rules his fathers have passed down to him. Says Kernan:

He [the satiric persona] views life in social terms and exhorts his audience to return to the ways of their fathers, to live with fortitude, reason, chastity, honor, justice, simplicity, the virtues which make for the good life and the good society.[46]

This satiric narrator persuades the reader that "things are so bad, vice so arrant, the world so overwhelmingly wicked" that he is forced to attack these conditions because "he regards himself and his satire . . . as the only method of correction left, the last hope of mankind." Since the satirist wishes to persuade us "that vice is both ugly and rampant," says Kernan, "he deliberately distorts, excludes, and slants" his portrait of society, implying that "distortion of literal reality is necessary in order to get at the truth." Thus, paradoxically, the pose of simple, honest, and artless man is at variance with the fact that he "turns out to be the most cunning of rhetoricians, highly skilled in all the tricks of persuasion."

Returning to Eisinger, we learn that the "frustration of the Jeffersonian and Whitmanian ideal is the heart of Dos Passos' criticism of the New Deal," depicted as a corporate state that "humilitates people while professing to help them," that contains "almost vicious portraits" of those connected with the Roosevelt administration, and that ends "with the bitter charge that the President . . . has misused his power in redesigning a world in which men's freedoms are left out." Or, returning to the twenties, when Dos Passos espoused different politics, one might again quote Edmund Wilson, who questioned whether the motivation for Dos Passos' "repulsive" portrait of New York City might not be "some stubborn sentimentalism . . . some deeply buried streak of hysteria of which his misapplied resentments represent the aggressive side." [47] Are not these slanted portraits of contemporary society, one might ask, motivated by the emotional frustration of the satirist?

The possible emotional causes underlying Dos Passos' attacks upon both real and imaginary authoritarian power structures have been of primary interest to the psychological critics of Dos Passos and his work. The first of these studies, Martin Kallich's analysis of Dos Passos' political attitudes, agrees with David Sanders' interpretation of Dos Passos' anarchism, but links this anarchism to an underlying "Oedipus complex." [48] Since Dos Passos' parents were members of the upperclass, says Kallich, his youthful anarchism did not result from poverty or economic exploitation, but from a neurotic rebellion against the authority of his father, the lawyer, John Randolph Dos Passos. To substantiate his theory, Kallich points out the recurrent pattern of the Vag hero who values "absolute or primitive liberty" above all and to the predominance of dead or absent father figures in Dos Passos' fiction. He characterizes Dos Passos' anarchism as passing through three fundamental stages: the individualist, the socialist, and the conservative. After his initial anarchistic revolt against parental authority, says Kallich, Dos Passos' quest for purpose and emotional security forsworn by his rejection of his family led him to accept "an authoritative complex of ideas associated with socialism" as a parental surrogate. But finding submission to the demands of "collectivist socialist discipline" too taxing upon his rugged-individualistic temperament, he ultimately rejected it and returned to the laissez-faire values of his father's class.

Kallich's psychological interpretation, although perhaps too simplistic in its approach to both Freud and Dos Passos, is useful in locating a possible neurotic basis for Dos Passos' political shifts and can be further substantiated by referring to probable psychological deprivations caused by Dos Passos' illegitimacy and his father's denial of open recognition and family name until he was sixteen years old. However, as Kallich himself seems to recognize, this kind of approach tends to oversimplify Dos Passos' motivational pattern so as to disregard important rational and moral considerations behind his social consciousness. It also leads Kallich to the oversimplified conclusion that "liberty, in reverse, has carried him from the class of the weak underdog to

that of the strong topdog." As Hicks more correctly
points out, Dos Passos has remained sympathetic to the
individual underdog, although, certainly, his villains
have changed along with his conception of which groups
represent the oppressive "topdog."

For example, in *Midcentury*, Dos Passos levels a
blistering attack against the bureaucratic structure of
large unions that he believes favors those who have
mediocre abilities and who perpetuate their own power
at the expense of the ordinary union member. But Dos
Passos, I believe, does not attack the idea of unionism.
In the narrative, the honest "underdog" union organizer,
Terry Bryant, is thrown out of one union and later
murdered by the hired killer of a corrupt taxicab syn-
dicate. Also in the narrative and through the autobiographical reflections of Blackie Bowman, the disillusioned ex-Wobbly (one of his most sympathetic and
successful portraits to date), Dos Passos exposes the
greed and favoritism of both big-business executives and
union officials (who, by the way, play the stock market
with their unearned incomes). Consistent with his intentions in *U.S.A.*, he still supports individual honesty
against the presumed villainous power groups that dominate a particular era.

A more satisfying blend of psychology and literary
criticism, though indebted to Kallich's analysis, is
Blanche Gelfant's important study of the "identity"
theme in Dos Passos' fiction.[49] Although Mrs. Gelfant
hesitates to make the "clear-cut equation" that Kallich
does between Dos Passos and his heroes, her examination of the recurrent behavioral pattern of Dos Passos'
"generic hero" (Howe, Andrews, Herf, Spotswood,
Perkins, Graves, Pignatelli) leads back by implication to
Dos Passos' own possible neurotic compulsions, and
ultimately becomes the basis for her appraisal of
his supposed historical inaccuracies. Starting with the
fragmentary images of the Camera Eye (*U.S.A.*) and
with Jay Pignatelli's memories (*Chosen Country*) —
commonly assumed to be Dos Passos' own autobiograph-

ical reflections—Mrs. Gelfant proceeds through Dos Passos' other works, describing the generic hero's futile attempts to find inner stability, belonging, and purpose, by surrendering his individuality to an authoritarian institution or by immersing himself in a social cause. The hero's early ambivalence towards his parents and their success values, his romantic adolescent fantasies about the freedom and virility of "low-class" muckers and vags, and his eventual revolutionary anarchism and actual attainment of freedom from parental restriction, offer no solution for his feelings of alienation, insecurity, and boredom. Consequently, he attempts to rid himself of his egotism and lack of purpose by conforming to the goals of some public institution or group such as the Army or the Communist Party. This pattern also ends in failure. The hero cannot reconcile either his personal needs with the requirements of authority, or his personal sense of morality with the group's institutional expediency.

Following Kallich's line of analysis, Mrs. Gelfant finds that Dos Passos' generic hero—and by implication, the author himself—later returns to the values of his father. She finds two kinds of resolutions to the hero's identity problem. First, in *The Grand Design* (1949), there is the shift of personal responsibility for the hero's failure to the outer—always oppressive—instutution, in this case, the corrupt New Deal administration. Thus, Dos Passos' generic hero (Perkins, Graves) "need no longer recriminate himself for his ineffectuality: he has been blamelessly overwhelmed by a political clique . . . which is his enemy as well as the enemy of his country, the obstacle to his self-fulfillment and the fulfillment of America's founding dreams." With this transfer of guilt and hatred from himself to the outer political and social sphere, the generic hero can now accept both his country and himself. Secondly, as depicted in *Chosen Country* (1951), the hero returns to the values of his father and his father's class, resolves his "success" ambivalence, and finds a renewed sense of belonging. Jay Pignatelli marries a girl who resembles his mother, chooses his father's profession of law, and identifies himself with the idealism of his American heritage.

Although Mrs. Gelfant focuses upon the compulsive pattern of the generic hero rather than upon Dos Passos himself, the close parallels between the attitudes of his heroes and the expressed statements and political shifts of Dos Passos himself suggest that Dos Passos has been projecting—indeed, almost working out—his emotional conflicts in his fiction. His shift of public roles—from destructive revolutionary critic to preserver of his country's democratic heritage, and the different writing styles that have characterized these roles—can be interpreted as changes in the writer's masks or personae: his poses or facades that hide an insecurity about his inner identity. This transference of his own emotional self-hatred, guilt, and frustration into the public arena of his fiction also provides a psychological explanation for the satirist's slanted interpretations of historical figures and events to which his critics have alluded.

The parallels between the attitudes of Dos Passos and his heroes are so close that even Mrs. Gelfant has a difficult time separating them. For example, at one point in her discussion it is ambiguous to the reader whether she is referring to the generic hero of *The Grand Design* or the "compulsive" Dos Passos himself when she says:

> There is then a new target for his pent-up resentments and frustrations—Roosevelt, his satellites, and the New Deal, the entire Democratic administration and its policies. His animosity against these frustrating elements can be no less than the hatred he has for so long borne against himself, and its expression can be no less vehement.

Thus, the generic hero (Dos Passos?) "loses perspective and objectivity" and becomes "less and less capable of making valid social judgments" because these judgments are increasingly affected by the psychological projection of the hero's personal problems. Mrs. Gelfant is careful, however, to qualify her views of the hero's psychic conflict to allow for the fact that his criticism might be to some extent valid:

> That these hatreds imply social and moral judgments which call for the reader's consideration must be recognized. But it must also be recognized that these hatreds are always implicated in the character's neurotic pattern of inner need and self-defeating conflict. The hero's inner compulsion to define himself through a social role in turn defines the novels . . . and it gives them also their pertinence and moving power, for this problem of achieving a whole and innerly motivated "real" identity is one of the characteristic and driving problems of our time.

Dos Passos is without doubt one of the most appropriate literary subjects of the post-World War I period for the comparative approach used by several critics and scholars in their studies of his work. More internationally minded than most of his contemporaries, Dos Passos was an astute observer of trends in various art forms, a competent painter, a dramatist and set designer, and one of the most skillful literary adaptors of technical innovations associated with such European avant-garde art movements as impressionism, cubism, expressionism, futurism, and surrealism. In the craft of fiction, the young Dos Passos' "true Penelope" of style was Flaubert (who also served as an important model for Henry James, Ernest Hemingway, and other American exiles abroad). But in addition to studying such literary models as Flaubert, Joyce, and the French symbolists, Dos Passos probably adapted many of the striking visual techniques of painters, dramatists, and film directors, and the staccato effects and harmonic dissonances of jazz music into his dynamic sight and sound panoramas of modern urban society.

Critics who have discovered interesting analogies be-

tween Dos Passos' fiction and the other arts point out
that Dos Passos' literary style was maturing during an
era of great revolutionary fervor and stimulating interaction among all the arts—a fervor resulting from,
among other things, the upheavals produced by the War
and the excitement about the revolutionary political
developments in Russia. With the models of Picasso's
cubism, Stieglitz's photography, the documentary and
expressionistic films of New York's mass culture created
by Paul Strand and Fritz Lang, the symbolic dramas
of O'Neill and Rice, and the montage techniques of
D. W. Griffith and Sergei Eisenstein before him, Dos
Passos created unique visual effects in an attempt to
produce a simultaneous visual-emotive impact upon the
reader analogous to the way Eisenstein, for example,
was using the technique of montage juxtaposition to
produce, through visual conflict, an ideological concept
in the minds of his viewers.

Besides the work of such perceptive French scholars as Claude-Edmonde Magny [50] and Georges-Albert
Astre,[51] the essays of Ben Stoltzfus, Richard Lehan,
Marshall McLuhan, and George Knox represent the
beginning of documentation of these relationships and
influences between Dos Passos' fiction and the other
arts.[52] On the basis of Dos Passos' own statements about
his literary indebtedness to the poets and painters of
the cubist and futurist schools and the statements of
Jean-Paul Sartre, the French existentialist, acknowledg-
ing the technical impact of Dos Passos' work upon the
generation of post-World War II French writers, Stoltzfus and Lehan have substantiated with some success
these French-American reciprocal influences. Stoltzfus
is concerned with the early European sources and influences upon Dos Passos, while Lehan places the texts
of the trilogies of Sartre and Dos Passos side by side and
examines the similarity of particular techniques and
themes.

Ben Stoltzfus emphasizes Dos Passos' internationally
cultivated sensibility, and thus disregards important

American influences.[53] First, he alludes, rather inconclusively, to possible technical antecedents in the works of Flaubert, Balzac, Zola, and Rolland. He then makes some interesting analogies between the "telegram" and "collage" poetry of Cendrars and Apollonaire which imitated the cubists' *simultanéisme* and the futurists' dynamism, and similar techniques used by Dos Passos in the prose-poems of *Manhattan Transfer*, and in the Camera Eyes, Newsreels, and biographies of *U.S.A.* More convincingly, Stoltzfus makes an extended comparison between the collectivist techniques of Jules Romains (his *unanimisme*) and Dos Passos. Comparing Romains' *Verdun* with Dos Passos' *Three Soldiers*, and *Les hommes de bonne volonté* with *U.S.A.*, Stoltzfus points out some interesting similarities, but acknowledges that neither Dos Passos nor Romains has recognized the other as an influence and that each has used the collectivist technique with an essentially different intention. Whereas Romains has stressed the social cohesiveness and spiritual unanimity possible among groups in emerging urbanism, Dos Passos has emphasized the spiritually destructive forces of isolation and alienation produced by the mass culture of the city. However, says Stoltzfus, both men are moralists, "architects of history," who have attempted to influence their generation by shaping the chaotic events of life into a coherent artistic form.

Richard Lehan [54] also discusses some similarities and differences in the collectivist techniques of Dos Passos and Sartre. Both men, he says, have adapted the film technique of montage juxtaposition as a means of relating the similar experiences of a variety of characters as they react to a common historical situation. Whereas Dos Passos depicts his characters as commonly immersed in the sexual abandonment and scramble for wealth that characterized the frenetic post-World War I period in the United States, Sartre portrays the collective "bad-faith" and inauthenticity of his characters during the crucial Munich conference in 1938, relating their individual moral failures to the collective moral decay of Europe, the rise of Hitler, and the beginning of World War II. Lehan also observes that Sartre probably borrowed Dos Passos' technique of simultaneously shifting between subjective and objective—the individual and the collective consciousness—as a means of dramatizing certain of his own existential concepts.

A probable literary influence upon Dos Passos that is often mentioned by critics and scholars is the work of James Joyce, perhaps the most technically influential novelist of our century. Dos Passos has mentioned several times that he read Joyce's *Portrait of the Artist as a Young Man* and *The Dubliners* while at Harvard, and *Ulysses* aboard ship returning from the Near East to New York in 1921.[55] Also, in a preface to a later edition of *Three Soldiers* (1932) Dos Passos has acknowledged the important example of Joyce's work to contemporary writers who wish to contribute anything of lasting value to their own age. While Joseph Warren Beach and others have suggested the influence of Joyce's "abstract composition" and "stream of consciousness" style, much remains to be examined and systematically documented in this area. Marshall McLuhan's interesting comparison between the two writers, though providing some information about their technical similarities, is more concerned with the way their different cultural backgrounds affect their treatment of man in modern society.[56]

McLuhan starts with the perhaps too confident assumption that because their impressionistic treatments of the modern city as a "discontinuous landscape" are strikingly similar, Dos Passos' fiction would not exist in its present form if he had not read Joyce. But his main point is that Joyce's vision of the human condition is more profound and his characterizations more convincing than those of Dos Passos. Joyce, says McLuhan, accepts evil as a universal principle of all human society, and is therefore able to manipulate a continuous parallel between the historical past and present to make the characters of modern Dublin representatives of the human condition. Joyce's method is therefore truly impersonal and "analogical."

But, says McLuhan, Dos Passos' view of man, conditioned by transcendental optimism and Jeffersonian idealism, is more limited. He cannot accept evil as being intrinsic to human nature and therefore attributes the suffering of his urban inhabitants to the mechanized impersonality of the city and to the shortcomings of centralized government, besides blaming his characters for failing to be true to the Jeffersonian dream. His treatment of the present age is not truly analogical as is Joyce's because he refers to the past only to expose the moral degeneration of contemporary America. Though Dos Passos' technique, like Joyce's, is impressionistic and his method impersonal, Dos Passos' intention, says McLuhan, is satirical, a fact which limits both his emotional response to, and his ethical view of, his characters. Although valuable in calling attention to some differences between the methods and intentions of these two writers, McLuhan's essay tends to judge the supposed shortcomings of Dos Passos' work on the basis of a Joycean standard of realism with its accompanying objectivity and impersonality (no doubt oversimplifying Joyce's intentions in the process, for example, his satirical way of pointing up the diminished significance of man in the modern epoch). His distinctions fail to consider Dos Passos' effectiveness as a satirist, and the fact that his different intention necessarily called for a different treatment of both character and environment.

George Knox's imaginative essay points out some of the many interesting pictorial analogies in Dos Passos' poetry and fiction in order to suggest the likely possibility that Dos Passos' experiences as an amateur painter and careful student of the visual arts were incorporated into his writing style.[57] His essay also contributes much toward substantiating the often vague generalizations others have made about poetry-painting analogies in Dos Passos' work and toward clarifying just how such indis-

criminately used terms as "impressionistic" and "expressionistic" really apply to his fiction.

Knox traces Dos Passos' stylistic development from
his early impressionistic treatment of light and shadow
for its own sake, to the broken color, distorted surfaces,
and syncopated rhythms of his later symbolic and social
mode of penetrating through the object in order to link
image and idea. Thus, Dos Passos' stylistic development
is shown to parallel historical changes in the pictorial
arts from impressionism to expressionism, cubism, and
surrealism. After comparing Knox's pictorial treatment
and Mrs. Gelfant's literary treatment of Dos Passos'
"abstract realism," one appreciates Dos Passos' virtuosity in creating visual images—objective correlatives
—that symbolically suggest the spiritual wasteland of
the modern city (as the imagery of Baudelaire, Joyce,
and Eliot had suggested earlier).

Finally, Knox's discussion of George Grosz's satirical
method is especially relevant to the consideration of the
style and intention of Dos Passos' fiction. Iconoclastic
in attitude and revolutionary in form, Grosz's work
depicted the greed, cruelty, and violence of postwar
German urban life in the disjunctive and distorted perspectives of the cubists and surrealists. He used, says
Knox, "a kind of abstractionist sectioning that Dos
Passos may have simulated in *Manhattan Transfer*
and *U.S.A.*" In this connection it is important to remember that Dos Passos once declared that his discovery
of Grosz's work in Paris during World War I "was
finding a brilliant new weapon. . . . Looking at his
work was a release from hatred, like hearing well-im-
agined and properly balanced strings of cusswords." [58]
Grosz, said Dos Passos, was a satirist and moralist who,
like Swift, "was full of the horror of life." Consequently,
he felt compelled to force his nightmare vision of man's
irrationality upon his audience in order to relieve his
anger and cut through the kind of moral complacency
that allows violence and injustice to exist. Dos Passos'
enthusiasm for Grosz's work suggests that he, too,

Introduction lxi

wished to combine a "visual freshness with a bitter satirical intensity that few complacencies can survive."

I wish to thank the Humanities Committee of the Desert Research Institute for financial assistance that allowed me some time off from teaching duties during summer 1968, to work on this book. Thanks also to the reference and circulation staffs of the Getchell Library at the University of Nevada, Reno, for helping me locate materials on Dos Passos found in this book. I am especially grateful to Professor Charlton Laird for reading the first draft of this Introduction and contributing pertinent suggestions, and to Professors Bruce R. McElderry and Charles Metzger at the University of Southern California for their knowledgeable guidance through Dos Passos' work some years back. Finally, I wish to thank Meredith Hoffman and Lynn Herman for their help in typing parts of the manuscript, and my wife, Francine, for bearing the discomforts of solitude and for many helpful suggestions concerning the manuscript.

ALLEN BELKIND

Reno, Nevada
Fall, 1970

Dos Passos, the Critics,
and the Writer's Intention

Dos Passos and the "Lost Generation"

ALFRED KAZIN

A chapter in the moral history of modern American writing does come to an end with Hemingway and the lost generation, and nowhere can this be more clearly seen than in the work of John Dos Passos, who rounds out the story of that generation and carries its values into the social novel of the thirties. For what is so significant about Dos Passos is that though he is a direct link between the post-war decade and the crisis novel of the depression period, the defeatism of the lost generation has been slowly and subtly transferred by him from persons to society itself. It is society that becomes the hero of his work, society that suffers the anguish and impending sense of damnation that the lost-generation individualists had suffered alone before. For him the lost generation becomes all the lost generations from the beginning of modern time in America—all who have known themselves to be lost in the fires of war or struggling up the icy slopes of modern capitalism. The tragic "I" has become the tragic inclusive "we" of modern society; the pace of sport, of the separate peace and the separate death, has become the pounding rhythm of the industrial machine. The central beliefs of his generation, though they have a different source in Dos Passos and a different expression, remain hauntingly the same. Working in politics and technology as Fitzgerald worked in the high world and Hemingway

From *On Native Grounds*, copyright, 1942, by Alfred Kazin. Reprinted by permission of Harcourt, Brace & World, Inc.

in war and sport, Dos Passos comes out with all his equations zero. They are almost too perfectly zero, and always uneasy and reluctantly defeatist. But the record of his novels from *One Man's Initiation* to *Adventures of a Young Man*, whatever the new faith revealed in his hymn to the American democratic tradition in *The Ground We Stand On*, is the last essential testimony of his generation, and in many respects the most embittered.

Dos Passos's zero is not the "nada hail nada full of nada" of Hemingway's most famous period, the poetically felt nihilism and immersion in nothingness; nor is it the moody and ambiguous searching of Fitzgerald. The conviction of tragedy that rises out of his work is the steady protest of a sensitive democratic conscience against the tyranny and the ugliness of society, against the failure of a complete human development under industrial capitalism; it is the protest of a man who can participate formally in the struggles of society as Hemingway and Fitzgerald never do. To understand Dos Passos's social interests is to appreciate how much he differs from the others of his generation, and yet how far removed he is from the Socialist crusader certain Marxist critics once saw in him. For what is central in Dos Passos is not merely the fascination with the total operations of society, but his unyielding opposition to all its degradations. He cannot separate the "I" and society absolutely from each other, like Hemingway, for though he is essentially even less fraternal in spirit, he is too much the conscious political citizen. But the "I" remains as spectator and victim, and it is that conscientious intellectual self that one hears in all his work, up to the shy and elusive autobiography in the "Camera Eye" sections of *U.S.A.* That human self in Dos Passos is the Emersonian individual, not Hemingway's agonist; he is the arbiter of existence, always a little chill, a little withdrawn (everything in Dos Passos radiates around the scrutiny of the camera eye), not the sentient, suffering center of it. He is man believing and trusting in the Emersonian "self-trust" when all else fails him, man taking his stand on individual integrity against the pressures of society. But he is not Hemingway's poetic man. What Emerson once said of himself in his journal is particularly true of Dos Passos: he likes Man, not men.

Dos Passos certainly came closer to Socialism than most artists in his generation; yet it is significant that no novelist in America has written more somberly of the dangers to individual integrity in a centrally controlled society. Spain before the war had meant for Hemingway the bullfighters, Pamplona, the golden wine; for Dos Passos it had meant the Spanish Anarchists and the Quixotic dream he described so affectionately in his early travel book, *Rosinante to the Road Again.* Yet where Hemingway found his "new hope" in the Spanish Civil War, Dos Passos saw in that war not merely the struggle into which his mind had entered as a matter of course, the agony of the Spain with which he had always felt spiritual ties, but the symbolic martyrdom of Glenn Spotswood, the disillusioned former Communist, at the hands of the OGPU in Spain in *Adventures of a Young Man.* Hemingway could at least write *For Whom the Bell Tolls* as the story of Robert Jordan's education; Dos Passos had to write his Spanish novel as the story of Glenn Spotswood's martyrdom. And what is so significant in Dos Passos's work always is individual judgment and martyrdom, the judgment that no fear can prevent his heroes from making on society, the martyrdom that always waits for them at its hands. That last despairing cry of Glenn Spotswood's in the prison of the Loyalists—"I, Glenn Spotswood, being of sound mind and emprisoned body, do bequeath to the international working-class my hope of a better world"—is exactly like the cry of the poilu in Dos Passos's callow first novel, *One Man's Initiation*—"Oh, the lies, the lies, the lies, the lies that life is smothered in! We must strike once more for freedom, for the sake of the dignity of man. Hopelessly, cynically, ruthlessly, we must rise and show at least that we are not taken in; that we are slaves but not willing slaves." From Martin Howe to Glenn Spotswood, the Dos Passos hero is the young man who fails and is broken by society, but is never taken in. Whatever else he loses—and the Dos Passos characters invariably lose, if they have ever possessed, almost everything that is life to most people —he is not taken in. Hemingway has "grace under pressure," and the drama in his work is always the inherently passionate need of life: the terrible insistence on the individual's need of survival, the drumming fear that he may not survive. Dos Passos, though he has so intense an imagination, has not Hemingway's grace, his need to make so dark and tonal a poetry of defeat; he centers everything around the inviolability of the individual, his sanctity. The separation of the individual from society in Hemingway may be irrevocable, but it is tragically felt; his cynicism can seem so flawless and dramatic only because it mocks itself. In Dos Passos that separation is organic and self-willed: the mind has made its refusal, and the fraternity that it seeks and denies in the same voice can never enter into it.

It is in this concern with the primacy of the individual, with his need to save the individual from society rather than to establish him in or over it, that one can trace the conflict that runs all through Dos Passos's work— between his estheticism and strong social interests; his profound absorption in the total operations of modern society and his overscrupulous withdrawal from all of them; the iron, satirical prose he hammered out in U.S.A. (a machine prose for a machine world) and the youthful, stammering lyricism that pulses under it. Constitutionally a rebel and an outsider, in much of his work up to U.S.A. a pale and self-conscious esthete, Dos Passos is at once the most precious of the lost-generation writers and the first of the American "technological" novelists, the first to bring the novel squarely into the Machine Age and to use its rhythms, its stock piles of tools and people, in his books.

Dos Passos has never reached the dramatic balance of

Hemingway's great period, the ability to concentrate all the resources of his sensibility at one particular point. The world is always a gray horror, and it is forever coming undone; his mind is forever quarreling with itself. It is only because he has never been able to accept a mass society that he has always found so morbid a fascination in it. The modern equation cancels out to zero, everything comes undone, the heroes are always broken, and the last figure in *U.S.A.*, brooding like Dos Passos himself over that epic of failure, is a starving and homeless boy walking alone up the American highway. Oppression and inequity have to be named and protested, as the democratic conscience in Dos Passos always does go on protesting to the end. Yet what he said of Thorstein Veblen in one of the most brilliantly written biographies in *U.S.A.* is particularly true of himself: he can "never get his mouth round the essential yes." The protest is never a Socialist protest, because that will substitute one collectivity for another; nor is it poetic or religious, because Dos Passos's mind, while sensitive and brilliant in inquiry, is steeped in materialism. It is a radical protest, but it is the protest against the status quo of a mind groping for more than it can define to itself, the protest of a mind whose opposition to capitalism is no greater than his suspicion of all societies.

In Dos Passos's early work, so much of which is trivial and merely preparatory to the one important work of his career, *U.S.A.*, this conflict means the conflict between the esthete and the world even in broadly social novels like *Three Soldiers* and *Manhattan Transfer*. But under the surface of preciosity that covers those early novels, there is always the story of John Roderigo Dos Passos, grandson of a Portuguese immigrant, and like Thorstein Veblen—whose mordant insights even more than Marx's revolutionary critique give a base in social philosophy to *U.S.A.*—an outsider. Growing up with all the advantages of upper-middle-class education and travel that his own father could provide for him, Dos Passos nevertheless could not help growing up with the sense of difference which even the sensitive grandsons of immigrants can feel in America. He went to Choate and to Harvard; he was soon to graduate into the most distinguished of all the lost generation's finishing schools, the Norton-Harjes Ambulance Service subsidized by a Morgan partner; but he was out of the main line, out just enough in his own mind to make the difference that can make men what they are.

It is not strange that Dos Passos has always felt such intimate ties with the Hispanic tradition and community, or that in his very revealing little travel book, *Rosinante to the Road Again,* he mounted Don Quixote's nag and named himself Telemachus, as if to indicate that his postwar pilgrimage in Spain was, like Telemachus's search for Ulysses, a search for his own father-principle, the continuity he needed to find in Hispania. It was in Spain and in Latin America that Dos Passos learned to prize men like the Mexican revolutionary Zapata, and the libertarian Anarchists of Spain. As his travel diaries and particularly the biographical sketches that loom over the narrative in *U.S.A.* tell us, Dos Passos's heart has always gone out to the men who are lonely and human in their rebellion, not to the victors and the politicians in the social struggle, but to the great defeated—the impractical but human Spanish Anarchists, the Veblens, the good Mexicans, the Populists and the Wobblies, the Bob La Follettes, the Jack Reeds, the Randolph Bournes, all defeated and uncontrolled to the last, most of them men distrustful of too much power, of centralization, of the glib revolutionary morality which begins with hatred and terror and believes it can end with fraternity. So even the first figure in *U.S.A.,* the itinerant Fenian McCreary, "Mac," and the last, "Vag," are essentially Wobblies and "working stiffs"; so even Mary French, the most admirable character in the whole trilogy, is a defeated Bolshevik. And it is only the defeated Bolsheviks whom Dos Passos ever really likes. The undefeated seem really to defeat themselves.

The grandson of the Portuguese immigrant was also,

however, the boy who entered college, as Malcolm Cowley has pointed out, "at the beginning of a period which was later known as that of the Harvard esthetes." The intellectual atmosphere there was that of "young men who read Pater and *The Hill of Dreams,* who argued about St. Thomas in sporting houses, and who wandered through the slums of South Boston with dull eyes for 'the long rain slanting on black walls' and eager eyes for the face of an Italian woman who, in the midst of this squalor, suggested the Virgin in Botticelli's Annunciation." Dos Passos went to the slums; and he could find the Botticelli Virgin there. The *Harvard Monthly* was publishing his first pieces: a free-verse poem, an editorial, and an essay on industrialism entitled "A Humble Protest." "Are we not," asked the young author, "like men crouching on a runaway engine? And at the same time we insensately shovel in the fuel with no thought as to where we are being taken." It was but one step from this to *One Man's Initiation,* published in England in 1920, and significantly subtitled 1917. For this first of his two antiwar novels made no pretense to the hardboiled realism of *Three Soldiers.* It was the very boyish and arty memoir of a young architect-poet whose chief grievance against the war, in a way, seems to have been that he could not admire the Gothic cathedrals in France for the clamor of the guns in his ears. The hero, consciously posing himself against a Europe ravaged by war, was a pale imitation of all the pale heroes in fin-de-siècle fiction, a hand-me-down Huysmans torn between a desire to enter a monastery, a taste for architecture, and a need to write a ringing manifesto for all the embittered artist-revolutionaries in the world. "God!" exclaims Martin Howe in the trenches, "if only there were somewhere nowadays where you could flee from all this stupidity, from all this cant of governments, and this hideous reiteration of hatred, this strangling hatred."

By 1921, with *Three Soldiers,* the esthete had become something more of the social novelist. The rhetorical petulance of *One Man's Initiation* had given way to a dull, gritty hatred. No longer could Dos Passos write a sentence such as "Like the red flame of the sunset setting fire to opal sea and sky, the old exaltation, the old flame that would consume to ashes all the lies in the world, the trumpet-blast under which the walls of Jericho would fall down, stirs and broods in the womb of his grey lassitude." He was a realist whose odyssey of three buck privates—Fuselli from the West, Chrisfield from the South, John Andrews the musician from New York —was an attempt to tell in miniature the national story in the A.E.F. Yet for all the grimness of *Three Soldiers*, the sounding in it of the characteristically terse and mocking tone of Dos Passos's later social novels, it was essentially as flaky and self-consciously romantic as *One Man's Initiation*. There are three protagonists in the book, but only one hero, John Andrews; and it is his humiliation and agony in war that finally dominate the book. It is interesting to note that in this first important novel Dos Passos had already shown that interest in the type, the mass as central protagonist, that would distinguish *U.S.A.*; and certainly nothing is so good in the book as his ability to suggest the gray anonymity, the treadmill, the repeated shocks and probings of the private's experience, the hysterical barroom jokes and conclusive brothel loves, the boredom and weariness.

Yet it is even more significant that Dos Passos did sacrifice his inclusive design to John Andrews. For Andrew is what he cares most for; Andrews is a sadder and older brother to Martin Howe, the shy and esthetic and fumbling Dos Passos hero, and like the hedonists of 1919, he survives the war only to die—at least symbolically, at the hands of the military police—in the peace. Where the enemy in *One Man's Initiation* was abstract, the society at war in *Three Soldiers* is a bureaucratic horror. But the war does exist still only as something oppressive to John Andrews; the artist is against the world, and when Andrews speaks out of his full heart at the end of the book, it is to say to Jeanne: "We must live very much, we who are free to make up for all the people who are still . . . bored." The artist has no place in war, as in a sense he has no place in the industrial mass society Dos Passos has not yet discovered; war seems only the last brazen cruelty of the enemy, the outrage inflicted upon those who would live bravely and be passionately free—for art. The army is the public self (Dos Passos can never accept the public self); the artist can only conceal himself in it or die by it. "This sentient body of his, full of possibilities and hopes and desires, was only a pale ghost that depended on the other self, that suffered for it and cringed for it." And the public self wins; it always will in Dos Passos. So John Andrews, who deserted to write a great orchestral poem (around the Queen of Sheba), is captured after all; and when the police take him away, the sheets of music flutter slowly into the breeze.

Thirteen years after he had completed *Three Soldiers*, Dos Passos wrote that it was a book that had looked forward to the future. For all its bitterness, he had written it as an epilogue to the war from which men in 1919 seemed to be turning to reconstruction or even revolution. "Currents of energy seemed breaking out everywhere as young guys climbed out of their uniforms . . . in every direction the countries of the world stretched out starving and angry, ready for anything turbulent and new." He himself had gone on to Spain, Telemachus looking for the father and teasing himself because he was so callow. Spain was where the old romantic castles still remained; Spain had been neutral during the war; in Spain one might even be free of the generation "to which excess is a synonym for beauty." In Spain there were the Anarchists and tranquillity without resignation, and the kind of life that would develop a Pío Baroja, physician and baker and novelist of revolution. "It's always death," cries the friend in *Rosinante to the Road Again*, "but we must go on. . . . Many years ago I should have set out to right wrong—for no one but a man, an individual alone, can right a wrong; organization merely substitutes one wrong for another—but now. . . ." But now Telemachus is listening to Pío Baroja, whose characters, as he describes them, are so much like the characters in *Manhattan Transfer* and *U.S.A.*—"men whose nerve has failed, who live furtively on the outskirts, snatching a little joy here and there, drugging their hunger with gorgeous mirages." Baroja is a revolutionary novelist as Dos Passos only seems to be, but as Dos Passos reports Baroja's conception of the middle-class intellectual, one can see his own self-portrait:

He has not undergone the discipline which can only come from common slavery in the industrial machine, necessary for a builder. His slavery has been an isolated slavery which has unfitted him forever from becoming truly part of a community. He can use the vast power of knowledge which training has given him only in one way. His great mission is to put the acid test to existing institutions, and to strip the veils off them.

By 1925, when he published *Manhattan Transfer*, Dos Passos had come to a critical turn in his career. He had been uprooted by the war, he had fled from the peace; but he could not resolve himself in flight. More than any other American novelist of the contemporary generation, Dos Passos was fascinated by the phenomenon of a mass society in itself; but his mind had not yet begun to study seriously the configuration of social forces, the naturalism and social history, which were to become his great subject in *U.S.A.* Like so much that he wrote up to 1930, *Manhattan Transfer* is only a preparation for *U.S.A.*, and like so many of those early works, it is a mediocre, weakly written book. He had as yet no real style of his own; he has not even in *Manhattan Transfer*. But he was reaching in that book for a style and method distinctively his own; and just as the Sacco-Vanzetti case was two years later to crystallize the antagonism to American capitalist society that is the base of *U.S.A.*, so the experimental form of *Manhattan Transfer*, its attempt to play on the shuttle of the great city's life dozens of human stories representative of the mass scene (and, for Dos Passos, the mass agony), was to lead straight into the brilliantly original technique of *U.S.A.*

Yet the achievement in style and technique of *Manhattan Transfer* is curiously inconclusive and muddy. The book seems to flicker in the gaslight of Dos Passos's own confusion. Out of the endlessly changing patterns of metropolitan life he drew an image that was collective. He was all through this period working in expressionist drama, as plays like *The Garbage Man, Airways, Inc.,* and *Fortune Heights* testify; and as in the expressionist plays of Georg Kaiser and Ernst Toller, he sketched out in his novel a tragic ballet to the accompaniment of the city's music and its mass chorus. Most significantly, he was working out a kind of doggerel prose style completely removed from his early lushness, full of the slangy rhythms he had picked up in *Three Soldiers* by reproducing soldier speech, and yet suggestive of a wry and dim poetry. This new style Dos Passos evidently owed in part to contemporary poetry, and like his trick of liquefying scenes together as if in a dream sequence and fusing words to bring out their exact tonal reverberation in the mind, to James Joyce. But what this meant in *Manhattan Transfer* was that the romantic poet, the creator and double of Martin Howe and John Andrews and the novel's Jimmy Herf, had become fascinated with a kind of mass and pictorial ugliness. The book was like a perverse esthetic geometry in which all the colors of the city's scenes were daubed together madly, and all its frames jumbled. What one saw in *Manhattan Transfer* was not the broad city pattern at all, but a wistful absorption in monstrousness. The poet-esthete still stood against the world, and rejected it completely. Characteristically even the book's hero (*U.S.A.* was to have no heroes, only symbols), Jimmy Herf, moons through it only to walk out into the dawn after a last party in Greenwich Village, bareheaded and alone, to proclaim his complete disgust with the megalopolis of which he was, as the Dos Passos poet-heroes always are, the victim.

So Dos Passos himself, though torn between what he had learned from Pío Baroja and his need to take refuge in "the esthete's cell," was ready to flee again. The conflict all through his experience between the self and the world, the conflict that he had been portraying with growing irony and yet so passionately in all his works, was coming to a head. And now the social insights he had been gathering from his own personal sense of isolation, from his bitterness against the war, from Spain, were kindled by the martyrdom of Sacco and Vanzetti. More perhaps than any other American writer who fought to obtain their freedom, it can be said, Dos Passos was really educated and toughened, affected as an artist, by the long and dreary months he spent working for them outside Charlestown Prison. For many writers the Sacco-Vanzetti case was at most a shock to their acquiescent liberalism or indifference; for Dos Passos it provided immediately the catalyst (he had never been acquiescent or indifferent) his work had needed, the catalyst that made *U.S.A.* possible. It transformed his growing irritable but persistently romantic obsession with the poet's struggle against the world into a use of the class struggle as his base in art. The Sacco-Vanzetti case gave him, in a word, the beginnings of a formal conception of society; and out of the bitter realization that this society—the society Martin Howe had mocked, that John Andrews had been crushed by, that Jimmy Herf had escaped—could grind two poor Italian Anarchists to death for their opinions, came the conception of the two nations, the two Americas, that is the scaffolding of *U.S.A.*

Dos Passos knew where he stood now: the old romantic polarity had become a social polarity, and America lay irrevocably split in his mind between the owners and the dispossessed, between those who wielded the police power and the great masses of people. He began to write *The 42nd Parallel*, the first volume in *U.S.A.*, after the Sacco-Vanzetti case; and the trilogy itself draws to its end after Mary French's return from their execution in *The Big Money*. The most deeply felt writing in all of *U.S.A.* is Dos Passos's own commentary on the Sacco-Vanzetti case in the "Camera Eye," where he speaks in his own person, an eloquent hymn of compassion and rage that is strikingly different from the low-toned stream-of-consciousness prose that is usually found in the "Camera Eye" sections, and which lifts it for a moment above the studied terseness and coldness of the whole work:

> they have clubbed us off the streets   they are stronger   they are rich   they hire and fire the politicians the newspapereditors the old judges the small men with reputations the collegepresidents the wardheelers (listen businessmen collegepresidents judges America will not forget her betrayers) they hire the men with guns the uniforms the policecars the patrolwagons
>
> all right you have won   you will kill the brave men our friends tonight . . .
>
> America our nation has been beaten by strangers who have turned our language inside out who have taken the clean words our fathers spoke and made them slimy and foul
>
> their hired men sit on the judge's bench they sit back with their feet on the tables under the dome of the State House they are ignorant of our beliefs they have the dollars the guns the armed forces the powerplants
>
> they have built the electricchair and hired the executioner to throw the switch
>
> all right we are two nations

All right we are two nations. It is the two nations that compose the story of *U.S.A.* But it was the destruction of two individuals, symbolic as they were, that brought out this polarity in Dos Passos's mind, their individual martyrdom that called the book out. From first to last Dos Passos is primarily concerned with the sanctity of the individual, and the trilogy proper ends with Mary

French's defeat and growing disillusionment, with the homeless boy "Vag" alone on the road. It is not Marx's two classes and Marx's optimism that speak in *U.S.A.* at the end; it is Thorstein Veblen, who like Pío Baroja could "put the acid test to existing institutions and strip the veils off them," but "couldn't get his mouth round the essential yes." And no more can Dos Passos. *U.S.A.* is a study in the history of modern society, of its social struggles and great masses; but it is a history of defeat. There are no flags for the spirit in it, and no victory save the mind's silent victory that integrity can acknowledge to itself. It is one of the saddest books ever written by an American.

Technically *U.S.A.* is one of the great achievements of the modern novel, yet what that achievement is can easily be confused with its elaborate formal structure. For the success of Dos Passos's method does not rest primarily on his schematization of the novel into four panels, four levels of American experience—the narrative proper, the "Camera Eye," the "Biographies," and the "Newsreel." That arrangement, while original enough, is the most obvious thing in the book and soon becomes the most mechanical. The book lives by its narrative style, the wonderfully concrete yet elliptical prose which bears along and winds around the life stories in the book like a conveyor belt carrying Americans through some vast Ford plant of the human spirit. *U.S.A.* is a national epic, the first great national epic of its kind in the modern American novel; and its triumph is not the pyrotechnical display that the shuttling between the various devices seems to suggest, but Dos Passos's power to weave so many different lives together in narrative. It is possible that the narrative sections would lose much of that power if they were not so craftily built into the elaborate framework of the book. But the framework holds the book together and encloses it; the narrative makes it. The "Newsreel," the "Camera Eye," and even the very vivid and often brilliant "Biographies" are meant to lie a little outside the book always; they speak with the formal and ironic voice of History. The "Newsreel" sounds the time; the "Biographies" stand above time, chanting the stories of American leaders; the "Camera Eye" moralizes shyly in a lyric stammer upon them. But the great thing about *U.S.A.* is that though it sweeps up so many human lives together and intones their waste and illusion and defeat so steadily, we seem to be swept along with them and to see each life perfectly at the moment it passes by us.

The brilliance of the structure lies therefore not so much in its external surface design as in its internal one, in the manifold rhythms of the narrative. Each of the various narrative sections has its dominant musical mode, as it were; each of the characters is encased in his characteristic prose. Thus at the very beginning of *The 42nd Parallel*, when the "Newsreel" blares in a welcome to the new century, while General Miles falls off his horse and Senator Beveridge's toast to the new imperialist America is heard, the story of Fenian McCreary, "Mac," begins with the smell of whale-oil soap in the printer's house in Middletown. That smell, the clatter of the presses, the political arguments, the muddy streets and saloons, give the tone of Mac's life from the first, as his life—Wobbly, tramp, working stiff—sounds the emergence of labor as a dominant force in the new century. So the story of Eleanor Stoddard begins with "When she was small she hated everything," a sentence that calls up the thin-lipped rebellion and superciliousness, the artiness and desperation, of her loveless life before we have gone into it. *The 42nd Parallel* is a study in youth, of the youth of the new century, the "new America," and of all the human beings who figure in it; and it is in the world of Mac's bookselling and life on freights, of Eleanor Stoddard's rebellion against her father and Janey Williams's picnic near the falls at Georgetown, of J. Ward Moorehouse's Wilmington and the railroad boarding house Charley Anderson's mother kept in North Dakota, that we move. The narrator behind his "Camera Eye" is a little boy holding to his mother's hand, listening to his father's boasts (at the end of the book he will be on his way to France); the "Newsreel" sings out the headlines and popular songs of 1900–1916; the "Biographies" are of the magnates (Minor C. Keith, Carnegie), the wonder men of the new century (Steinmetz, Edison, Burbank), the rebels (Bryan, Debs, Bob La Follette, Big Bill Haywood).

We have just left the world of childhood behind us in *The 42nd Parallel*, but we can already hear the clatter of the conveyor belt pushing all these lives along. Everyone is sparring hard for position; the fences of life are going up. There is no expectancy in this youth, not even the sentimental poetry of adolescence. The "Newsreel" singing the lush ballads of 1906 already seems very far away; the "Biographies" are effigies in stone. The life in the narrative has become dominant; the endless pulsing drowns everything else out. Everything is hard, dry, and already a little outrageous. Johnny Moorehouse falls in love only to learn that the socially prominent girl whom he needs for his ambition is a whore. When Eleanor Stoddard's father announces his plan to marry again, he tells her it will be to a "Mrs. O'Toole, a widow with five children who kept a boardinghouse out Elsdon way." Mac, after his bitterly hard youth, leaves the Wobblies with whom he has found comradeship and the joy of battle to marry a girl who drives him almost insane; then leaves her and is thrown into the Mexican revolutions of the period. Janey Williams's life has already taken on the gray color of the offices in which she will spend her life. There are no refuges in this world, no evasions, and above all no second starts. The clamps have been laid down early, and for all time.

Yet we can feel the toneless terror of all these lives, the oppression and joylessness that seem to beat down upon us from the first, only because every narrative section is so concrete and every sentence, as Delmore Schwartz pointed out, "can expand in the reader's mind to include a whole context of experience." *U.S.A.* is perhaps the first great naturalistic novel that is primarily a triumph of style. Everything that lives in the book is wound up on the spool of that style; from the fragments of popular songs in the "Newsreel" and the clean verse structure of the "Biographies" down to the pounding beat of the narrative, the book seems to be propelled by one dynamic rhythm. The Dos Passos prose, once so uncertain and self-conscious, has here been whittled down to a sharpness that can kill; but it has by no means lost its old wistful rhetoric in *U.S.A.*, which is particularly conspicuous in the impressionist "Camera Eye" sections, and generally gives a kind of secret and mischievous color to the severely reportorial prose. Scrubby, slangy, with a kind of grim straightforwardness, it is the style of a very cunning artisan who seems to be working in these human materials as another might work in stone or wood—forever carving away, forever whittling, but never without subtle turns and a loving sense of design. It is never a "distinguished" style, beautiful in its own right; never as prismatic as Fitzgerald's or as delicately molded as Hemingway's, and there is always something fundamentally mechanical about it. But it is the style Dos Passos needs to turn the motor of the conveyor belt; it is the reportorial and satiric style needed to push along and circumscribe all these lives. With *The 42nd Parallel* we have entered into a machine world in which the rhythm of the machine has become the primal beat of all the people in it; and Dos Passos's hard, lean, mocking prose, forever sounding that beat, calling them to their deaths, has become the supreme expression of his conception of them.

Perhaps nowhere in the trilogy, save in the descending spiral of Charley Anderson's life in the first half of *The Big Money*, is Dos Passos's use of symbolic rhythm so brilliant as in the story of Joe Williams in 1919. For Joe, Janey Williams's sailor brother, is the leading protagonist of the war and the early postwar period, as J. Ward Moorehouse's ambitiousness marked the pattern of *The 42nd Parallel*. Joe's endless shuttling between the continents on rotting freighters has become the migration and rootlessness of the young American generation whom we saw growing up in *The 42nd Parallel*; and the growing stupor and meaninglessness of his life became the leit-motif of the waste and death that hold everyone in the book as in a ghostly vise. The theme of death, of the false optimism immediately after the Armistice, are sounded immediately by the narrator behind his "Camera Eye" reporting the death of his mother and the notation on the coming of peace—"tomorrow I hoped would be the first day of the first month of the first year." The "Biographies" are all studies in death and defeat, from Randolph Bourne to Wesley Everest, mutilated and lynched after the Centralia shootings in Washington in 1919; from the prose poem commemorating the dozens of lives the Unknown Soldier might have led to the death's-head portrait of J. P. Morgan ("Wars and panics on the stock exchange,/machinegunfire and arson/ . . . starvation, lice, cholera and typhus"). The "Camera Eye" can detect only "the almond smell of high explosives sending singing éclats through the sweetish puking grandiloquence of the rotting dead." And sounding its steady beat under the public surface of war is the story of Joe Williams hurled between the continents—Joe, the supreme Dos Passos cipher and victim and symbol, suffering his life with dumb unconsciousness of how outrageous his life is, and continually loaded and dropped from one ship to another like a piece of cargo.

> Twentyfive days at sea on the steamer *Argyle*, Glasgow, Captain Thompson, loaded with hides, chipping rust, daubing red lead on steel plates that were sizzling hot griddles in the sun, painting the stack from dawn to dark, pitching and rolling in the heavy dirty swell; bedbugs in the bunks in the stinking focastle, slumgullion for grub, with potatoes full of eyes and mouldy beans.

All through 1919 one can hear death being sounded. Every life in it, even J. Ward Moorehouse's, has become a corrosion, a slow descent. Richard Ellsworth Savage goes back on his early idealism and becomes a cynical but willing abetter in Moorehouse's schemes. Eveline Hutchins and Eleanor Stoddard lose all their genteel pretense to art and grapple for Moorehouse's favor. "Daughter," the Texas girl Savage has betrayed, falls to her death in an airplane. Even Ben Compton, the New York radical, soon finds himself rotting away in prison. The war for almost all of them has become an endless round of drink and travel; they have brought nothing to it and learned nothing from it save a growing consciousness of their futility. And when they all slip into the twenties and the boom with *The Big Money*, the story of Charley Anderson's precipitate rise and fall becomes the last mad parable of their existence, a carnival of greed and corruption. Beginning with Dick Savage's life on ambulances and trains over France and Italy in 1919, the pace of the trilogy has become faster and faster; now, as the war world empties into the pleasure world of *The Big Money*—New York and Detroit, Hollywood and Miami at the height of the boom—it has become a death ride. There is money in the air, money and power for Charley Anderson and Margo Dowling and Dick Savage; but as they come closer to this material triumph, their American dream, the machine has begun to spin them too rapidly. Charley Anderson can kiss the bright new century notes in his wallet, Margo can rise higher and higher in Hollywood, Dick Savage, having sold out completely, can enjoy his power at the hands of J. Ward Moorehouse; the machine has begun to strangle them; there is no joy here for anyone. All through *The Big Money* we wait for the balloon to collapse, for the death cry we hear in that last drunken drive of Charley Anderson's and his smashup.

What Waldo Frank said of Mencken is particularly relevant to Dos Passos: he brings energy to despair. Not merely does the writing in the trilogy become richer and firmer as the characters descend into the pit, but Dos Passos himself seems so imbued with an almost mystical conviction of failure that he rises to new heights in those last sections of *The Big Money* which depict the last futile efforts of the liberals and radicals to save Sacco and Vanzetti, and their later internecine quarrels. The most moving scene in all of *U.S.A.* is the scene in which Mary French, the only counterpoise to the selfishness of the other characters in *The Big Money*, becomes so exhausted by her labors for Sacco and Vanzetti that when she goes to bed she dreams that her whole world is forever coming apart, that she is climbing up a shaky hillside "among black guttedlooking houses pitching at crazy angles where steelworkers lived" and being thrown back. The conflicting hopes of Mary French, who wanted socialism, and of Charley Anderson, who wanted the big money, have brought two different kinds of failure; but it is failure that broods over them and over everyone else in *U.S.A.* in the end—over the pompous fakes like J. Ward Moorehouse, the radicals like Ben Compton, the grasping little animals like Eleanor Stoddard and Eveline Hutchins, the opportunists like Richard Ellsworth Savage. The two survivors are Margo Dowling, supreme for the moment in Hollywood, and the homeless boy "Vag," who stands alone on the Lincoln Highway, gazing up at the transcontinental plane above winging its way west, the plane full of solid and well-fed citizens glittering in the American sun, the American dream. *All right we are two nations.* And like the scaffolding of hell in *The Divine Comedy,* they are frozen into eternity; for Dos Passos there is nothing else, save the integrity of the camera eye that must see this truth and report it, the integrity and sanctity of the individual locked up in the machine world of modern society.

With *The Big Money,* published at the height of the nineteen-thirties, the story of the twenties comes to a close; but even more does it bring the story of the lost generation to a close, that generation which has stood at the peak of modern time in America as no other has. Here in *U.S.A.*, in the most ambitious of all its works, is its measure of the national life, its conception of history—and it is a history of struggle that is vain, of failure that is irrevocable, and of final despair. There is strength in *U.S.A.*, Dos Passos's own strength, the strength of the craft that can weld so many lives together and make them live so intensely before us as they pass. But for the rest it is a brilliant hetacomb, and one of the coldest and most mechanical of tragic novels. By the time we have come to the end of *U.S.A.* we begin to feel that Edmund Wilson could detect in Dos Passos before it appeared, that "his disapproval of capitalistic society becomes a distaste for all the human beings who compose it." The protest, the lost-generation "I," has taken all of them into his vision; he has given us his truth. Yet if it intones anything affirmative in the end, it is the pronouncement of young Orestes Brownson—"There is no such thing as reforming the mass without reforming the individuals who compose it." It is this conviction, rising to a bitter crescendo in *Adventures of a Young Man*, this unyielding protest against modern society on the part of a writer who has now turned back to the roots of "our storybook democracy" in works like *The Ground We Stand On* and his projected life of Thomas Jefferson, that separates Dos Passos from so many of the social novelists who follow after him in the thirties. Where he speaks of sanctity, they speak of survival; where he lives by the truth of the camera eye, they live *in* the vortex of that society which Dos Passos has always been able to measure, with hatred but not in panic, from the outside. Dos Passos is the first of the new naturalists, and *U.S.A.* is the dominant social novel of the thirties; but it is not merely a vanished social period that it commemorates: it is an individualism, a protestantism, a power of personal disassociation, that seem almost to speak from another world.

John Dos Passos
The Poet and the World

John Dos Passos is in reality two novelists. One of them is a late-Romantic, an individualist, an esthete moving about the world in a portable ivory tower; the other is a collectivist, a radical historian of the class struggle. These two authors have collaborated in all his books, but the first had the larger share in *Three Soldiers* and *Manhattan Transfer*. The second, in his more convincing fashion, has written most of *The 42nd Parallel* and almost all of *1919*. The difference between the late-Romantic and the radical Dos Passos is important not only in his own career: it also helps to explain the recent course of American fiction.

The late-Romantic tendency in his novels goes back to his years in college. After graduating from a good preparatory school, Dos Passos entered Harvard in 1912, at the beginning of a period which was later known as that of the Harvard esthetes. I have described this period elsewhere, in reviewing the poems of E. E. Cummings, but I did not discuss the ideas which underlay its picturesque manifestations, its mixture of incense, patchouli and gin, its erudition displayed before barroom mirrors, its dreams in the Cambridge subway of laurel-crowded Thessalian dancers. The esthetes themselves were not philosophers; they did not seek to define

From Malcolm Cowley, *Think Back on Us* (Carbondale and Edwardsville: Southern Illinois University Press, 1967) pp. 212–18, 298–301. Reprinted by permission of the author and publisher.

their attitude; but most of them would have subscribed to the following propositions:

That the cultivation and expression of his own sensibility are the only justifiable ends for a poet.

That originality is his principal virtue.

That society is hostile, stupid and unmanageable: it is the world of the philistines, from which it is the poet's duty and privilege to remain aloof.

That the poet is always misunderstood by the world. He should, in fact, deliberately make himself misunderstandable, for the greater glory of art.

That he triumphs over the world, at moments, by mystically including it within himself: these are his moments of *ecstasy*, to be provoked by any means in his power—alcohol, drugs, madness or saintliness, venery, suicide.

That art, the undying expression of such moments, exists apart from the world; it is the poet's revenge on society.

That the past has more dignity than the present.

There are a dozen other propositions which might be added to this unwritten manifesto, but the ideas I have listed were those most generally held, and they are sufficient to explain the intellectual atmosphere of the young men who read *The Hill of Dreams*, and argued about St. Thomas in Boston bars, and contributed to *The Harvard Monthly*. The attitude was not confined to one college and one magazine. It was often embodied in *The Dial*, which for some years was almost a postgraduate edition of *The Monthly*; it existed in earlier publications like *The Yellow Book* and *La Revue Blanche*; it has a history, in fact, almost as long as that of the upper middle class under capitalism. For the last half-century it has furnished the intellectual background of poems and essays without number. It would seem to preclude, in its adherents, the objectivity that is generally associated with good fiction; yet the esthetes themselves sometimes wrote novels, as did their predecessors all over the world. Such novels, in fact, are still being published, and favorably criticised: "Mr. Zed has written the absorbing story of a talented musician tortured by the petty atmosphere of the society in which he is forced to live. His wife, whom the author portrays with witty malice, prevents him from breaking away. After an unhappy love affair and the failure of his artistic hopes, he commits suicide. . . ."

Such is the plot forever embroidered in the type of fiction that ought to be known as the art novel. There are two essential characters, two antagonists, the Poet and the World. The Poet—who may also be a painter, a violinist, an inventor, an architect or a Centaur—is generally to be identified with the author of the novel, or at least with the novelist's ideal picture of himself. He tries to assert his individuality in despite of the World, which is stupid, unmanageable and usually victorious. Sometimes the Poet triumphs, but the art novelists seem to realize, as a class, that the sort of hero they describe is likely to be defeated in the sort of society which he must face. This society is rarely presented in accurate terms. So little is it endowed with reality, so great is the author's solicitude for the Poet, that we are surprised to see him vanquished by such a shadowy opponent. It is as if we were watching motion pictures in the darkhouse of his mind. There are dream pictures, nightmare pictures; at last the walls crash in and the Poet disappears without ever knowing what it was all about; he dies by his own hand, leaving behind him the memory of his ecstatic moments and the bitter story of his failure, now published as a revenge on the world of the philistines.

The art novel has many variations. Often the World is embodied in the Poet's wife, whose social ambitions are the immediate cause of his defeat. Or the wife may be painted in attractive colors: she is married to a mediocre Poet who finally and reluctantly accepts her guidance, abandons his vain struggle for self-expression, and finds that mediocrity has its own consolations, its country clubs and business triumphs—this is the form in which the art novel is offered to readers of *The Saturday*

Evening Post. Or again the Poet may be a woman who fights for the same ambitions, under the same difficulties, as her male prototypes. The scene of the struggle may be a town on the Minnesota prairies, an English rectory, an apartment on Washington Square or Beacon Hill; but always the characters are the same; the Poet and the World continue their fatal conflict; the Poet has all our sympathies. And the novelists who use this plot for the thousandth time are precisely those who believe that originality is a writer's chief virtue.

Many are unconscious of this dilemma. The story rises so immediately out of their lives, bursts upon them with such freshness, that they never recognize it as a family tale. Others deliberately face the problem and try to compensate for the staleness of the plot by the originality of their treatment. They experiment with new methods of story-telling—one of which, the stream of consciousness, seems peculiarly fitted to novels of this type. Perhaps they invest their characters with new significance, and rob them of any real significance, by making them symbolic. They adopt new manners, poetic, mystical, learned, witty, allusive, or obfuscatory; and often, in token of their original talent, they invent new words and new ways of punctuating simple declarative sentences. Not all their ingenuity is wasted. Sometimes they make valuable discoveries; a few of the art novels, like *The Hill of Dreams*, are among the minor masterpieces of late-Romantic literature; and a very few, like *A Portrait of the Artist as a Young Man*, are masterpieces pure and simple.

Dos Passos' early books are neither masterpieces nor are they pure examples of the art novel. The world was always real to him, painfully real; it was never veiled with mysticism and his characters were rarely symbolic. Yet consider the plot of a novel like *Three Soldiers*. A talented young musician, during the War, finds that his sensibilities are being outraged, his aspirations crushed, by society as embodied in the American Army. He deserts after the Armistice and begins to write a great orchestral poem. When the military police come to arrest him, the sheets of music flutter one by one into the spring breeze; and we are made to feel that the destruction of this symphony, this ecstatic song choked off and dispersed on the wind, is the real tragedy of the War. Some years later, in writing *Manhattan Transfer*, Dos Passos seemed to be undertaking a novel of a different type, one which tried to render the color and movement of a whole city; but the book, as it proceeds, becomes the story of Jimmy Herf (the Poet) and Ellen Thatcher (the Poet's wife), and the Poet is once again frustrated by the World: he leaves a Greenwich Village party after a last drink of gin and walks out alone, bare-headed, into the dawn. It is obvious, however, that a new conflict has been superimposed on the old one: the social ideas of the novelist are now at war with his personal emotions, which remain those of *The Dial* and *The Harvard Monthly*. Even in 1919, this second conflict persists, but less acutely; the emotional values themselves are changing, to accord with the ideas; and the book as a whole belongs to a new category.

1919 is distinguished, first of all, by the very size of the project its author has undertaken. A long book in itself, containing 473 pages, it is merely the second chapter, as it were, of a novel which will compare in length with *Ulysses*, perhaps even with *Remembrance of Things Past*. Like the latter, it is a historical novel dealing with the yesterday that still exists in the author's memory. It might almost be called a news novel, since it uses newspaper headlines to suggest the flow of events, and tells the story of its characters in reportorial fashion. But its chief distinction lies in the author's emphasis. He is not recounting the tragedy of bewildered John Smith, the rise of ambitious Mary Jones, the efforts of sensitive Richard Robinson to maintain his ideals against the blundering malice of society. Such episodes recur in this novel, but they are seen in perspective. The real hero of *The 42nd Parallel* and *1919* is society itself, American society as embodied in forty or fifty representative characters who drift along with it, struggle to change its course, or merely to find a secure footing—perhaps they build a raft of wreckage, grow fat on the refuse floating about them; perhaps they go under in some obscure eddy—while always the current sweeps them onward toward new social horizons. In this sense, Dos Passos has written the first American collective novel.

The principal characters are brought forward one at a time; the story of each is told in bare, straightforward prose. Thus, J. Ward Moorehouse, born in Wilmington, Delaware, begins his business career in a real-estate office. He writes songs, marries and divorces a rich woman, works for a newspaper in Pittsburgh—at the end of fifty-seven pages he is a successful public-relations counselor embarked on a campaign to reconcile labor and capital at the expense of labor. Joe and Janey Williams are the children of a tugboat captain from Washington, D. C.; Janey studies shorthand; Joe plays baseball, enlists in the Navy, deserts after a brawl and becomes a merchant seaman. Eleanor Stoddard is a poor Chicago girl who works at Marshall Field's; she learns how to speak French to her customers and order waiters about "with a crisp little refined moneyed voice." All these characters, first introduced in *The 42nd Parallel*, reappear in 1919, where they are joined by others: Richard Ellsworth Savage, a Kent School boy who goes to Harvard and writes poetry; Daughter, a warm-hearted flapper from Dallas, Texas; Ben Compton, a spectacled Jew from Brooklyn who becomes a Wobbly. Gradually their careers draw closer together, till finally all of them are caught up in the War.

"This whole goddam war's a gold brick," says Joe Williams. "It ain't on the level, it's crooked from A to Z. No matter how it comes out, fellows like us get the shitty end of the stick, see? Well, what I say is all bets is off . . . every man go to hell in his own way . . . and three strikes is out, see?" Three strikes is out for Joe, when his skull is cracked in a saloon brawl at St.

Nazaire, on Armistice night. Daughter is killed in an airplane accident; she provoked it herself in a fit of hysteria after being jilted by Dick Savage—who for his part survives as the shell of a man, all the best of him having died when he decided to join the Army and make a career for himself and let his pacifist sentiments go hang. Benny Compton gets ten years in Atlanta prison as a conscientious objector. Everybody in the novel suffers from the War and finds his own way of going to hell—everybody except the people without bowels, the empty people like Eleanor Stoddard and J. Ward Moorehouse, who stuff themselves with the proper sentiments and make the right contacts.

The great events that preceded and followed the Armistice are reflected in the lives of all these people; but Dos Passos has other methods, too, for rendering the sweep of history. In particular he has three technical devices which he uses both to broaden the scope of the novel and to give it a formal unity. The first of these consists of what he calls "Newsreels," a combination of newspaper headlines, stock-market reports, official communiqués and words from popular songs. The Newsreels effectively perform their function in the book, that of giving dates and atmospheres, but in themselves, judged as writing, they are not successful. The second device is a series of nine biographies interspersed through the text. Here are the lives, briefly told, of three middle-class rebels, Jack Reed, Randolph Bourne and Paxton Hibben; of three men of power, Roosevelt, Wilson and J. P. Morgan; and of three proletarian heroes. All these are successful both in themselves and in relation to the novel as a whole; and the passage dealing with the Wobbly martyr, Wesley Everest, is as powerful as anything Dos Passos has ever written.

The "Camera Eye," which is the third device, introduces more complicated standards of judgment. It consists in the memories of another character, presumably the author, who has adventures similar to those of his characters, but describes them in a different style, one which suggests Dos Passos' earlier books. The "Camera Eye" gives us photographs rich in emotional detail:

Ponte Decimo   in Ponte Decimo ambulances were parked in a moonlit square of bleak stone working-people's houses   hoarfrost covered everything   in the little bar the Successful Story Writer taught us to drink cognac and maraschino half and half
havanuzzerone
it turned out he was not writing what he felt he wanted to be writing   What can you tell them at home about the war?   it turned out he was not wanting what he wrote he wanted to be feeling cognac and maraschino   was no longer young (It made us damn sore we greedy for what we felt we wanted tell 'em all they lied see new towns go to Genoa)   havanuzzerone?   it turned out that he wished he was a naked brown shepherd boy sitting on a hillside playing a flute in the sunlight

Exactly the same episode, so it happens, is described in Dos Passos' other manner, his prose manner, during the course of a chapter dealing with Dick Savage:

That night they parked the convoy in the main square of a godforsaken little burg on the outskirts of Genoa. They went with Sheldrake to have a drink in a bar and found themselves drinking with the Saturday Evening Post correspondent, who soon began to get tight and to say how he envied them their good looks and their sanguine youth and idealism. Steve picked him up about everything and argued bitterly that youth was the lousiest time in your life, and that he ought to be goddam glad he was forty years old and able to write about the war instead of fighting in it.

The relative merit of these two passages, as writing, is not an important question. The first is a good enough piece of impressionism, with undertones of E. E. Cummings and Gertrude Stein. The style of the second passage, except for a certain conversational quality, is almost colorless; it happens to be the most effective way of recording a particular series of words and actions; it aspires to no other virtue. The first passage might add something to a book in which, the plot being hackneyed or inconsequential, the emphasis had to be placed on the writing, but 1919 is not a novel of that sort. Again, the Camera Eye may justify itself in the next volume of this trilogy—or tetralogy—by assuming a closer relation to the story and binding together the different groups of characters; but in that case, I hope the style of it will change. So far it has been an element of disunity, a survival of the art novel in the midst of a different type of writing, and one in which Dos Passos excels.

He is, indeed, one of the few writers in whose case an equation can accurately and easily be drawn between social beliefs and artistic accomplishments. When he writes individualistically, with backward glances toward Imagism, Vorticism and the Insurrection of the Word, his prose is sentimental and without real distinction. When he writes as a social rebel, he writes not flawlessly by any means, but with conviction, power and a sense of depth, of striking through surfaces to the real forces beneath them. This last book, in which his political ideas have given shape to his emotions, and only the Camera Eye remains as a vestige of his earlier attitude, is not only the best of all his novels; it is, I believe, a landmark in American fiction.

Four years ago in reviewing 1919, the second volume of Dos Passos' trilogy, I tried to define two types of fiction that have been especially prominent since the War. An *art novel*, I said, was one that dealt with the opposition between a creatively gifted individual and the community surrounding him—in brief, between the Poet and the World. Usually in books of this type the Poet gets all the attention; he is described admiringly, tenderly, and yet we learn that he is nagged and broken and often, in the end, driven to suicide by an implacably stupid World. Dos Passos' earlier novels had applied this formula, but *The 42nd Parallel* and *1919* belonged to a second category: they were *collective novels*, whose real hero was American society at large, and this fact helped to explain their greater breadth and vigor. I added, however, that certain elements in these later books—and notably the autobiographical passages called the "Camera Eye"—suggested the art novel and therefore seemed out of place.

But after reviewing *The Big Money* and rereading the trilogy as a whole, it seems to me that this judgment has to be partly revised. I no longer believe that the art novel is a "bad" type of fiction (though the philosophy behind it is a bad philosophy for our times), nor do I believe that the collective novel is necessarily a "good" type (though it has advantages for writers trying to present our period of crisis). With more and more collective novels published every year, it is beginning to be obvious that the form in itself does not solve the writer's problems. Indeed, it raises new problems and creates new disadvantages. The collective novelist is tempted to overemphasize the blindness and impotence of individuals caught in the rip tides of history. He is obliged to devote less space to each of his characters, to relate their adventures more hastily, with the result that he always seems to be approaching them from the outside. I can see now that the Camera Eye is a device adopted by Dos Passos in order to supply the "inwardness" that is lacking in his general narrative.

I can see too that although the device is borrowed from the art novel—and indeed is a series of interior monologues resembling parts of Joyce's *Ulysses*—it is not in the least alien to the general plan of the trilogy. For the truth is that the art novel and the collective novel as conceived by Dos Passos are not in fundamental opposition: they are like the two sides of a coin. In the art novel, the emphasis is on the individual, in the collective novel it is on society as a whole; but in both we get the impression that society is stupid and all-powerful and fundamentally evil. Individuals ought to oppose it, but if they do so they are doomed. If, on the other hand, they reconcile themselves with society and try to get ahead in it, then they are damned forever, damned to be empty, shrill, destructive insects like Dick Savage and Eleanor Stoddard and J. Ward Moore-house.

In an earlier novel, *Manhattan Transfer*, there is a paragraph that states one of Dos Passos' basic perceptions. Ellen Herf, having divorced the hero, decides to marry a rich politician whom she does not love:

> Through dinner she felt a gradual icy coldness stealing through her like novocaine. She had made up her mind. It seemed as if she had set the photograph of herself in her own place, forever frozen into a single gesture. . . . everything about her seemed to be growing hard and enameled, the air bluestreaked with cigarettesmoke, was turning to glass.

She had made up her mind. . . . Sometimes in reading Dos Passos it seems that not the nature of the decision but the mere fact of having reached it is the unforgivable offense. Dick Savage, the ambulance driver, decided not to be a pacifist, not to escape into neutral Spain, and from that moment he is forever frozen into a single gesture of selfishness and dissipation. Don Stevens, the radical newspaper correspondent, decides to be a good Communist, to obey party orders, and immediately he is stricken with the same paralysis of the heart. We have come a long way from the strong-willed heroes of the early nineteenth century—the English heroes, sons of Dick Whittington, who admired the world of their day and climbed to the top of it implacably; the French heroes like Julien Sorel and Rastignac and Monte Cristo who despised their world and yet learned how to press its buttons and pull its levers. To Dos Passos the world seems so vicious that any compromise with its standards turns a hero into a villain. The only characters he seems to like instinctively are those who know they are beaten, but still grit their teeth and try to hold on. That is the story of Jimmy Herf in *Manhattan Transfer*; to some extent it is also the story of Mary French and her father and Joe Askew, almost the only admirable characters in *The Big Money*. And the same lesson of dogged, courageous impotence is pointed by the Camera Eye, especially in the admirable passage where the author remembers the execution of Sacco and Vanzetti:

> America our nation has been beaten by strangers who have turned our language inside out who have taken the clean words our fathers spoke and made them slimy and foul
>
> their hired men sit on the judge's bench they sit back with their feet on the tables under the dome of the State House they are ignorant of our beliefs they have the dollars the guns the armed forces the power-plants . . .
>
> all right we are two nations

"The hired men with guns stand ready to shoot," he says in another passage, this one dealing with his visit to the striking miners in Kentucky. "We have only words against POWER SUPERPOWER." And these words that serve as our only weapons against the machine guns and tear gas of the invaders, these words of the vanquished nation are only that America in developing from pioneer democracy into monopoly capitalism has followed a road that leads toward sterility and slavery. Our world is evil, and yet we are powerless to change or direct it. The sensitive individual should cling to his own standards, and yet he is certain to go under. Thus, the final message of Dos Passos' three collective novels is similar to that of his earlier novels dealing with maladjusted artists. Thus, for all the vigor of 1919 and *The*

Big Money, they leave us wondering whether the author hasn't overstated his case. For all their scope and richness, they fail to express one side of contemporary life—the will to struggle ahead, the comradeship in struggle, the consciousness of new men and new forces continually rising. Although we may be for the moment a beaten nation, the fight is not over.

The America of John Dos Passos

LIONEL TRILLING

U.S.A. is far more impressive than even its three impressive parts—*42nd Parallel*, *1919*, *The Big Money*—might have led one to expect. It stands as the important American novel of the decade, on the whole more satisfying than anything else we have. It lacks any touch of eccentricity; it is startlingly normal; at the risk of seeming paradoxical one might say that it is exciting because of its quality of cliché: here are comprised the judgments about modern American life that many of us have been living on for years.

Yet too much must not be claimed for this book. Today we are inclined to make literature too important, to estimate the writer's function at an impossibly high rate, to believe that he can encompass and resolve all the contradictions, and to demand that he should. We forget that, by reason of his human nature, he is likely to win the intense perception of a single truth at the cost of a relative blindness to other truths. We expect a single man to give us all the answers and produce the "synthesis." And then when the writer, hailed for giving us much, is discovered to have given us less than everything, we turn from him in a reaction of disappointment: he has given us nothing. A great deal has been claimed for Dos Passos and it is important, now that *U.S.A.* is completed, to mark off the boundaries of its

From *Partisan Review*, 4 (April 1938), 26–32. Reprinted by permission of the author and the editor of *Partisan Review*.

enterprise and see what it does not do so that we may know what it does do.

One thing *U.S.A.* does not do is originate; it confirms but does not advance and it summarizes but does not suggest. There is no accent or tone of feeling that one is tempted to make one's own and carry further in one's own way. No writer, I think, will go to school to Dos Passos, and readers, however much they may admire him will not stand in the relation to him in which they stand, say, to Stendhal or Henry James or even E. M. Forster. Dos Passos' plan is greater than its result in feeling; his book *tells* more than it *is*. Yet what it tells, and tells with accuracy, subtlety and skill, is enormously important and no one else has yet told it half so well.

Nor is *U.S.A.* as all-embracing as its admirers claim. True, Dos Passos not only represents a great national scene but he embodies, as I have said, the cultural tradition of the intellectual Left. But he does not encompass—does not pretend to encompass in this book—all of either. Despite his title, he is consciously selective of his America and he is, as I shall try to show, consciously corrective of the cultural tradition from which he stems.

Briefly and crudely, this cultural tradition may be said to consist of the following beliefs, which are not so much formulations of theory or principles of action as they are emotional tendencies: that the collective aspects of life may be distinguished from the individual aspects; that the collective aspects are basically important and are good; that the individual aspects are, or should be, of small interest and that they contain a destructive principle; that the fate of the individual is determined by social forces; that the social forces now dominant are evil; that there is a conflict between the dominant social forces and other, better, rising forces; that it is certain or very likely that the rising forces will overcome the now dominant ones. *U.S.A.* conforms to some but not to all of these assumptions. The lack of any protagonists in the trilogy, the equal attention given to many people, have generally been taken to represent Dos Passos' recognition of the importance of the collective idea. The book's historical apparatus indicates the author's belief in social determination. And there can be no slightest doubt of Dos Passos' attitude to the dominant forces of our time: he hates them.

But Dos Passos modifies the tradition in three important respects. Despite the collective elements of his trilogy, he puts a peculiar importance upon the individual. Again, he avoids propounding any sharp conflict between the dominant forces of evil and the rising forces of good; more specifically, he does not write of a class struggle, nor is he much concerned with the notion of class in the political sense. Finally, he is not at all assured of the eventual triumph of good; he pins no faith on any force or party—indeed he is almost alone of the novelists of the Left (Silone is the only other one that comes to mind) in saying that the creeds and idealisms of the Left may bring corruption quite as well as the greeds and cynicisms of the established order; he has refused to cry "Allons! the road lies before us," and, in short, his novel issues in despair.—And it is this despair of Dos Passos' book which has made his two ablest critics, Malcolm Cowley and T. K. Whipple, seriously temper their admiration. Mr. Cowley says: "They [the novels comprising *U.S.A.*] give us an extraordinarily diversified picture of contemporary life, but they fail to include at least one side of it—the will to struggle ahead, the comradeship in struggle, the consciousness of new men and new forces continually rising." And Mr. Whipple: "Dos Passos has reduced what ought to be a tale of full-bodied conflicts to an epic of disintegration."

These critics are saying that Dos Passos has not truly observed the political situation. Whether he has or not, whether his despair is objectively justifiable, cannot, with the best political will in the world, be settled on paper. We hope he has seen incorrectly; he himself must hope so. But there is also an implicit meaning in the objections which, if the writers themselves did not intend it, many readers will derive, and if not from Mr. Whipple and Mr. Cowley then from the book itself: that the emotion in which *U.S.A.* issues is negative to the point of being politically harmful.

But to discover a political negativism in the despair of *U.S.A.* is to subscribe to a naïve conception of human emotion and of the literary experience. It is to assert that the despair of a literary work must inevitably engender despair in the reader. Actually, of course, it need do nothing of the sort. To rework the old Aristotelian insight, it may bring about a catharsis of an already existing despair. But more important: the word "despair" all by itself (or any other such general word or phrase) can never characterize the emotion the artist is dealing with. There are many kinds of despair and what is really important is what goes along with the general emotion denoted by the word. Despair with its wits about it is very different from despair that is stupid; despair that is an abandonment of illusion is very different from despair which generates tender new cynicisms. The "heartbreak" of *Heartbreak House,* for example, is the beginning of new courage and I can think of no more useful *political* job for the literary man today than, by the representation of despair, to cauterize the exposed soft tissue of too-easy hope.

Even more than the despair, what has disturbed the radical admirers of Dos Passos' work is his appearance of indifference to the idea of the class struggle. Mr. Whipple correctly points out that the characters of *U.S.A.* are all "midway people in somewhat ambiguous positions." Thus, there are no bankers or industrialists (except incidentally) but only J. Ward Moorehouse, their servant; there are no factory workers (except, again, incidentally), no farmers, but only itinerant workers, individualistic mechanics, actresses, interior decorators.

This, surely, is a limitation in a book that has had claimed for it a complete national picture. But when we say limitation we may mean just that or we may mean falsification, and I do not think that Dos Passos has falsified. The idea of class is not simple but complex. Socially it is extremely difficult to determine. It cannot be determined, for instance, by asking individuals to what class they belong; nor is it easy to convince them that they belong to one class or another. We may, to be sure, demonstrate the idea of class at income-extremes or function-extremes, but when we leave these we must fall back upon the criterion of "interest"—by which we must mean *real* interest ("real will" in the Rousseauian sense) and not what people say or think they want. Even the criterion of action will not determine completely the class to which people belong. Class, then, is a useful but often undetermined category of political and social thought. The political leader and the political theorist will make use of it in ways different from those of the novelist. For the former the important thing is people's perception that they are of one class or another and their resultant action. For the latter the interesting and suggestive things are likely to be the moral paradoxes that result from the conflict between real and apparent interest. And the "midway people" of Dos Passos represent this moral-paradoxical aspect of class. They are a great fact in American life. It is they who show the symptoms of cultural change. Their movement from social group to social group—from class to class, if you will—makes for the uncertainty of their moral codes, their confusion, their indecision. Almost more than the people of fixed class, they are at the mercy of the social stream because their interests cannot be clear to them and give them direction. If Dos Passos has omitted the class struggle, as Mr. Whipple and Mr. Cowley complain, it is only the external class struggle he has left out; within his characters the class struggle is going on constantly.

This, perhaps, is another way of saying that Dos Passos is primarily concerned with morality, with personal morality. The national, collective, social elements of his trilogy should be seen not as a bid for completeness but rather as a great setting, brilliantly delineated, for his moral interest. In his novels, as in actual life, "conditions" supply the opportunity for personal moral action. But if Dos Passos is a social historian, as he is so frequently said to be, he is that in order to be a more complete moralist. It is of the greatest significance that for him the barometer of social breakdown is not suffering through economic deprivation but always moral degeneration through moral choice.

This must be said in the face of Mr. Whipple's description of Dos Passos' people as "devoid of will or purpose, helplessly impelled hither and yon by the circumstances of the moment. They have no strength of resistance. They are weak at the very core of personality, the power to choose." These, it would seem, are scarcely the characters with which the moralist can best work. But here we must judge not only by the moral equipment of the characters (and it is not at all certain that Mr. Whipple's description is correct: choice of action is seldom made as the result of Socratic dialectic) but by the novelist's idea of morality—the nature of his judgments and his estimate of the power of circumstance.

Dos Passos' morality is concerned not so much with the utility of an action as with the quality of the person who performs it. *What* his people do is not so important as *how* they do it, or what they become by doing it. We despise J. Ward Moorehouse not so much for his creation of the labor-relations board, his support of the war, his advertising of patent-medicines, though these are despicable enough; we despise him rather for the words he uses as he does these things, for his self-deception, the tone and style he generates. We despise G. H. Barrow, the labor-faker, not because he betrays labor; we despise him because he is mealy-mouthed and talks about "the art of living" when he means concupiscence. But we do not despise the palpable fraud, Doc Bingham, because, though he lies to everyone else, he does not lie to himself.

The moral assumption on which Dos Passos seems to work was expressed by John Dewey some thirty years ago; there are certain moral situations, Dewey says, where we cannot decide between the ends; we are forced to make our moral choice in terms of our preference for one kind of character or another: "What sort of an agent, of a person shall he be? This is the question finally at stake in any genuinely moral situation: What shall the agent *be*? What sort of character shall he assume? On its face, the question is what he shall *do*, shall he act for this or that end. But the incompatibility of the ends forces the issue back into the questions of the kind of selfhood, of agency, involved in the respective ends." One can imagine that this method of moral decision does not have meaning for all times and cultures. Although dilemmas exist in every age, we do not find Antigone settling her struggle between family and state by a reference to the kind of character she wants to be, nor Orestes settling his in that way; and so with the medieval dilemma of wife vs. friend, or the family oath of vengeance vs. the feudal oath of allegiance. But for our age with its intense self-consciousness and its uncertain moral codes, the reference to the quality of personality does have meaning, and the greater the social flux the more frequent will be the interest in qualities of character rather than in the rightness of the end.

The modern novel, with its devices for investigating the quality of character, is the aesthetic form almost specifically called forth to exercise this modern way of judgment. The novelist goes where the law cannot go; he tells the truth where the formulations of even the subtlest ethical theorist cannot. He turns the moral values inside out to question the worth of the deed by looking not at its actual outcome but at its tone and style. He is subversive of dominant morality and under his influence we learn to praise what dominant morality condemns; he reminds us that benevolence may be aggression, that the highest idealism may corrupt. Finally, he gives us the models of the examples by which, half-unconsciously, we make our own moral selves.

Dos Passos does not primarily concern himself with the burly sinners who inherit the earth. His people are those who sin against themselves and for him the wages of sin is death—of the spirit. The whole Dos Passos morality and the typical Dos Passos fate are expressed in Burns' quatrain:

> I *waive the quantum o' the sin,*
> *The hazard of concealing;*
> *But, och! it hardens a' within*
> *And petrifies the feeling!*

In the trilogy physical death sometimes follows upon this petrifaction of the feeling but only as its completion. Only two people die without petrifying, Joe Williams and Daughter, who kept in their inarticulate way a spark of innocence, generosity and protest. Idealism does not prevent the consequences of sinning against oneself and Mary French with her devotion to the working class and the Communist Party, with her courage and "sacrifice" is quite as dead as Richard Savage who inherits Moorehouse's mantle, and she is almost as much to blame.

It is this element of blame, of responsibility, that exempts Dos Passos from Malcolm Cowley's charge of being in some part committed to the morality of what Cowley calls the Art Novel—the story of the Poet and the World, the Poet always sensitive and right, the World always crass and wrong. An important element of Dos Passos' moral conception is that, although the World does sin against his characters, the characters themselves are very often as wrong as the world. There is no need to enter the theological purlieus to estimate how much responsibility Dos Passos puts upon them and whether this is the right amount. Clearly, however, he holds people like Savage, Fainy McCreary and Eveline Hutchins accountable in some important part for their own fates and their own ignobility.

The morality of Dos Passos, then, is a romantic morality. Perhaps this is calling it a bad name; people say they have got tired of a morality concerned with individuals "saving" themselves and "realizing" themselves. Conceivably only Dos Passos' aggressive contemporaneity has kept them from seeing how very similar is his morality to, say, Browning's—the moment to be snatched, the crucial choice to be made, and if it is made on the wrong (the safe) side, the loss of human quality, so that instead of a man we have a Success and instead of two lovers a Statue and a Bust in the public square. But too insistent a cry against the importance of the individual quality is a sick cry—as sick as the cry of "Something to live for" as a motivation of political choice. Among members of a party the considerations of solidarity, discipline and expedience are claimed to replace all others, and moral judgment is left to history; among liberals, the idea of social determination, on no good ground, appears tacitly to exclude the moral concern: witness the nearly complete conspiracy of silence or misinterpretation that greeted Silone's *Bread and Wine,* which said not a great deal more than that personal and moral—and eventually political—problems were not settled by membership in a revolutionary party. It is not at all certain that it is political wisdom to ignore what so much concerns the novelist. In the long run is not the political choice fundamentally a choice of personal quality?

The Gullivers of Dos Passos

During the Forties and the Fifties John Dos Passos has very nearly achieved the rank of a neglected novelist. In the Twenties with the publication of *Three Soldiers* (1921) and *Manhattan Transfer* (1925) he was one of the promising young novelists, *Three Soldiers* particularly striking its period as a daring and realistic novel. In the thirties the three novels that constitute *U.S.A.* gave him the reputation of having written "the American collective novel" at a time when everyone took the collective novel pretty seriously. These reputations were all misleading.

Three Soldiers is mainly an "art novel," the story of a young man too sensitive and esthetically aware to endure the crude world, who is defeated by that world; it is only incidentally the exposé of the Army in the First World War, which gave it its initial reputation with a decade very much concerned to come to terms with the war. *U.S.A.* is something different—and better—than the collective novel in which, as the fashion of the Thirties required, "the real hero . . . is society itself." The real hero of the book is a state of mind, a moral attitude toward our society and, by clear implication, all social organization. And a very "uncollective" state of mind it is, too ("when you try to find the people, always in the end it comes down to somebody").

From *The Saturday Review of Literature*, 34 (June 30, 1951), 6–7, 34–35. Reprinted by permission of the author and Saturday Review, Inc.

Probably the Thirties' decision that *U.S.A.* was a collective novel was as unavoidable as the former decision that *Three Soldiers* was a realistic novel about the war. The form of the collective novel had been adumbrated by fashionable critics and proved in theory to be the one demanded by the times. They were nearly as certain to turn up a collective novel as was the eighteenth century to turn up a noble savage; and Dos Passos has suffered about as much from his selection for the first honor as Omai did from his selection for the second.

As Dos Passos has gone on producing the kind of novel he started to develop with *Manhattan Transfer*, his work has been less and less well received. The professional Left found *Adventures of a Young Man* (1938) grossly offensive; here, believe it or not, was the collective novelist himself passionately damning the conduct of the Communist Party in the Spanish Civil War and generally conducting himself like a Trotskyite. *Number One* (1943) was deplored as a journalistic novel about Huey Long. *The Grand Design* (1949) seemed painfully unenlightened to the numerous and influential liberals who had gone into the New Deal; think of Dos Passos setting up a prosperous businessman, almost a "malefactor of great wealth," as his hero and then having him defeated by the confusion, the egotism, and the selfishness of New-Deal liberals! This was unkind; this was betrayal. It has been a final misfortune for Dos Passos during these years that his kind of novel must carefully avoid the minute shading of character and the sensitive poetical style which have been the main current fashions in the novel, so that even the people who ought to have been reading and admiring him quietly while the liberals disowned him have (with a few honorable exceptions like Alfred Kazin) neglected him.

It was apparently useless to protest these irrelevant but damaging judgments during the Thirties and Forties; when T. K. Whipple remarked of *U.S.A.* in 1938 that in it "the class struggle is presented as a minor theme; the major theme is the vitiation and degradation of character in such a civilization," nobody minded him. But enough time has passed now so that we ought to be able to see—instead of debating whether he takes a political position we happen at the moment to agree with or whether he writes in a style more or less like Virginia Woolf's—what Dos Passos has been doing. To look at him thus seeingly is, I believe, to discover that Dos Passos is a good novelist of a kind almost unique in our time.

What we need to recognize above all is the kind of novel Dos Passos is writing, the genre to which his work belongs. The best way to do that is to approach it by way of the tradition of comedy exemplified in slightly different ways by Ben Jonson and Swift. Dos Passos is not, I assume, consciously working in a literary tradition; neither was Swift. And Jonson is a great writer not because he had read and borrowed from the classics but because of the intensity of his vision of human experience. "He invades [classical] authors like a monarch," as Dryden put it; "and what would be theft in other poets is only victory in him." Yet Jonson, like Dos Passos, has suffered from the charge that—in his case because of slavish imitation of the classics—he is full of typed characters without the charm and warmth that romantically inclined people think is the whole value of Shakespeare's characters (and never know what to do with Timon and Coriolanus). Jonson, we are told, did not allow his characters to come alive and be human because he was too anxious to manipulate them like puppets in order to prove some commonplace moral fetched from the classics.

It is true, of course, that Jonson's characters are two-dimensional, calculatedly and necessarily, and that the moral values of his plays are, in one sense, familiar. Yet, for all their familiarity, they have hardly impressed themselves on us deeply enough to make humanity live by them. Doctor Johnson, speaking of another kind of romantic taste, made the best defense of Jonson's kind of poetry. "Those writers who lay on the watch for novelty," he said, "could have little hope of greatness; for great things cannot have escaped former observation." What matters finally in any kind of literature is not the novelty of its attitudes and values or the superficial charm and colorfulness of its characters but the realized and communicated passion for "the great things."

If a writer sees people, as writers like Jonson and Dos Passos do, not as aggregations of charming eccentricities, as "characters," but as representative cases, each of whom contributes in his way to our understanding of the drift of the community's life, and if he sees them thus with passion and intelligence, then he will produce neither romance nor tragedy but the most serious kind of satiric comedy, works like *Bartholomew Fair* or *Le Misanthrope* or *Gulliver's Travels* or *Adventures of a Young Man*. Such a work is immediately ironic about the shortcomings of its own society and, beyond that, about the permanent defects of humanity; it will seem to writers like these the most serious kind of work they can produce. "For if men will impartially, and not asquint, look toward the offices and functions of a poet," as Ben Jonson put it about his own work, "they will easily conclude to themselves the impossibility of any man's being a good poet, without first being a good man . . . it being the office of a comic poet to imitate justice, and instruct to live. . . ."

Therefore Jonson, basing his attack on the humanistic and Christian attitude professed by his age, held up to deadly ridicule the capitalist acquisitiveness and puritan pretentiousness of the early seventeenth century. Therefore Swift, basing his attack on the Christian reason and the benevolence professed by the eighteenth century, attacked (at least on the whole; he is a more complicated case than Jonson) the functionless ritual and the brutality of his society. With both writers the ultimate object of attack was man himself, that "most pernicious race of little odious vermin," as the King of

Brobdingnag put it, "that nature ever suffered to crawl upon the surface of the earth." In the same way Dos Passos, taking quite seriously the anarchistic individualism and the egalitarianism of the American democratic tradition, attacks with satire the institutionalized corruption and the disintegrated private lives produced by the two mighty opposites of our society—industry and politics.

The characteristic novel form for comedy of this kind is the picaresque tale which carries its hero through a series of socially representative adventures (*The Adventures of*—Joseph Andrews, Roderick Random, A Young Man—is the formula for the title of the picaresque novel). This hero may be a young man of innocent and incurable good will, like the early Gulliver; or he may be the equally innocent rascal who believes that happiness is to be obtained by being smart and financially successful, like Volpone (except that after almost two centuries of benevolence Dos Passos's Volpones and Jonathan Wilds tend to be pathetic as well as vicious). In either case he is finally destroyed or at least defeated, if possible by the most pretentiously righteous institution of his society.

As in all fiction of this kind, there is in Dos Passos's work a lively, almost journalistic interest in the manners and customs of the Several Remote Nations into which his Gullivers travel. Just as Ben Jonson never overlooked a chance to work into his comedies a "humorous" portrait of an Elizabethan rascal or fool, so Dos Passos's work is full of comic portraits of American types, of bootleggers and Vassar girls, hillbillies and bankers, movie stars and labor bosses, radio pundits and merchant seamen; it would be difficult to name a type in our society which does not appear in Dos Passos. But always, from the day Fainy McCreary had to decide between his feelings for Maisie and his loyalty to the IWW, the core of Dos Passos's work has been an isolating, individual struggle between stubborn idealism and the corrupting forces of an organized society which demands conformity.

The passion of Swift's work comes to its sharpest focus in his hatred of the organized selfishness and hypocrisy of society: "I have ever hated all nations, professions, and communities, and all my love is toward individuals. . . . Principally I hate and detest that animal called man, although I heartily love John, Peter, Thomas, and so forth. . . ." The passion of Dos Passos's work is of exactly this kind. People may suppress the John, Peter, Thomas in themselves, as does Dick Savage when he sacrifices Daughter to conformity and success; but they die inside. Or they may insist on preserving it at any cost, as does Glenn Spotswood. In Dos Passos this cost is always not less than everything; these people are always destroyed by organized society, by the organized middle class, by organized business or labor or politics (standard American, which destroyed Tyler Spotswood, or CP, which destroyed Glenn).

Dos Passos was some time in arriving at the picaresque form which would allow full play to all these feelings, but he began to work toward it in *Manhattan Transfer.* In the book's wonderful panorama of representative American lives, of manners and customs, the lives of Ellen Thatcher and Jimmy Herf stand out. The last we see of Ellen she is on her way to meet George Baldwin, for whom she is divorcing Jimmy. "There are lives to be lived," she thinks, "if only you didn't care. Care for what, for what; the opinion of mankind, money, success, hotel lobbies, health, umbrellas, Uneeda biscuits. . . ? As she goes through the shining soundless revolving door . . . there shoots through her a sudden pang of something forgotten. . . . What did I forget in the taxicab?" What she forgot was her life. But the last we see of Jimmy Herf he is pulling out, down to his last three cents and hitching a ride with a redheaded truck driver. " 'How fur ye goin?' 'I dunno. . . . Pretty far.' "

Through *The 42nd Parallel* and *Nineteen Nineteen* the magnificent panorama of American lives continues. In construction, in the controlled and integrated organization of an immense variety of characters Dos Passos goes way beyond Swift. This is structure as Jonson understood it in *The Alchemist,* the kind of organization Coleridge was thinking of when he said *The Alchemist* had one of the three perfect plots in the world. But it is only, I believe, with *The Big Money* that Dos Passos achieves the fully developed form of his kind of fiction. In *The Big Money* the attitude of tragic satire, the unwavering sense of the hero's essential innocence, the grim humor of his defeat dominate the novel; and there emerges the full picaresque form in which the hero's life is central and the ironic account of the manners of his world, however detailed, becomes the circumstance of his destruction. As Malcolm Cowley remarked of the book when it was first published, "We are likely to remember it as a furious and somber poem written in a mood of revulsion even more powerful than that which T. S. Eliot expressed in *The Waste Land.*" The effect of *U.S.A.* as a whole is the effect of a world in which no one wins, whether he "succeeds," as do Richard Savage and Margo Dowling and Charley Anderson, or fails, as do Mary French and Ben Compton and Eveline Hutchins. Their defeat in either case is a defeat beyond social or political redress, perhaps beyond human redress of any kind.

Since *The Big Money* Dos Passos has continued to write satiric comedies like it. The Gullivers change from novel to novel. Counting both Charley Anderson and Tyler Spotswood there are two innocent—and therefore finally pathetic—rascals who, like Ellen Thatcher, discover too late that they have left something in the taxicab ("I want to talk like we used to when, you know, up the Red River fishin' when there wasn't any," says the dying Charley Anderson). And there are two stubbornly innocent idealists.

In *Adventures of a Young Man,* Glenn Spotswood really believes in the ideals of Communism and is therefore excommunicated and eventually murdered by the Party. In *Grand Design* Millard Carroll believes in the same way in the ideals of the New Deal and is thrown into the discard along with it when the war comes along. The stubborn esthetic resistance to the world of John Andrews in *Three Soldiers* has gradually changed through the course of Dos Passos's work to the stubborn unworldliness of the Good American. Each of these heroes is the predestined victim of all the forces of compromise and corruption in his immediate society. Like the comic victims of all works of this kind—like Don Quixote and Alceste and Candide, like Sir Fopling Flutter and Joseph Andrews and Gulliver—the hero allows his author to show how greed and lust in their various local American forms operate to destroy the virtues American society is supposed to live by. Each has the innocence and the incurable purity of motive of the genuine idealist ("Tyler, what I'd started to write you about was not letting them sell out too much of the for the people and by the people part of the old-time United States way"). Each has, too, the primness, for Dos Passos can, like all good comic writers, see that his hero's stubborn goodness is not only touching but in the circumstances grimly funny.

Around each of these heroes Dos Passos constructs his wonderfully varied, satiric representation of a segment of American society, of the business world, of the labor movement, of professional politics, of New-Deal Washington. Each subordinate character fits his part in the whole by being what Jonson would have called a "humor." You cannot easily forget Marice Gulick or Comrade Irving Silverstone or Chuck Crawford or Herbert Spotswood; you remember them not because they seem "real" to you but because, like Sir Epicure Mammon, they are classic representations of their types, warmed to the kind of life all great satirists can create by the anger and grief of their author at finding them what they are. "Who but must laugh, if such a man there be? / Who would not weep, if Atticus were he?"

All these characters are held together by the beautifully integrated action. From the point of view of strict verisimilitude Dos Passos's story has far too many coincidences, just as it has far too many type characters. Glenn Spotswood, for instance, meets the Gulicks when he is a student and even lives in their house for a while; Tyler meets them when he is working for Chuck Crawford; Millard Carroll begins his career in Washington by having dinner with them. If your standards are those of the realistic novel you will be annoyed to find that every liberal academic economist no matter where he turns up is always Mike Gulick. But you might as well protest against Swift that of all the possible men in boats it is always Lemuel Gulliver who gets stranded on odd islands. Each of Dos Passos's minor characters leads a representative life; that life is related to other representative lives in typical ways. If we are to see Dos Passos's world whole, we must see how each of these lives impinges on every other one. In a fiction where the characters are typical, such coincidents—as long as they are individually plausible—are truer than random events would be. Dos Passos's greatest imaginative achievement is to have constructed this complex, minutely detailed, and yet tightly interlocked pattern of lives; it is the equivalent in his work of Faulkner's genealogy.

Just as the pattern of the story is designed to emphasize the representative nature of the characters, so is Dos Passos's style. Except for the Camera Eye in U.S.A. and the interspersed prose poems of direct moralizing in the later novels, which seem to me a mistake, he writes in a flat, deadly accurate, and devastating prose which reduces events and motives to what seems to Dos Passos their essential horror. These qualities are particularly evident in the last three novels, from the moment when Glenn defies the concentratedly fatuous Dr. Talcott at Camp Winnesquam to the final scene between Paul Graves and Walker Watson. They are most brilliantly demonstrated in the dialogue, in Joe Yerkes's wonderfully banal CP jargon, in Marice's fashionable drawing-room Freudian chatter, in Chuck Crawford's quintessential demagoguery, in Jerry Evans's bullying businessman's jocularity. Dos Passos's characters do not speak the language of the unique and special, the "interesting" personality; they speak with the voices of whole kinds, concentrated to cliché and glowing with Dos Passos's sad scorn for their terrible inadequacy. His novels are a nightmare of people damned to go on muttering forever "our beautiful lake . . . our lifegiving air," "wanted to observe complexes in various social stratifications," "hadn't been able to restrain her bourgeois possessive feelings," "this great worldwide effort to block the advance of tyranny and barbarism," "the case of those poor damned oil men."

To say that the talk and the feelings of Dos Passos's people are commonplace is to miss altogether the governing irony of his work: one might as well say that Polonius or The Citizen in "Ulysses" are not always so intelligent or original as they might be. To say that Dos Passos's judgment of our world is the application to it of perfectly familiar values is to ignore what makes his work the imposing indictment it is, that is, the passionate sincerity of his hatred of our failure, of humanity's failure, to be what it professes—and what it ought —to be.

Manhattan Transfer
Collectivism and Abstract Composition

JOSEPH WARREN BEACH

Dos Passos went into the War as a man of letters, and in the end his contribution was bound to be in the form of literature. The satisfactions of John Andrews took the line of artistic expression; he was bent on giving voice in music to "these thwarted lives, the miserable dulness of industrialized slaughter." Martin Howe was no more resigned than the relief worker who complained of the people being forced to fight and die like cattle driven to the slaughterhouse. "I am going to do something some day, but first I must see. I want to be initiated in all the circles of hell." He was soon initiated; and what he did was *Three Soldiers*. The compelling realities of the present took the place of the figures of ballet and harlequinade. His subject was given him. It may not have been to his liking, but he had no choice. It was still a work of art and skill which he labored to fashion. But he had to use the stuff at hand; and the taste which might have been informed by delight and love was guided and compelled by the reactions of disgust and repulsion.

Three Soldiers was the first important American novel, and one of the first in any language, to treat the War in the tone of realism and disillusion. It made a deep impression, and may be counted the beginning of

Condensed from Joseph Warren Beach, *American Fiction: 1920–1940* (New York: Macmillan, 1941). Reprinted by permission of the estate of Dagmar Doneghy Beach.

strictly contemporary fiction in the United States. Stephen Crane had come before him with *The Red Badge
of Courage*. But Crane's war was imagined, not experienced, and there is about his work an air of the
archaic and synthetic. Norris and Dreiser and Lewis
are honorable names in American realism, but in many
points of tone and technique they belong to the past
rather than to the present.

So it was the War that determined the bent of Dos
Passos' genius. But the war was just the beginning. The
"lies" that made the War were the creation of our society as it operates in time of "peace." And his great
work was destined to be the representation of American
life on a grand scale, in which the War is shown as a
mere incident.

He began with a relatively limited subject. *Manhattan Transfer* (1925) is a survey of life in New York City
during the period from about 1890 to about 1925.[1] It
consists of a kaleidoscopic succession of moments from
the lives of a large number of persons chosen to represent the various classes who may be taken to make up
society in the metropolis. If there is one character more
central than another it is the newspaperman Jimmy
Herf, who may be assumed to represent the general attitude and point of view of Dos Passos. The other
characters are largely such as would make the front page
of a newspaper, the tacit assumption being, rightly
enough perhaps, that the newspaper is the best single in-
dex of the American mind. Ellen Thatcher, daughter
of a registered accountant who plays the market, a
second-rate but successful actress in musical shows,
married successively to the actor Jo-Jo, to the newspaperman Herf, and to the lawyer Baldwin; George
Baldwin, rising lawyer with a somewhat shady practice,
who finally throws over his labor-union friends to run
for district attorney on the reform ticket; Jeff Merivale, Jimmy's uncle, who has made his way to the top in
banking, and his son James, who goes into business with
the same firm; labor organizers and politicians; bootleg-

gers made wealthy by prohibition; theatrical producers —these hold the center of the stage, and represent the classes that prosper most under the set-up. Along with these is a scattering of vocations essential to modern life—realtors, architects, sanitary engineers, theatrical people living from hand to mouth, together with other types of businessmen whose prosperity is great but precarious—promoters of wildcat schemes, who have to take to their heels, large importers and exporters, who go down for millions in a market crash.

These represent the upper and middle layers of metropolitan society—those who know how to take advantage of conditions, and make up the glittering figures in the social tapestry. And then, weaving in and out among these foreground figures, are the obscure shadows of those who cannot take care of themselves—the misfits, the exploited masses, those thrown off on the slagheap from the great industrial machine. There is Bud Korpenning, from upstate, who slew his father in a moment of frenzied revolt against ill treatment, who seeks to lose himself in the great city, but he is haunted by men in derbies and finally throws himself off Brooklyn Bridge. There is Joe Harland, drunken bum, who could not maintain his favored position in the business world. There is Dutch Robertson, private back from the wars, who cannot make an honest living and keep his girl; he goes in for crime and the law soon catches up with him. There are Jewish garment workers zealous for the union which will win them a decent living. There is Anna Cohen, milliner's employee, who has no place to take her man, and who loses her life in the fire at Mme. Soubrine's.

These are obscure and dreary figures, wisps and straws on the churning surface of our industrial maelstrom; but each one has his moment of spotlight on the front page, which daily serves up for our general entertainment a selection of the disasters and tragedies that grace the progress of civilization. Throughout the book the steady rising lines of those who prosper are crossed in a regular pattern by the falling lines of those who are drifting slowly downward, or plunging suddenly into the darkness like falling stars.

No one's story is told consecutively or with completeness; but the characters reappear from time to time at significant moments so that we can trace the general outline of their lives. The fragmentary moments are shown with startling vividness in circumstance, and with a certain intimacy in the rendering of sensations and moods. We never question the reality of the character or the situation. But so rapid is the shift from situation to situation, from character to character, so wide are the intervals between appearances, that we cannot quite grasp the thread which binds together the psychic life of the individual. They are individuals, for they have particular bodies and vocations and social status, and they have names and addresses in the telephone book. But they are not quite *persons*; for we are not made to feel that they are self-directing spirits. We are not shown the ideal nucleus round which their emotional life is organized. And so in spite of their vivid reality, they do not have the sentimental *importance* of characters in fiction.

This is no doubt intentional and deliberate on the part of the author. The standard novel of an earlier period was either biographical or dramatic in structure. That is, it followed through the life-history of one person, bringing in as many other characters as were important in relation to him; or it took up a group of characters at the moment in which their story came to a climax and carried it through to its dénouement. In either case, there was a high degree of continuity in storytelling. Our interest was centered continuously on the character and affairs of the leading person; or it was focused sharply on the problem of a group of persons with more or less conflicting interests and objectives. In either case, there were certain issues to be determined, problems to be faced, either in the successive moments of a single career, or in the urgent pressures of a special dramatic situation. The leading persons were faced with difficulties to be met, decisions to be made, and the way the problem was resolved depended largely on the character of the persons involved, their aims and ideals, their moral prepossessions, their ruling passions. Sometimes they could not have what they wanted because of circumstances that might not be overcome, because of weakness in their own make-up; but character is fate, as Novalis says, and the direction of their effort, at any rate, was determined by the objectives held by the persons of the drama.

This may, in the last analysis, be the case with the characters in *Manhattan Transfer*; but such is not the impression made upon the reader. The manner of narrative is not of a sort to emphasize ideal objectives at all as a determinant of action, but rather to suggest that the whole thing is a matter of stimulus and response. It is true that individuals are differentiated according to gift and vocation, and this is not wholly the result of circumstances. Somewhere along the line there comes in presumably the individual "set" in a certain direction, determined at least in part by the native temper of the individual. But the differentiation is more outward than inward. Human beings have different ways of securing their gratifications; but the gratifications are limited in number and kind. The impulse to make one's way in the world (here measured primarily in terms of money), the craving for "love," for entertainment, and for the avoidance of discomfort—human behavior is pretty well determined by these four considerations; and the word "craving" is perhaps too positive in its implications to suit the case. The working of the human organism would appear to be automatic—certain conditions set going certain types of behavior. The presence of a given organism within the field of vision provokes the response of "love"; discomfort drives one to a more comfortable attitude; a feeling of emptiness provokes boredom and sets one on the track of entertainment and novelty; a business opportunity releases effort and ambition.

Now, this is not a romantic view of human behavior and does not appeal to the ordinary reader of novels. He does not readily identify himself with characters whose behavior is determined in this accidental and piecemeal way. He thinks of himself as *after* something in life, as moved to action by certain ideal aims, which operate continuously, and in reference to which all his effort is organized. There is, accordingly, more coherence to his behavior, and more drama. Many are the difficulties in the way of success in the pursuit of ideal ends: our own weakness, conflict among our ideals, adverse circumstance, misunderstanding, opposing wills. There are odds to be overcome, intricate issues to be resolved. It is in the meeting of such difficulties that the personality makes itself known. And that is one reason why we are fond of drama, even in literature that makes a point of being "realistic."

There are probably several distinct reasons for Dos Passos' denying himself the method of storytelling which is most in favor and which has the great advantage of impressing the reader with the importance, and so—in the last analysis—with the essential truth of his characters. His project is obviously not to present human nature as it might be, as it may have been under favoring conditions, as it may actually be in exceptional cases, but rather as it impresses him in the main as being today under the conditions actually prevailing. He is himself a sensitive idealist grossly offended and disillusioned by what he finds to be the prevailing tone of human feeling in the world that made the War.

There are some faint indications in his characters of ideal objectives which have been missed and which survive obscurely in the depths of souls not strong enough to make headway against the main currents of the time. None of the characters are happy; few are altogether content with the way of life which they feel compelled to follow. Gus McNiel is a milk-wagon driver; he is destined to become a prosperous politician. He has his dream of taking up free land in North Dakota and raising wheat—"pretty curlyheaded Nellie feeding chickens at the kitchen door." This is his feeble tribute to the ideal. For several of the men, it is "love" that symbolizes the ideal values which they have missed in the pursuit of success. Harry Goldweiser, the theatrical producer, takes Ellen for an evening's entertainment. He remembers the raptures of boyhood taking a girl to Coney Island. "What I want to do is get that old feelin back, understand?" When Baldwin has divorced his wife and is going to marry Ellen, he assures the latter that "life's going to mean something for me now. God if you knew how empty life had been for so many years. I've been like a tin mechanical toy, all hollow inside." Stan, the reckless Harvard boy, who literally set himself on fire in a drunken fit, had meant something of this sort to Ellen. It was doubtless from Stan that she had learned the Shelleyan formula—"Darkly, fearfully afar from this nonsensical life, from this fuzzy idiocy and strife. . . ." In the midst of her successes and triumphs professional and personal, she has to remind herself to relax and not "to go round always keyed up so that everything is like chalk shrieking on a blackboard." She has been caught in a whirl of meaningless activities and empty gratifications. She knows: "There are lives to be lived if only you didn't care. Care for what, for what; the opinion of mankind, money, success, hotel lobbies, health, umbrellas, Uneeda biscuits . . . ? It's like a busted mechanical toy the way my mind goes brrr all the time."

There is one person in the book who has never let the machine quite run over him; has not delivered himself to Mammon. At the age of sixteen, through some perverse streak in him, Jimmy Herf refused to go in business with his Uncle Jeff; he would not be fed like tape in and out of revolving doors. He has been a newspaper reporter; he has gone to Europe as a Red Cross worker; he has been married to the enchanting Ellen, but has neither converted her from futile worldliness nor been subdued to it himself; he has tasted of dead sea apples but will not make them his daily fare. At length he throws over even his newspaper job; he will no longer stay "pockmarked with print." He turns his back on the city of destruction like the one good man of Sodom. He gets a lift on a furniture truck headed South. He doesn't know how far he's going, but it's "pretty far." Such is the protest of the self-determining individual against a world that would make of him a sensual automaton.

But there is another consideration leading Dos Passos to his employment of a method which ignores the personal drama dear to fiction. *Manhattan Transfer* is one of the earliest of that type of novel which has come to be known as "collectivistic." The idea is to present a cross-section of the social structure, the social organism; an "over-view" of the subject in which the details of individual lives merge in the general picture of "society." For this purpose, he requires a larger number of characters than can conveniently be featured in the usual storytelling manner; a number and variety of characters such as to suggest general conclusions. The interest is not in the individual dramas of these people, in their personal joys and sorrows, their hole-in-the-corner moral problems; these are of interest only in so far as they are the cellular stuff, the protoplasmic basis, of all social structures. But it is the structure itself which interests the collectivist, the pattern made from innumerable individual cases; the interplay, the working together—the "organic filaments" (as Carlyle calls them) that bind together man to man, and class to class, in the orderly complex of "society." It is the social nexus which the collectivist is seeking.

But the paradox of Dos Passos' world is that the social nexus is just what is lacking. These people live in the same world, the same city. They are subject to the same natural laws, the same economic stresses, and to the same legal statutes. There is a constituted city government—traffic regulations, fire department, milk delivery, sewage disposal—a material organization of the prettiest and most efficient. But for the social nexus binding man to man—affection, gratitude, obligation, cooperation—this is nowhere to be seen. It is every man for himself and the devil take the hindmost. There is hardly a suggestion of any motivation but the four sluggish impulses above referred to, none of which has any but the vaguest reference to interests shared, sentiments reciprocated, ideals held in common. It is an atomistic world, a moral chaos, set in a frame of cosmic order. Society is of necessity collective where so many material needs are served for so many people by so many common agencies, where the stopping of the railroads or the water-supply would result in instant catastrophe and starvation. But in men's relations to man the collectivistic logic is ignored and denied; society is organized on individualistic lines, which means that in effect it is not organized at all.

Everyone denies the connections with his fellows though inevitably bound up with them in the same pattern. Ellen cannot have her hats without the labor of Anna Cohen, but it is only the tragic fire and the death of Anna that bring her briefly to Ellen's mind. Captain James Merivale returns with private Dutch Robertson from the same AEF; but the one prospers in finance while the other drifts into crime; and the only connection between them is the possibility that Merivale may read in the paper of Robertson's getting twenty years. Merivale's banking depends on the commerce of Blackhead and Densch; but Blackhead and Densch fail for ten million dollars, while the bankers still have money to handle. "That's the thing about banking. Even in a deficit there's money to be handled. These commercial propositions always entail a margin of risk. We get 'em coming or else we get 'em going. . . ." George Baldwin is carrying on with Gus McNiel's wife while he is wangling twelve thousand dollars damages for Gus. His going in for political reform means throwing over his friends. The code of the political clansman is simpler. "You know how [Gus] likes to stand by his friends and have his friends stand by him." In marriage people change partners as easily as they change trains at Manhattan Transfer in Jersey; and children are no complication in the world of the abortionist.

Manhattan Transfer is a picture of chaos moral and social; and the narrative technique corresponds to the theme. Each chapter is a loose bundle of incidents from the lives of many different persons or groups, anywhere from four to sixteen in number, completely unrelated save in time and their common involvement in the chaos of Manhattan. There is no effort to mark transitions; each slide replaces the preceding one without preparation or apology, but with something like the flicker of the early silent movies. We pass from the midst of one situation to the midst of another. The characters reappear at wide intervals, without connection or reintroduction. We find ourselves plunged into a situation years later in time and pick up as we can the dropped threads. If Ellen has changed her name to Elaine or Elena, we find this out for ourselves; we piece things together and make our inferences without slowing down, as we read traffic signs on a dark night in unfamiliar country. Within scenes the narrative is often elliptical, with sudden changes from objective action to subjective comment, from what happens to what the character says about it to himself, from third person to first, as the character dramatizes his own experience. The characters' thoughts are not presented formally and consecutively, but by flashes and allusions, as in actual thinking, and with free association of ideas, which do not follow a steady and logical course.

This technique, often suggestive of James Joyce or Virginia Woolf, is dictated by many considerations purely esthetic. There is the instinct to get rid of the author, with his fussy explanations and intrusive comments; to let the situation come to the reader directly with its impact of immediacy and intimacy. But this technique is symbolic too, and corresponds to the philosophical theme. It underlines the discontinuity in the psychic life of the characters. We have the sense of persons not persons—of individuals made up of separate and unrelated moments—at best, a succession of stimuli followed by their responses. What occurs in the intervals does not matter, for the personality is not bound together by a consistency of aim or objective; it is simply uniform in its responses to stimuli of a certain order. Thus the technique contributes to the effect of life as sensation, of thinking as non-purposive, of human beings as puppets on a string. And since the human mind has difficulty in thinking of itself in such purely mechanical terms, we have the effect of bewilderment and futility which is so characteristic of contemporary literature represented physically in the very structure of the narrative.

Again, this technique serves the social theme. So many separate lives are shown being led simultaneously, as it were. There is no need to carry each incident through to its completion, to follow each individual into all the ramifications of his private life. What is called for is a representative section, enough of the tissue in each case to determine its structure; and of such representative bits a vast number, typical and comprehensive. Each one must be reduced in scale so that all may be brought under a single survey, as specimens are assembled under the view of a laboratory worker whose business is to characterize the whole.

But the whole in this case is a social whole; in a social whole the important thing should be the connections, the social relations. And this narrative discontinuity serves again to emphasize the paradox of social beings ignoring the connections, denying the relations, without which they could not exist. So that what appears at first a mere eccentricity in technique turns out to be a peculiarly fitting symbol of something primary in the author's philosophy.

Manhattan Transfer we have found to be a representation of chaos. But in such an undertaking, the danger is that the representation should itself be chaotic, which would be in direct contradiction to the aims of art. In the fiction of Dos Passos there is much to suggest want of form to readers accustomed to the sort of form which prevails in standard novels of the past centuries. In the standard novel the chief element of form is the plot, with its Aristotelian beginning, middle and end. It is the dramatic issue which is continuous throughout the successive occasions shown and whose resolution determines the dénouement with the strictest of logic. In *Manhattan Transfer* there is no plot in the traditional sense, no dramatic issue to give relevance to each successive incident and leave us with a sense of progress and unity. In the standard novel, pattern is provided by the close interrelation of the several characters. But the very point of *Manhattan Transfer* is that the multitudinous characters who represent the city of New York are in the deepest sense unrelated; and by the conditions of the case the author has denied himself this element of pattern.

Or so it seems throughout the first half of the story. As things move forward in time, we begin to realize that the people are not so completely unrelated as we thought. In the deepest sense they are unrelated still; for they continue to ignore and deny the moral bonds that unite them. But it is inevitable, even in so big a world, that some of these people should make contact with one another. Jimmy Herf, the newspaperman, is bound sooner or later to make acquaintance with the popular actress Ellen Thatcher; and once within the orbit of this stellar being he is bound to revolve about her for a certain period. Such a prominent lawyer as George Baldwin is bound to meet with Ellen, if only in the establishment of a world-famous bootlegger; and he too will be drawn within her powerful influence. So it is that some of the more prominent characters are brought together toward the end of the book in contacts more or less casual, and a semblance of plot is produced. More significant perhaps are the connections not positively made but implied; for this is an art that lives by implications more than by front-stage business. When Ellen visits the millinery shop of Mme. Soubrine on the very day that Anna Cohen loses her life in the fire and sees them carry in the stretcher for the dead girl, humanity asserts itself through all the layers of selfish indifference. "Ellen can hardly breathe. She stands beside the ambulance behind a broad blue policeman. She tries to puzzle out why she is so moved; it is as if some part of her were going to be wrapped in bandages, carried away on a stretcher."

It is by touches like this, rare indeed and faint enough so far as action is concerned, that the reader has a sense of progress, if not in the story then in understanding of the author's intention. Formally, however, this book is to be thought of not in terms of plot or dramatic issue, but in terms of themes. The author is not at liberty to develop his themes by personal intrusion and comment in the course of the story; but he has another means of making his comment—that is, in the chapter-headings and in the prose poems prefixed to each chapter in place of the ancient quotations from the classics. Certain chapter-headings, like "Ferryslip" and "Nine Days' Wonder," have reference to something that happens within the particular chapter. But more often the title—"Metropolis," "Dollars"—might as well stand at the head of any chapter in the book, and taken all together—Ferryslip, Metropolis, Dollars, Tracks, Steamroller, Rollercoaster, Revolving Doors, Skyscraper, with the poems attached—they are one continual reminder of the unsettlement and casualness of life in the great city, its hard commercialism, its crazy pace and the sheer mechanical force of compulsion on all its victims—fed in and out of revolving doors, crushed beneath the anonymous weight of its steamroller.

Under "Metropolis" is a brief enumeration of the great cities of antiquity, with the materials of which they were built, long since fallen to dust, concluding with the steel, glass, tile and concrete of the modern skyscrapers. One chapter is headed with a Sandburgian poem on metropolitan themes—trade (selling out; we have made a terrible mistake), entertainment (dancers in a chop-suey joint), and religion (Salvation Army), the last coming as a consolation for the meagerness of the others, but yielding to the dominant commercial theme repeated. One chapter, entitled "Went to the Animals' Fair," has a fantasy on the stop-go signals, red and green lights, and the endless streams of automobiles mechanically controlled. "Rejoicing City that Dwelt Carelessly" develops the war motives: flags of the nations, bullion-gold (interspersed with soldiers' songs), death and apocalypse, the lure of the French woman (Madymoselle from Armenteers), the Liberty Loan and Red Cross drives, the hospital ships, and again the flags of the nations covering all the other themes with their patriotic glamour. There are glimpses of the suburbs, of the city after office hours, of the streams of people homeward or office bound. "Nickelodeon" introduces a wistful review of the people's pleasures, the cheap pleasures that can be bought for a nickel, newspaper extras, cup of coffee in the automat, popular love songs, naughty peep shows . . . "wastebasket of torn-up daydreams."

These prose poems, like the titles, seldom have particular application to the chapters they head. Their reference is general and universal; they have a backward and a forward glance. They build up the physical background of Manhattan. They are summary and symbolic. Once these themes are sounded, they go on reverberating through every incident of the story, like the jazzy jingle of popular songs. They are cumulative, with the titles they accompany. Dollars after Metropolis is incremental; and then Steamroller, Rollercoaster, Revolving Doors. They reach their climax in Skyscraper (suggesting the Tower of Babel) and their nemesis in The Burthen of Nineveh. And if there is no one else to note the crescendo and heed the warning, there is Jimmy Herf, wise man of Sodom, who takes the ferry to Jersey and shakes the dust of the doomed city from his heels.

Oh, yes, there is progress, direction, in the development of these themes; there is composition in the arrangement of incidents from the private lives of Gotham. The thing has form in its modernistic manner; by suggestion, by implication, by contrast and irony. The more one examines it, the more one finds of studied implication. It has throughout its own hard, bright, clean, crisp realism of presentation. It has its vividness and splendor in recording sensations and pictures. Here is perhaps the most pervasive of the ironies that dominate its tone. The world of Manhattan is so painfully bright and glittering, so garishly magnificent—the colors and sounds and smells so perpetually in evidence; and the moral lives of its people so dull and drab, so lacking in imagination, in daring and splendor. The moral world is so thrown in the shade by the world of material things.

Manhattan Transfer is not a story in the traditional sense. It is an abstract composition of story elements made to develop a series of themes. It would be fun to list the possible influences affecting Dos Passos in the conception of this work. There would be Joyce's *Ulysses*, itself an abstract composition of the utmost daring and complexity, and with a thousand technical inventions to which all subsequent writers are free to help themselves. There were perhaps Dorothy Richardson and Virginia Woolf. There would be Eliot's *Waste Land*, with its thematic development, its discontinuity and ironic implications. There would be the poems of Sandburg. There would be perhaps some of the earlier work of Jules Romains, most famous of collectivists. Above all there would be Gertrude Stein and whatever gates she opened to the young artist when he frequented her circle in Paris shortly after the War. That would mean, more than anything else, the French cubists and post-impressionists—men who chose to paint not one landscape literally, but to pick and choose among the visual objects before them, manipulate them, present them in fragments, arrange them in esthetic patterns, use them as freely as composers in music use the themes they put together. There was also the Salle Gaveau and the modern music of the day, with techniques analogous to those of the painters and the poets. There was the Russian Ballet, with its symbolism, its daring, its free manipulation of human living for visual effect and abstract theme. And then there was the moving picture with its lightning shifts of scene, flash backs and bizarre juxtapositions, double and multiple projection, retarded and accelerated motion, its large facilities for thematic treatment and manifold tricks of magic and legerdemain.

Such models would have been most helpful in freeing the young artist from the conventions of the novel. But no number of influences can abate the originality, the conceptual daring, the technical skill, the freshness, the novelty, the realism and the intellectual power of this performance. Readers were not at first impressed, or knew not what to make of this strange offering. The critics in general were not much better off. Some of the writers had an inkling of its importance; and one of them, the most famous of the time, had the discernment and the generosity to welcome it with warm enthusiasm. One of the most honorable incidents in the career of Sinclair Lewis was his public recognition, in the *New York Times* review,[2] of the signal importance for American letters of *Manhattan Transfer*, published in the same year with his own *Arrowsmith*. But the stature of Sinclair Lewis has all along manifested itself in his readiness to recognize and welcome what is novel and promising among the younger writers.

John Dos Passos and *1919*

JEAN-PAUL SARTRE

A novel is a mirror. So everyone says. But what is meant by *reading* a novel? It means, I think, jumping into the mirror. You suddenly find yourself on the other side of the glass, among people and objects that have a familiar look. But they merely look familiar. We have never really seen them. The things of our world have, in turn, become outside reflections. You close the book, step over the edge of the mirror and return to this honest-to-goodness world, and you find furniture, gardens and people who have nothing to say to you. The mirror that closed behind you reflects them peacefully, and now you would swear that art is a reflection. There are clever people who go so far as to talk of distorting mirrors.

Dos Passos very consciously uses this absurd and insistent illusion to impel us to revolt. He had done everything possible to make his novel seem a mere reflection. He has even donned the garb of populism. The reason is that his art is not gratuitous; he wants to prove something. But observe what a curious aim he has. He wants to show us this world, our own—to *show* it only, without explanations or comment. There are no revelations about the machinations of the police, the imperialism of the oil kings or the Ku Klux Klan, no cruel pictures of poverty. We have already seen everything he wants to show us, and, so it seems at first

From Jean-Paul Sartre, *Literary Essays*, trans. Annette Michelson (New York: Philosophical Library, 1957), pp. 88–96. Reprinted by permission of the Hutchinson Publishing Group Ltd.

glance, seen it exactly as he wants us to see it. We recognize immediately the sad abundance of these untragic lives. They are our own lives, these innumerable, planned, botched, immediately forgotten and constantly renewed adventures that slip by without leaving a trace, without involving anyone, until the time when one of them, no different from any of the others, suddenly, as if through some clumsy trickery, sickens a man for good and throws a mechanism out of gear.

Now, it is by depicting, as we ourselves might depict, these too familiar appearances with which we all put up that Dos Passos makes them unbearable. He arouses indignation in people who never get indignant, he frightens people who fear nothing. But hasn't there been some sleight-of-hand? I look about me and see people, cities, boats, the war. But they aren't the real thing; they are discreetly queer and sinister, as in a nightmare. My indignation against this world also seems dubious to me; it only faintly resembles the other indignation, the kind that a mere news item can arouse. I am on the other side of the mirror.

Dos Passos' hate, despair and lofty contempt are real. But that is precisely why his world is not real; it is a created object. I know of none—not even Faulkner's or Kafka's—in which the art is greater or better hidden. I know of none that is more precious, more touching or closer to us. This is because he takes his material from our world. And yet, there is no stranger or more distant world. Dos Passos has invented only one thing, an art of story-telling. But that is enough to create a universe.

We live in time, we calculate in time. The novel, like life, unfolds in the present. The perfect tense exists on the surface only; it must be interpreted as a present *with aesthetic distance*, as a stage device. In the novel the dice are not loaded, for fictional man is free. He develops before our eyes; our impatience, our ignorance, our expectancy are the same as the hero's. The tale, on the other hand, as Fernandez has shown, develops in the past. But the tale explains. Chronological order, life's order, barely conceals the causal order, which is an order for the understanding. The event does not touch us; it stands half-way between fact and law. Dos Passos' time is his own creation; it is neither fictional nor narrative. It is rather, if you like, historical time. The perfect and imperfect tenses are not used simply to observe the rules; the reality of Joe's or of Eveline's adventures lies in the fact they are now part of the past. Everything is told as if by someone who is remembering.

> *The years Dick was little* he never heard anything about his Dad. . . . All Eveline thought about *that winter* was going to the Art Institute. . . . They waited two weeks in Vigo while the officials quarrelled about their status and they got pretty fed up with it.

The fictional event is a nameless presence; there is nothing one can say about it, for it develops. We may be shown two men combing a city for their mistresses, but we are not told that they "do not find them," for this is not true. So long as there remains one street, one café, one house to explore, it is not yet true. In Dos Passos, the things that happen are named first, and then the dice are cast, as they are in our memories.

> Glen and Joe only got ashore for a few hours and couldn't find Marcelline and Loulou.

The facts are clearly outlined; they are ready for *thinking about*. But Dos Passos never thinks them. Not for an instant does the order of causality betray itself in chronological order. There is no narrative, but rather the jerky unreeling of a rough and uneven memory, which sums up a period of several years in a few words only to dwell languidly over a minute fact. Like our real memories, it is a jumble of miniatures and frescoes. There is relief enough, but it is cunningly scattered at random. One step further would give us the famous idiot's monologue in *The Sound and the Fury*. But that would still involve intellectualizing, suggesting an explanation in terms of the irrational, suggesting a Freudian order beneath this disorder. Dos Passos stops just in time. As a result of this, past things retain a flavour of the present; they still remain, in their exile, what they once were, inexplicable tumults of color, sound and passion. Each event is irreducible, a gleaming and solitary *thing* that does not flow from anything else, but suddenly arises to join other things. For Dos Passos, narrating means adding. This accounts for the slack air of his style. "And . . . and . . . and . . ." The great disturbing phenomena — war, love, political movements, strikes — fade and crumble into an infinity of little odds and ends which can just about be set side by side. Here is the armistice:

> In early November rumors of an armistice began to fly around and then suddenly one afternoon Major Wood ran into the office that Eleanor and Eveline shared and dragged them both away from their desks and kissed them both and shouted, "At last it's come." Before she knew it Eveline found herself kissing Major Moorehouse right on the mouth. The Red Cross office turned into a college dormitory the night of a football victory: It was the Armistice.
>
> Everybody seemed suddenly to have bottles of cognac and to be singing, *There's a long long trail awinding* or *La Made-lon pour nous n'est pas sévère.*

These Americans see war the way Fabrizio saw the battle of Waterloo. And the intention, like the method, is clear upon reflection. But you must close the book and reflect.

Passions and gestures are also things. Proust analyzed them, related them to former states and thereby made them inevitable. Dos Passos wants to retain only their factual nature. All he is allowed to say is, "In that place and at that time Richard was that way, and at another time, he was different." Love and decisions are great spheres that rotate on their own axes. The most we can grasp is a kind of *conformity* between the psychological state and the exterior situation, something resembling a color harmony. We may also suspect that explanations are *possible*, but they seem as frivolous and futile as a spider-web on a heavy red flower. Yet, never do we have the feeling of fictional freedom: Dos Passos imposes upon us instead the unpleasant impression of an indeterminacy of detail. Acts, emotions and ideas suddenly settle within a character, make themselves at home and then disappear without his having much to say in the matter. You cannot say he submits to them. He experiences them. There seems to be no law governing their appearance.

Nevertheless, they once did exist. This lawless past is irremediable. Dos Passos has purposely chosen the perspective of history to tell a story. He wants to make us feel that the stakes are down. In *Man's Hope*, Malraux says, more or less, that "the tragic thing about death is that it transforms life into a destiny." With the opening lines of his book, Dos Passos settles down into death. The lives he tells about are all closed in on themselves. They resemble those Bergsonian memories which, after the body's death, float about, lifeless and full of odors and lights and cries, through some forgotten limbo. We constantly have the feeling that these vague, human lives are destinies. Our own past is not at all like this. There is not one of our acts whose meaning and value we cannot still transform even now. But beneath the violent colors of these beautiful, motley objects that Dos Passos presents there is something petrified. Their significance is fixed. Close your eyes and try to remember your own life, try to remember it *that way*; you will stifle. It is this unrelieved stifling that Dos Passos wanted to express. In capitalist society, men do not have lives, they have only destinies. He never says this, but he makes it felt throughout. He expresses it discreetly, cautiously, until we feel like smashing our destinies. We have become rebels; he has achieved his purpose.

We are rebels *behind the looking-glass*. For that is not what the rebel of this world wants to change. He wants to transform Man's *present* condition, the one that develops day by day. Using the past tense to tell about the present means using a device, creating a strange and beautiful world, as frozen as one of those Mardi-Gras masks that become frightening on the faces of real, living men.

But whose memories are these that unfold through the novel? At first glance, they seem to be those of the heroes, of Joe, Dick, Fillette, and Eveline. And, on occasion, they are. As a rule, whenever a character is sincere, whenever he is bursting with something, no matter how, or with what:

> When he went off duty he'd walk home achingly tired through the strawberry-scented early Parisian morning, thinking of the faces and the eyes and the sweat-drenched hair and the clenched fingers clotted with blood and dirt.

But the narrator often ceases to coincide completely with the hero. The hero could not quite have said what he does say, but you feel a discreet complicity between them. The narrator relates from the outside what the hero would have wanted him to relate. By means of this complicity, Dos Passos, without warning us, has us make the transition he was after. We suddenly find ourselves inside a horrible memory whose every recollection makes us uneasy, a bewildering memory that is no longer that of either the characters or the author. It seems like a chorus that remembers, a sentable chorus that is accessory to the deed.

> All the same he got along very well at school and the teachers liked him, particularly Miss Teazle, the English teacher, because he had nice manners and said little things that weren't fresh but that made them laugh. Miss Teazle said he showed real feeling for English composition. One Christmas he sent her

a little rhyme he made up about the Christ Child and the three Kings and she declared he had a gift.

The narration takes on a slightly stilted manner, and everything that is reported about the hero assumes the solemn quality of a public announcement: ". . . she declared he had a gift." The sentence is not accompanied by any comment, but acquires a sort of collective resonance. It is a *declaration*. And indeed, whenever we want to know his characters' thoughts, Dos Passos, with respectful objectivity, generally gives us their declarations.

Fred . . . said the last night before they left he was going to tear loose. When they got to the front he might get killed and then what? Dick said he liked talking to the girls but that the whole business was too commercial and turned his stomach. Ed Schuyler, who'd been nicknamed Frenchie and was getting very continental in his ways, said that the street girls were too naive.

I open *Paris-Soir* and read, "*From our special correspondent*: Charlie Chaplin declares that he has put an end to Charlie." Now I have it! Dos Passos reports all his characters' utterances to us in the style of a statement to the Press. Their words are thereby cut off from thought, and become pure utterances, simple reactions that must be registered as such, in the behaviorist style upon which Dos Passos draws when it suits him to do so. But, at the same time, the utterance takes on a social importance; it is inviolable, it becomes a maxim. Little does it matter, thinks the satisfied chorus, what Dick had in mind when he spoke that sentence. What matters is that it has been uttered. Besides, it was not formed inside him, it came from afar. Even before he uttered it, it existed as a pompous sound, a taboo. All he has done is to lend it his power of affirmation. It is as if there were a Platonic heaven of words and commonplaces to which we all go to find words suitable to a given situation. There is a heaven of gestures, too. Dos Passos makes a pretense of presenting gestures as pure events, as mere exteriors, as free, animal movements. But this is only appearance. Actually, in relating them, he adopts the point of view of the chorus, of public opinion. There is no single one of Dick's or of Eleanor's gestures which is not a public demonstration, performed to a humming accompaniment of flattery.

> At Chantilly they went through the château and fed the big carp in the moat. They ate their lunch in the woods, sitting on rubber cushions. J. W. kept everybody laughing explaining how he hated picnics, asking everybody what it was that got into even the most intelligent women that they were always trying to make people go on picnics. After lunch they drove out to Senlis to see the houses that the Uhlans had destroyed there in the battle of the Marne.

Doesn't it sound like a local newspaper's account of an ex-servicemen's banquet? All of a sudden, as the gesture dwindles until it is no more than a thin film, we see that it *counts*, that it is sacred in character and that, at the same time, it involves commitment. But for whom? For the abject consciousness of "everyman," for what Heidegger calls "das Mann." But still, where does it spring from? Who is its representative as I read? *I* am. In order to understand the words, in order to make sense out of the paragraphs, I first have to adopt his point of view. I have to play the role of the obliging chorus. This consciousness exists only through me; without me there would be nothing but black spots on white paper. But even while I *am* this collective consciousness, I want to wrench away from it, to see it from the judge's point of view, that is, to get free of myself. This is the source of the shame and uneasiness with which Dos Passos knows how to fill the reader. I am a reluctant accomplice (though I am not even sure that I am reluctant), creating and rejecting social taboos. I am, deep in my heart, a revolutionary again, an unwilling one.

In return, how I hate Dos Passos' men! I am given a fleeting glimpse of their minds, just enough to see that they are living animals. Then, they begin to unwind their endless tissue of ritual statements and sacred gestures. For them, there is no break between inside and outside, between body and consciousness, but only between the stammerings of an individual's timid, intermittent, fumbling thinking and the messy world of collective representations. What a simple process this is, and how effective! All one need do is use American journalistic technique in telling the story of a life, and like the Salzburg reed, a life crystallizes into the Social, and the problem of the transition to the typical— stumbling-block of the social novel—is thereby resolved. There is no further need to present a working man type, to compose (as Nizan does in *Antoine Bloyé*) an existence which represents the exact average of thousands of existences. Dos Passos, on the contrary, can give all his attention to rendering a single life's special character. Each of his characters is unique; what happens to him could happen to no one else. What does it matter, since Society has marked him more deeply than could any special circumstance, since *he is* Society? Thus, we get a glimpse of an order beyond the accidents of fate or the contingency of detail, an order more supple than Zola's physiological necessity or Proust's psychological mechanism, a soft and insinuating constraint which seems to release its victims, letting them go only to take possession of them again without their suspecting, in other words, a statistical determinism. These men, submerged in their own existences, live as they can. They struggle; what comes their way is not determined in advance. And yet, neither their efforts, their faults, nor their most extreme violence can interfere with the regularity of births, marriages, and suicides. The pressure exerted by a gas on the walls of its container does not depend upon the individual histories of the molecules composing it.

We are still on the other side of the looking-glass. Yesterday you saw your best friend and expressed to him your passionate hatred of war. Now try to relate this conversation to yourself in the style of Dos Passos. "And they ordered two beers and said that war was hateful. Paul declared he would rather do anything than fight and John said he agreed with him and both got excited and said they were glad they agreed. On his way home, Paul decided to see John more often." You will start hating yourself immediately. It will not take you long, however, to decide that you *cannot* use this tone in talking about yourself. However insincere you may have been, you were at least living out your insincerity, playing it out on your own, continuously creating and extending its existence from one moment to the next. And even if you got caught up in collective representations, you had first to experience them as personal resignation. We are neither mechanical objects nor possessed souls, but something worse; we are free. We exist either entirely *within* or entirely *without*. Dos Passos' man is a hybrid creature, an interior-exterior being. We go on living with him and within him, with his vacillating, individual consciousness, when suddenly it wavers, weakens, and is diluted in the collective consciousness. We follow it up to that point and suddenly, before we notice, we are on the outside. The man behind the looking-glass is a strange, contemptible, fascinating creature. Dos Passos knows how to use this constant shifting to fine effect. I know of nothing more gripping than Joe's death.

> Joe laid out a couple of frogs and was backing off towards the door, when he saw in the mirror that a big guy in a blouse was bringing down a bottle on his head held with both hands. He tried to swing around but he didn't have time. The bottle crashed his skull and he was out.

We are inside with him, until the shock of the bottle on his skull. Then immediately, we find ourselves outside with the chorus, part of the collective memory,

". . . and he was out." Nothing gives you a clearer feeling of annihilation. And from then on, each page we turn, each page that tells of other minds and of a world going on without Joe, is like a spadeful of earth over our bodies. But it is a behind-the-looking-glass death: all we really get is the fine *appearance* of nothingness. True nothingness can neither be felt nor thought. Neither you nor I, nor anyone after us, will ever have anything to say about our real deaths.

Dos Passos' world—like those of Faulkner, Kafka, and Stendhal—is impossible because it is contradictory. But therein lies its beauty. Beauty is a veiled contradiction. I regard Dos Passos as the greatest writer of our time.

Dos Passos and Naturalism

CHARLES C. WALCUTT

Although I deal with him briefly, John Dos Passos is a tremendously significant figure in the development of naturalism, particularly as an end-point in the evolution of naturalistic forms. We have looked at many of the ways in which the writer struggles to force his materialistic philosophy into a fictional structure that will represent it adequately while it permits him also to explore his characters; and we have seen one form after another discarded because it has brought obvious inconsistencies or taken the vitality and inwardness away from the characters. Dos Passos is a culmination and an end-point of the dark matter-dominated trends which have been explored in this volume; he has written almost as if he intended to carry these tendencies to their extremest possibility.

His early structure embodies and demonstrates the fractured lives and fractured values of the twentieth century. He writes a kaleidoscope, a pattern that always changes and never repeats because the possible combinations and permutations are endless; and this structure perfectly states its meaning because it is its meaning. It is a picture of chaos, a blind, formless, struggling, frantic world moving in so many directions at once that it would be impossible for anyone to imagine an intelligent control of its energies. In this whirling chaos

From Charles C. Walcutt, *American Literary Naturalism: A Divided Stream* (Minneapolis: University of Minnesota Press, 1956), pp. 280–89. Reprinted by permission of the publisher.

the characters work on their destinies—they do not work them out—and the reader is interested in the quality of their experiences as he shares the energy and variety of their lives. Here is a perfect naturalistic form, in which the envelope of chaos contains, physically and meta-phorically, the busy volitions of the individuals who move back and forth to weave its web. This form renders a picture of chaos: there is no suggestion that any event is demonstrated as inevitable because the picture does not consider a purposeful form in the world. That premise is not apparent.

In *Manhattan Transfer* (1925) Dos Passos is just leaning toward these effects. The title suggests the form, which is a sort of musical chairs. Characters appear and are described to the point where the reader begins to see them as people, only to be set aside while other char-acters are introduced and partially developed. As new people are introduced, the earlier ones fade into the background, and some of them disappear, so that there seem always to be about the same number involved in the game. In another figure, it is as if a wave passed over Manhattan, carrying three or four characters across the island and picking up half-a-dozen others whom it abandons successively as it picks up still others in its path.

The central characters, Jimmy Herf and Ellen Thatcher, have a hard time of it, whereas others become big-time mobsters, politicians, businessmen, and opera-tors. The effect of the continual shift of scene and character is to fix them in a series of positions; we have to accept these positions as evidence of their fates, but we cannot follow in detail the steps by which they came to be. Here is clearly a device that eliminates the will and shows the characters riding along on or under the wave of time and event that sweeps over the city. Psychologically, it depicts persons who are not persons but a succession of reactions to stimuli. The fragmented presentation suggests that life is not integrated by purpose or order, that it is a flow of sensation, that man is controlled by his basic physical responses. Since we do not like to think of ourselves in such purely physiological and mechanistic terms, the effect of the book is bewilderment.

It cannot be accident that many of the characters have father fixations. At the bottom of this totem is Bud, from Cooperstown, who has killed his father with a hoe in revenge for many beatings with a chain, and fled to New York. Ellen has a full-scale Oedipus complex; she drifts from man to man and does not "love anybody for long unless they're dead." Hovering in the background is her father with whom she had a relation so close as almost to displace the mother whom they both rejected. Jimmy Herf, too, breaks away from a widowed mother who oppresses him with her morbid devotion. Ellen for a while is a beautiful and successful actress, married to a homosexual, while Jimmy watches her with doglike devotion from a distance. After a divorce, and a couple of her affairs have dwindled away, she marries Jimmy and has a child; but then Jimmy loses his job, and when Ellen goes back to work she drifts into a new affair with an old friend. Presently she divorces Jimmy to marry this rising politician, and Jimmy stumbles off somewhere into the country. Harried people waver from disillusion to despair; the very successful are not much less desperate than the failures. Nobody seems able to help or to care about others. Starvation, abortion, crooked finance, hijacking, money panics, and general aimlessness fill this portrait of a city, and the tone is grim as it is sensational. The idealism of the American Dream is present as indignation and bitterness at the conditions which have thwarted that Dream, but this is so only if the reader deduces it from the ironic juxtapositions and from the overtones of Dos Passos' language, which shows the city always incredibly bright and polished, while its lives are dull and morally sterile. Traditional values may be scorned, both by the characters and their author, but there is no feeling here that science has the answer. A mad world of finance, sex, crime, and personal search is not a background against which the idea of scientific progress glows brightly.

Manhattan Transfer went through numerous editions in a few years after its publication. It owes a very great deal to Joyce's *Ulysses*, from which it takes the method of showing the life of a city by flash after flash of incident and personal experience. Dos Passos is more sentimentally aware of his people than Joyce is: he shows their agonies and fears and defeats in passages of considerable force—as when Ellen is preparing herself to accept George Baldwin, for security, after she has set Jimmy Herf aside:

> She had made up her mind. It seemed as if she had set the photograph of herself in her own place, forever frozen into a single gesture. . . . Beyond the plates, the ivory pink lamp, the broken pieces of bread, his face above the blank shirtfront jerked and nodded; the flush grew on his cheeks; his nose caught the light now on one side, now on the other, his taut lips moved eloquently over his yellow teeth. Ellen felt herself sitting with her ankles crossed, rigid as a porcelain figure under her clothes, everything about her seemed to be growing hard and enameled, the air bluestreaked with cigarettesmoke, was turning to glass. His wooden face of a marionette waggled senselessly in front of her.

He is also sampling a larger city than Joyce's Dublin, over several years (centering at about 1920) rather than a single day. Although *Ulysses* is tremendously complex, its Dublin is snug and intimately familiar, whereas Dos Passos' Manhattan is a screaming turmoil of machines and people—a clouded vortex in which the characters are arrested for poignant moments and then disappear again into the whirling background. Yet there is an improbable amount of interplay among them; nearly every character crosses the paths of several of the others or even becomes more or less involved with them, and since they come from all parts of the country and move from Greenwich

Village to Uptown, so much interplay has a special effect. It suggests that the form of this novel is consciously made to embody and express its naturalistic philosophy. Joyce, who is neither cold nor sentimental in *Ulysses*, had much more to say and a much more intimate control of his material. Aimlessness, whirl, and coincidence, expressed in the form of *Manhattan Transfer*, do not add up to a novel that says much, although its frantic picture is vivid and sensational. What it says is that social and personal chaos weaves a pattern that is no pattern but rather an unstopping movement—back and forth, in and out, up and down—whether it be in transit, sex, business, or life. It is a movement of agony, of a society in its death throes.

In spite of these conclusions, the technique of *Manhattan Transfer* is inconspicuous beside that of the trilogy *U.S.A.* (1937), composed of three huge novels, *The 42nd Parallel* (1930), *Nineteen Nineteen* (1932), and *The Big Money* (1936). In these novels Dos Passos has extended his method of projecting the kaleidoscope to the point where he fashions his pattern out of three elaborately contrived elements which interrupt and supplement the central narratives—the Newsreel, the Camera Eye, and the Biography. With this invention he seeks to find styles that are appropriate to the various types of material treated and that in blending give the effect of variousness, energy, and turmoil that we saw in a simpler way in *Manhattan Transfer*.

The body of the trilogy is devoted to the careers of a dozen representative people through the years from about the turn of this century to the big money days of the twenties. The first novel approaches World War I, the second deals largely with civilian activities during the war, in New York and Paris, the third explores the big money boom after the war. There is no central character in *U.S.A.* Each novel deals with about four of the dozen, and there is a slight carry-over from one novel to the next. In *The 42nd Parallel* the main characters are Mac McCreary, son of a laborer, who struggles through the labor movement, joins and leaves the I.W.W. in the Northwest, and ends by living with a Mexican girl and comfortably selling radical books from their shop; J. Ward Moorehouse, from Delaware, who marries wealthy women, rises through business and public relations into politics, where he pompously mediates between capital and labor with the purpose of keeping the latter in line, and has a long platonic relation with Eleanor Stoddard, who is a frigid, frustrated, artistic, ambitious bitch from Chicago, comes to New York, where she prospers as an interior decorator, has an important position in the Red Cross in Paris (this is in the second volume), and finally marries a Russian prince; and Janey Williams, mousey and fearful, who becomes the devoted secretary of J. Ward Moorehouse.

Nineteen Nineteen adds the career of Janey's brother, Joe Williams, an ignorant bloke trying to get along, who joins the Navy, deserts, and brawls his way purposelessly through the action; Richard Ellsworth Savage, cultured and personable, who somehow drifts down into opportunism and debasement of his literary talents in J. Ward Moorehouse's employment, a kind of unhappy playboy; Eveline Hutchins, daughter of a Chicago minister who terrifies her, seduced by a Mexican painter, who joins Eleanor Stoddard for a while as interior decorator, goes with her to Paris, is jilted by the man she loves, has a brief affair with Moorehouse and another with a soldier named Paul, and later dies from a lethal dose of sleeping pills; and Daughter, a wild Texas tomboy who has a gay and frantic life spending her father's money and running from men, traveling abroad after the war, who transfers the early frustrated passion that has been the cause of her restlessness to Dick Savage, and who dies, pregnant and rejected by him, in an airplane crash.

The Big Money almost has a central character, Charley Anderson, aviator and war ace, who goes into business manufacturing airplanes and is on the way to riches when he is caught up in the fever of market speculation that takes his money as fast as he can make it. An airplane crash puts him out of circulation and he loses his part in the business; his drinking and gambling increase, and he dies in Florida after an automobile accident when he tried to beat a train to a crossing, going eighty-five miles an hour. Charley's is the grittiest and most desperate story in the whole trilogy. There are also Mary French, a spectacled student, drab and miserable, who devotes herself to Reform; and Margo Dowling, who works her busy, heartless way through a number of men to a fat contract in Hollywood.

These interweaving careers (all the characters know some of the others at one time or another) are given in larger segments than those in *Manhattan Transfer*; but always with a clinical detachment that makes them seem like figures on a screen compelled by drives the inwardness of which we never know, until finally we come to the conclusion that all their drives are instinctive or compulsive. The total effect is much like the strident chaos of the first novel.

The three devices which interrupt the central narratives and "formalize" the chaos depicted represent the ultimate stylistic expressiveness of the naturalistic movement. The Newsreel introduces a section with bits of headlines, advertisements, feature articles, and phrases of news, interwoven with lines of poetry which presumably represent some of the emotions—usually popular and sentimental—being experienced at the time. Superficially, it represents a world of fraud and sophistication, violence and treachery; it is a backdrop of hysteria behind which the serious business of society, if such it can be called, is concealed; for high finance and international relations continue to control the world while the public is engaged with sentiment and sensation.

The Biographies—there are twenty-five of them scattered through the three volumes—are condensed records of typical public figures of the time, from the fields of business, politics, technology, labor, and the arts. Such figures as Carnegie, Hearst, Insull, Rudolph Valentino, Isadora Duncan, William Jennings Bryan, and Eugene Debs constitute a sampling of specific figures who dominate the stage and also move the properties and scenes of our time. They are set forth ironically and bitterly, for the businessmen are greedy and unscrupulous, the entertainers are victims of their public as well as panders to its lusts and vanities, the liberal politicians are confused by their ambitions and the inadequacies of their idealism, and the efficiency expert (F. W. Taylor) is an inhuman machine who dies with a stop watch in his hand. If these are the public heroes, the images of greatness which they portray for the common man—through the jittery glittering Newsreel—show why "our storybook democracy" has not come true. The one figure presented by Dos Passos with a devotion approaching reverence is Thorstein Veblen, the lonely and satiric analyst of leisure-class conduct and the sabotage of efficiency by rapacious business, who could not fit into our academic world and who died leaving the request that his ashes be scattered into the sea and no monument or memorial of any sort be erected to his name.

The Camera Eye is Dos Passos' subjective and rather poetic commentary on this world. It occurs fifty-one times through the trilogy, revealing the character, interests, and life history of the artist—how he came out of Virginia, went to school abroad and at Harvard, drove an ambulance during the war, was disillusioned by the Versailles Treaty and the rampage of materialism which followed it, and lived as a newspaper reporter and radical through the big money days of the early twenties. He is an oversensitive and fastidious intellectual, recoiling from the grubby masses and yet seeing in them the backbone and heart of the America which the great sweep of his novel shows being corrupted, debauched, and enslaved by the forces of commercial rapacity. He sees America through the lens of a poetic tradition—Whitman, Sandberg, perhaps Hart Crane—which impels him to identify the physical elements of our nation with the dream of greatness and individual realization that it has always embodied for the transcendentalist.

Here the characteristics I have attributed to American idealism when it breaks away from its scientific discipline and control—of unfocused idealism and uncontrolled protest—become increasingly evident in the notions that virtue is in the people, waste is the natural expression of the exploiters, and wealth is in a long-term conspiracy to sabotage labor and destroy our resources. It is perhaps not extravagant to identify the perfectly expressive form of this work with the final division of the great stream of American idealism. The form expresses a chaos; it is a fractured world pictured in a novel fractured into four parts through four styles from four points of view. This division of the subject combines with the range and variety of the materials treated to give the impression that nothing can be done because the problem is too complex to take hold of. It can be watched in the frantic samples that Dos Passos gives us, but we get no sense of comprehensible process that might be analyzed and controlled by the application of scientific method, because it is, finally, a *moral* deterioration that Dos Passos depicts. Thus with the radical writer we come full circle to the conservative position.

The point can be illustrated by samples of the Camera Eye taken from *The Big Money*: returning from Europe,

throat tightens when the redstacked steamer churning the faintlyheaving slatecolored swell swerves shaking in a long green-marbled curve past the red lightship.

spine stiffens with the remembered chill of the offshore Atlantic

and the jag of framehouses in the west above the invisible land and spiderweb rollercoasters and the chewinggum towers of Coney and the freighters with their stacks way aft and the blur beyond Sandy Hook

and the vision spreads over the nation, to

the whine and shriek of the buzzsaw and the tipsy smell of raw lumber and straggling through slagheaps through fireweed through wasted woodlands the shantytowns the shantytowns

He refuses a profitable job because he cannot become part of the exploiting machine, talks with other seekers in Greenwich Village, listens skeptically to orators in Union Square, identifies himself in Whitmanesque fashion with hunters and adventurers in the West, and toward the end makes a pilgrimage to Plymouth to hear about Sacco and Vanzetti.

pencil scrawls in my notebook the scraps of recollection the broken halfphrases the effort to intersect word with word to dovetail clause with clause to rebuild out of mangled memories unshakably (Oh Pontius Pilate) the truth . . .

. . . how can I make them feel how our fathers our uncles haters of oppression came to this coast how say Don't let them scare you how make them feel who are your oppressors America

rebuild the ruined words worn slimy in the mouths of lawyers districtattorneys collegepresidents judges without the old words the immigrants haters of oppression brought to Plymouth how can you know who are your betrayers America

And the final cry of denunciation:

they have clubbed us off the streets they are stronger they are rich they hire and fire the politicians the newspapereditors the old judges . . . America will not forget her betrayers . . .

America our nation has been beaten by strangers who have bought the laws and fenced off the meadows and cut down the woods for pulp and turned our pleasant cities into slums and sweated the wealth out of our people . . .

we stand defeated America.

The trouble here is that the indictment has been torn loose from the facts. People are not virtuous because they are poor. If we choose to be sentimental about trees, it was the poor pioneer who cut down and burned the hardwood forests over half a continent, a fearful waste, whereas the big corporations that cut the pulpwood conserve their trees carefully and have over the decades increased their reserves beyond the nation's needs. The prairies were gulched by the poor farming and overgrazing of the pioneers, too, long before they were fenced and restored and protected by the avaricious big money farmers.

Particularly significant of this division and confusion is the fact that most of the central characters are sexually frigid, inhibited, deprived, or frustrated. Margo Dowling is unfeeling; Janey is terrified of sex; Eleanor Stoddard is apparently quite frigid; Daughter is confused and repressed, and her sudden passion for Dick Savage causes her destruction; Mary French is completely inhibited and neurotic. Where the sexual life is presumed to be satisfactory, Dos Passos ignores it, but with the others a substantial preoccupation of the author is to explore the fears, the desolation, and the guilty aimlessness which he relates to the sense of being unloved. This preoccupation gives the book a pervasive dreariness which combines with the fact that people seem always to be smoky, grimy, gritty, and tired to make a desolation that is, ultimately, wholly subjective. It is a literary effect contrived by careful selection of detail and control of language.

It is true that the possessors of great wealth and power have abused both, and yet he has loaded the dice so heavily in favor of the common man that the reader is skeptical when Dos Passos is most earnest. His idealism has lost its hold on fact. The result, as usual, shows the facts (in the stream of materialism) as grim, dark, and uncontrollable, whereas the optimism of spirit is dissipated in fierce but unreliable indignation. The form of this trilogy is a perfect embodiment of this division between nature and spirit: the main blocks of the narrative portray characters groping in a hopeless jungle of sensation and instinct, whereas the Camera Eye cries its somewhat irresponsible protest against the retreat from the American Dream, denouncing the wrong culprit as often as the right one.

Dos Passos's *U.S.A.*
The Words of the Hollow Men

JOHN LYDENBERG

Because James Baldwin, like Tocqueville a decade or more ago, has now become so fashionable that one cannot decently take a text from him, I shall start with Yevgeny Yevtushenko, in the hope that he has not quite yet reached that point. In one of his poems appear the simple lines: "Let us give back to words/Their original meanings." My other non-Dos Passos text is so classic that it cannot be over-fashionable. In *A Farewell to Arms*, Gino says, "What has been done this summer cannot have been done in vain." And, as you all know, Hemingway has Frederic Henry reply: "I did not say anything. I was always embarrassed by the words sacred, glorious, and sacrifice and the expression in vain. . . . Abstract words such as glory, honor, courage, or hallow were obscene."

These quotations suggest the concern of writers with abstract words representing the ideals and values of their society. Both Yevtushenko and Hemingway say that these words have lost their glory, their true meaning. But they take diametrically opposed attitudes toward the role the words will play in their writings. Representing the party of Hope, Yevtushenko is the social and political idealist, the reformer, the artist who sees his art as a weapon in man's unceasing struggle for a

From Sidney J. Krause, ed., *Essays on Determinism in American Literature* (Kent, Ohio: Kent State University Press, 1964), pp. 97–107. Reprinted by permission of the author and publisher.

better world. Representing the party of Despair, Hemingway abjures political concerns, makes his separate peace, and develops an art unconcerned with social ideals. Thus they symbolize two extremes: writers at one pole—Yevtushenko's—will utilize the words, will insist on doing so; writers at the other—Hemingway's—will dispense with them altogether, or try to do so, as did Hemingway in most of his early fiction.

Dos Passos falls between the extremes, but instead of presenting us with a golden mean he gives something more like an unstable compound of the two. Hemingway abandons the words because he can see no relation between them and the realities, and creates a world stripped of the values represented by the words. By contrast, reformers—who are equally insistent on the disparity between the ideals and the realities—are unwilling to reject the words and strive, like Yevtushenko, to give back to them their original meanings. Dos Passos can neither abandon nor revivify the words. Like Hemingway he feels that they have been made obscene and he can find no way in his art to redeem them. Yet like any reformer he puts them at the center of his work.

Critics have often held that the protagonist of *U.S.A.* is society. I could almost maintain that it is, instead, "the words." Dos Passos seems obsessed by them: he cares about them passionately and cannot abandon them, but at the same time he is made sick at heart—nay at stomach—by the way they have been spoiled. So he concerns himself with problems of social values, ever returning to the words, "as a dog to his vomit" (to use the inelegant but expressive Biblical phrase). *U.S.A.* tastes sour because the words are tainted and indigestible, but neither here nor in his other fiction can Dos Passos spew them forth once and for all as could the Hemingways of our literature.

In two well-known passages, Dos Passos makes explicit his feeling about the words. These—the most eloquent and deeply felt parts of *U.S.A.*—are the Camera Eyes focused on the execution of Sacco and Vanzetti. In the first, immediately preceding the Mary French section on the last desperate days before the executions, he asks:

> how make them feel who are your oppressors
> America
> rebuild the ruined words worn slimy in the mouths
> of lawyers districtattorneys collegepresidents judges
> without the old words the immigrants haters of op-
> pression brought to Plymouth how can you know
> who are your betrayers America (*Big Money*, 437)

In the second, after the execution, he says:

> we the beaten crowd together . . . sit hunched
> with bowed heads on benches and hear the old words
> of the haters of oppression made new in sweat
> and agony tonight
> our work is over   the scribbled phrases   the nights
> typing releases the smell of the printshop the sharp
> reek of newprinted leaflets the rush for Western
> Union stringing words into wires the search for sting-
> ing words to make you feel who are your oppressors
> America
> America our nation has been beaten by strangers
> who have turned our language inside out who have
> taken the clean words our fathers spoke and made
> them slimy and foul (462) [1]

Just as Dos Passos makes the Sacco-Vanzetti affair symbolic of his vision of the state of the nation, so, in talking about the "old words," "the clean words our fathers spoke," and "the old American speech," he is alluding to his ideals, to the American dream, and in describing the words now as "ruined," "slimy and foul," and "turned . . . inside out," he is expressing his sense of the betrayal of the dream.

"Mostly U.S.A. is the speech of the people," says Dos Passos to conclude the prose poem he added as preface to the trilogy. Maybe. But U.S.A., the novel, in no way carries out that Sandburg-like suggestion of faith in the people and delight in their talk. It contains none of the salty talk, the boastful talk, the folksy talk, the "wise" talk that is the staple of much "realistic" American fiction. Actually, we discover, on re-examination of these novels, that dialogue plays a smaller role than we might have thought it did. What little talk there is is either purely functional, merely a way of getting on with the narrative: "Shall we go to bed?" "Where can I get a drink?" "God I feel lousy this morning." Or it is banal and stereotyped. Whenever his characters express anything resembling ideas they talk only in tired slogans; the words have been drained of meaning, and the characters mouthing them are empty puppets.

Here is one example. I would give many more, had I time, for the real effect is gained only through the continuous repetition of the vaporous phrases. This is from 1919, the novel written during the time Dos Passos was presumably most favorably inclined toward Marxism and the Communists. One might have expected that here if anywhere the words of a Communist, Don Stevens in this instance, would carry some conviction. Instead Dos Passos makes them sound mechanical, false, flat, like counterfeit coins. The effect is heightened here, as in many other places, by giving us the words in indirect dialog.

> He said that there wasn't a chinaman's chance that the U. S. would keep out of the war; the Germans were winning, the working class all over Europe was on the edge of revolt, the revolution in Russia was the beginning of the worldwide social revolution and the bankers knew it and Wilson knew it; the only question was whether the industrial workers in the east and the farmers and casual laborers in the middle west and west would stand for war. The entire press was bought and muzzled. The Morgans had to fight or go bankrupt. "It's the greatest conspiracy in history." (131)

This is the way the words sound in passage after passage. The ruined words dribble from the mouths of

Dos Passos's hollow men. Within is nothing but clichés, phrases having no meaning for the speaker and conveying none to the listener. *This* is the speech of the people in Dos Passos's *U.S.A.*, and it does much to establish the tone of the whole trilogy.

But if the words are often empty and meaningless, they often too have a very real meaning, vicious and perverted. The old words of the American dream have been "turned . . . inside out"; now they are the lies by which the new Americans live. The theme of the transformation of the clean words into lies had been badly stated in Dos Passos's first novel, *One Man's Initiation.* Early in the book, Martin Howe dreams romantically of his mission as the ocean steamer carries him "over there": "And very faintly, like music heard across the water in the evening, blurred into strange harmonies, his old watchwords echo a little in his mind. Like the red flame of the sunset setting fire to opal sea and sky, the old exaltation, the old flame that would consume to ashes all the lies in the world, the trumpet-blast under which the walls of Jericho would fall down, stirs and broods in the womb of his grey lassitude" (14). Then as Martin is first going up to the front, he comes to adopt a new conception in which the lies are all-inclusive, his "old watchwords" now no different from the rest of the world's lies. A stranger appears and explains it to him: "Think, man, think of all the oceans and lies through all the ages that must have been necessary to make this possible! Think of this new particular vintage of lies that has been so industriously pumped out of the press and the pulpit. . . . [The] lies are like a sticky juice over-spreading the world, a living, growing flypaper to catch and gum the wings of every human soul" (30). Finally, Martin talks in much the same way himself: " 'What terrifies me . . . is their power to enslave our minds. . . . America, as you know, is ruled by the press. . . . People seem to so love to be fooled. . . . We are slaves of bought intellect, willing slaves' " (144). And a French anarchist takes up the theme and makes the moral explicit: " 'Oh, but we are all such dupes. . . .

First we must fight the lies. It is the lies that choke us' "
(156).

In *U.S.A.*, Dos Passos does not *tell* us about the lies,
he makes us feel them. The Newsreels are his most
obvious device for showing us the "sticky juice" of lies
in which Americans are caught. The opening lines of
The 42nd Parallel are: "It was that emancipated
race/That was chargin up the hill;/Up to where them
insurrectos/Was afightin fit to kill." The hill is not San
Juan but a hill in the Philippines. And that first Newsreel
ends with Senator Beveridge's lucid bluster: "The
twentieth century will be American. American thought
will dominate it. American progress will give it color and
direction. American deeds will make it illustrious. . . .
The regeneration of the world, physical as well as
moral, has begun, and revolutions never move
backwards" (5).

One recognizable pattern keeps recurring in the shifting kaleidoscope of the Newsreels: that is—the official
lies disguised as popular truths. We see—and hear—the
rhetoric of the American Way drummed into the heads
of the American public, by advertisements, newspaper
headlines, newspaper stories, politicians' statements,
businessmen's statements. In contrast to these standardized verbalizations about happy, prosperous, good
America, the Newsreels give continual flashes of Dos
Passos's "real" America—of fads and follies, hardships
and horrors. More striking even than the contrasts within
these collages are those between the shimmering surface
of the Newsreels and the sardonic realities of the
Portraits, and above all the dreary lives of his fictional
characters.

The narratives of these lives take up the greater part
of the book, of course, and our reaction to it depends
to a great extent on our evaluation of the characters. My
suggestion is that it is by their use of "the words" that we
judge them. And here, *mirabile dictu*, we come at last
to the theme of "determinism."

That *U.S.A.* is strongly naturalistic and deterministic

is obvious to all. Readers who judge it a major work of fiction do so in part because of its success in portraying characters as helpless individuals caught in a world they have not made and can not control. Less admiring critics are apt to consider its weakness to be the weakness of the characters, sometimes even implying that Dos Passos's failure to create free, responsible heroes was a failure of execution. Whatever their assessment of the novel, all agree that *U.S.A.* is starkly deterministic. None of its characters has free will, none determines his fate, all move like automatons.

The chief way in which Dos Passos makes us feel that his characters—or non-characters—are determined is by showing their choices as non-choices. In *U.S.A.* Dos Passos's people do not make decisions. Or, if you insist that human beings all make decisions, choose one road over another, I will say instead that he presents his characters to us so that we do not feel their choices to be decisions. They simply are doing so and so, and continue thus until they find themselves, or we find them, doing something else.

Here are two examples. The first, a long one, includes two decisions, one a reversal of the other. Note here—for future reference—what the protagonist, Richard Ellsworth Savage, does with the words, and note also how the indirect dialogue accentuates the feeling of cliché and slogan. Dick is "deciding" what he should do about the war and about his college education.

In the Easter vacation, after the Armed Ship Bill had passed Dick had a long talk with Mr. Cooper who wanted to get him a job in Washington, because he said a boy of his talent oughtn't to endanger his career by joining the army and already there was talk of conscription. Dick blushed becomingly and said he felt it would be against his conscience to help in the war in any way. They talked a long time without getting anywhere about duty to the state and party leadership and highest expediency. In the end Mr.

Cooper made him promise not to take any rash step without consulting him. [Note that Dick has now "decided" that his "principles" forbid him to enter any war work.] Back in Cambridge everybody was drilling and going to lectures on military science. Dick was finishing up the four year course in three years and had to work hard, but nothing in the courses seemed to mean anything any more. He managed to find time to polish up a group of sonnets called Morituri Te Salutant that he sent to a prize competition run by *The Literary Digest*. It won the prize but the editors wrote back that they would prefer a note of hope in the last sestet. Dick put in the note of hope [so go the words!] and sent the hundred dollars to Mother to go to Atlantic City with. He discovered that if he went into war work he could get his degree that spring without taking any exams and went in to Boston one day without saying anything to anybody and signed up in the volunteer ambulance service. [Now he has "decided" that his "principles" no longer prevent him from war work.] (1919, 95–96)

And here is the sound of a Dos Passos character "deciding" to have an abortion:

Of course she could have the baby if she wanted to but it would spoil her usefulness in the struggle for several months and he didn't think this was the time for it. It was the first time they'd quarreled. She said he was heartless. He said they had to sacrifice their personal feelings for the workingclass, and stormed out of the house in a temper. In the end she had an abortion but she had to write her mother again for money to pay for it. (*Big Money*, 447)

These examples of important decisions presented as simply something that the character happened somehow to do are not exceptional; they are typical. I think I can say safely that there are *no* decisions in the three novels that are presented in a significantly different way.

To this extent, then, *U.S.A.* is systematically, rigidly, effectively deterministic. But there is a fault in its rigid structure, a softness in its determinism, and—in opposition to both the friendly and unfriendly critics of Dos Passos—I would suggest that a large part of the book's success comes precisely from the author's failure to be as consistently deterministic as he thinks he wants to be. True as it is that we never identify with any of his characters as we do with conventionally free characters, it is equally true that we do not regard them all with the nice objectivity required by the deterministic logic. Some we consider "good" and some "bad," just as though they were in fact responsible human beings making free choices. And these judgments that we make, however illogically, we base largely upon the way in which the different characters treat those crucial abstract words.

Some characters are essentially neutral—or perhaps I should say that we feel them to be truly determined. We look upon Margo Dowling, Eveline Hutchins, Eleanor Stoddard, and Charley Anderson with a coolly detached eye, even though we may feel that in their various ways the women are somewhat bitchy. And although Daughter, and Joe and Janey Williams tend to arouse our sympathies, we view them quite dispassionately. Certainly we do not consider any of these as responsible moral agents. And none of them shows any inclination to be concerned with the words.

In contrast to the neutral characters are Mac, Ben Compton, and Mary French. Dos Passos likes them and makes us like them because they affirm the values which he holds and wishes his readers to accept. Each of them uses the words, tries to uphold the true meaning of the "old words," and fights to rebuild the ruined words. Although their decisions are described in the same way that all other decisions are, we feel that their choices of the words are deliberate, and are acts of freedom for which they take the responsibility. Mac leaves his girl in San Francisco to go to Goldfield as a printer for the

Wobblies because he finds that his life is meaningless when he is not using and acting out the words. Later, after his marriage, he escapes again from the bourgeois trap because he can't bear not to be talking with his old comrades about their dream and ideals. Finally, unable to do anything but talk and unable to find a way to make the old words new or effective, he sinks back into the conventional rut of the other unfree characters. Ben Compton insists on talking peace and socialism after the United States has entered the war, freely choosing thereby to be taken by the police and imprisoned. During the war, it seems, the old words may not be used in public until they have been converted into the official lies.

Mary French is generally considered Dos Passos's most sympathetic character in *U.S.A.* She is certainly associated with the words throughout, and in her work with the 1919 steel strikers and the Sacco-Vanzetti committee she is actively engaged in the attempt to "renew" the words and make them effective in the fight for justice. But, significantly, she does not employ them much. Not only have they been worn slimy in the mouths of her enemies, but they are continually being perverted by her co-workers and supposed friends, the ostensible renovators of the words. So, in the final section of *The Big Money*, we find her collecting clothes for the struck coal miners, doing good, but not a good that goes beyond the mere maintenance of brute existence. Anything of more significance would demand use of the words, and at this point in his writing, the words, to Dos Passos, have been ruined beyond redemption.

And then there are the bad guys, J. Ward Moorehouse and Richard Ellsworth Savage. They are as hollow as any other Dos Passos men, their decisions, like all others, non-decisions. But where Joe and Janey Williams make us sad, these make us mad. We dislike them and blame them, just as though they had really chosen.

Dos Passos makes us feel that a character is responsible for the words he chooses. To explain just *how* Dos Passos does that is not easy, but I think it goes, in part, something like this. We don't blame Dick for drinking too much or for wenching, any more than we blame Charley Anderson or Joe Williams. These activities seem to be instinctive reactions, self-defeating but natural escapes from freedom. Part of the reason we feel Dick and the others determined in their dissipation, and consequently do not blame them, is because the characters blame themselves, regret what they do and feebly resolve not to do it again. Thus when they fall back into their old, familiar ways, we feel that they are doing what they do not want to do, do not will to do. But when we come to another sort of action, the choice of words, no character is shown regretting the abstract words he uses. Thus the character implicitly approves his choice of words, he seems to be acting freely, and we tend to hold him responsible.

To get back to our bad guys, Moorehouse and Savage are the successful exploiters in the trilogy, and on first thought we might assume that that fact would suffice to make them culpable. But they are not the usual exploiters found in proletarian novels: big bad businessmen gouging the workers, manufacturers grinding the faces of the poor. Indeed they don't seem to hurt anyone. They exploit not people but words, or people, impersonally, by means of the words. Their profession is "public relations." (We might look at them as precursors of the Madison Avenue villains of post-World War II fiction, and infinitely superior ones, at that.) Their job is to persuade people to buy a product or to act in a particular way. Their means of persuasion is words. And the words they use are to a great extent "the words," the words of the American dream. They talk cooperation, justice, opportunity, freedom, equality.

Here are two brief quotations from J. Ward Moorehouse. He and Savage are preparing a publicity campaign for old Doc Bingham's patent medicines—now called "proprietary" medicines. (You will remember that Doc was Mac's first employer at the beginning of the trilogy, as owner-manager of "The Truthseeker Literary Distributing Co., Inc.") The first quotation is part of J. W.'s argument to a complaisant senator: "But, senator, . . . it's the principle of the thing. Once government inter-ference in business is established as a precedent it means the end of liberty and private initiative in this country. . . . What this bill purports to do is to take the right of selfmedication from the American people" (505–6). And in this next one he is talking to his partner Savage about the advertising—no, publicity—campaign: "Of course selfservice, independence, individualism is the word I gave the boys in the beginning. This is going to be more than a publicity campaign, it's going to be a campaign for Americanism" (494).

Here at last we have arrived at the source—or at least one major source—of the cancerous evil that swells malignantly through the books. Here we observe the manufacturers of the all-pervasive lies busily at work, here we see the words being deliberately perverted. And we cannot consider the perverters of the words as merely helpless automatons or innocents; they deliberately choose their words and we judge them as villains.

So, in conclusion, Dos Passos finds that the old words of the immigrant haters of oppression, which should have set Americans free, have instead been worn slimy in their mouths. And these words are in effect central actors in *U.S.A.* They determine our attitudes toward the characters who use and misuse them, establish the tone of hollow futility that rings throughout the trilogy, and leave in our mouths the bitter after-taste of nausea. The novels that followed, to make the *District of Columbia* trilogy, emphasize Dos Passos's sick obsession with these words. In the first, the humanitarian socialist dream comes to us in the clichés and jargon of American Communists; in the second, the American dream is conveyed to us through the demagogery of a vulgar Louisiana dictator; in the third the dream of New Deal reform has been turned into a nightmare by cynical opportunists and time-serving bureaucrats who exploit the old words anew.

No longer able to imagine a way of giving to words

their original meanings, after *U.S.A.*, Dos Passos could still not abandon them for some more palatable subject. And so he seemed to take the worst part of the worlds of Yevtushenko and Hemingway. But in *U.S.A.* he could still write about Mac and Ben Compton and Mary French; he could still feel some hope that the ruined words might be rebuilt; he could still imagine the dream to be yet a possibility. In *U.S.A.* his despair was not yet total and his dual vision of the words brought to these novels a tension, a vitality, and a creative energy he would never be able to muster again.

The Politics of John Dos Passos

GRANVILLE HICKS

Somewhere on the face of the globe there is a bald, near-sighted, stoop-shouldered man in his early fifties, a stocky fellow with a pleasant, slightly apprehensive smile. He could be anywhere; a while back he was writing articles for *Life* from South America, but he may be at his home in Provincetown, or perhaps he is setting off for the Borneo Straits. Wherever he is, John Dos Passos is looking about him with the grim, puzzled honesty that has been his distinctive virtue, almost his trademark, for thirty years.

"All things are changing," the grandson of Charlemagne said, "and we change with them." No American novelist has written more directly about change, the great social changes, the characteristic and revolutionary changes of the twentieth century, than Dos Passos. He has been student and reporter and often poet of change. And he has been the victim of change, too. Twenty years ago he was as romantic a rebel as American letters had seen since the death of John Reed, passionate in his attack on capitalism, quick to support a radical cause. Today this pioneer fellow-traveler defends the profit motive, quarrels not merely with communism but also with the New Deal, looks in dismay at the program of the British Labor Party, and finds in Senator Taft the qualities of leadership he thinks America needs.

From *Antioch Review*, 10 (March 1950), 85–97. Reprinted by permission of the *Antioch Review*.

In its main parts—infatuation with communism and subsequent disillusionment—the case of Dos Passos is the case of dozens of his contemporaries. Fifty-one of those contemporaries, for instance, joined him in 1932 in signing a statement in support of William Z. Foster, Communist candidate for the presidency. Few of the fifty-one are fellow-travelers today, and several are as intransigently and articulately opposed to the Stalinist regime in Russia as is Dos Passos. The majority of the disillusioned, however, find themselves closer to Norman Thomas or Harry S. Truman than to Senator Taft. The trails of the ex-fellow-travelers go crisscrossing all over the map of American politics, and Dos Passos's is one of the few that lead straight to the right.

There are those who say that he has come to his senses —and high time, too. And there are those who grieve because he has turned into "a weary, cynical defender of vested interests." But few ask how it all happened— the movement to the left and the movement to the right. Yet Dos Passos, being first and foremost a writer, has left a detailed record of what, stage by stage, he has been thinking, and the record is worth looking at, not because he is merely or primarily a political writer but because his political development is a significant phenomenon of our time. I shall not attempt a literary evaluation in this article, nor discuss the problem—more complicated than some of the critics on both the Right and the Left seem to think—of the relationship between Dos Passos's political course and his development as a novelist. This is an attempt to set down the facts and to interpret them on the political level.

The printed record begins in the pages of the *Harvard Monthly* for 1916, when Dos Passos was twenty years old. After having lived in various parts of this country and Europe, he had entered Harvard in 1912, and had soon begun writing for the *Monthly* stories that were a little but not much better than the undergraduate average. It was not, however, until the end of his senior year that he stepped forward as a political thinker, with an editorial on the war and an article entitled "A Humble Protest."

"A Humble Protest" is directed against nothing less than the industrial revolution, "that bastard of science," which is cluttering up the world with "a silly claptrap of unnecessary luxuries" and smothering "the arts of life and the arts of creation." The article offers a dual indictment, moral and esthetic. "Millions of men," Dos Passos writes, "perform labor narrow and stultifying even under the best conditions, bound in the traces of mechanical industry without even a chance of self-expression, except in the hectic pleasures of suffocating lives in cities."

If we were to find that William Faulkner had begun his career with a sweeping attack on industrialism, we should not be surprised, for he has largely devoted himself to the unindustrialized segments of life in the backward South; nor would such a beginning seem inappropriate for the romantic, world-ranging Hemingway or for any of the other novelists who have managed to elude the principal consequences of the industrial revolution. It does startle us to discover that the man who, preeminently among his contemporaries, has refused to dodge industrialism began by repudiating it.

The first World War, in which Dos Passos participated as a member of private ambulance services and of the United States Medical Corps, exhibited to his eyes most of the characteristics he deplored in the civilization that had produced it. It was not blood and death that he wrote about in *One Man's Initiation* and *Three Soldiers*, but tyranny, exploitation, and purposelessness. The tasks of war, as he saw them, were not so much dangerous as "narrow and stultifying," and the destruction of the spirit was worse than the destruction of the flesh. The names that he selected for the sections of *Three Soldiers* established the identity of industrialism and war: "Making the Mould," "The Metal Cools," "Machines," "Rust," and "Under the Wheels."

The war was the first of the critical—one might almost say traumatic—experiences that can be picked out as the turning-points of Dos Passos's career. In *One Man's Initiation*, his trial flight, and, much more compellingly, in *Three Soldiers*, he was able to say what kind of shock the war had given him. First of the bitter, disillusioned, unpleasant novels about the war, *Three Soldiers* (1921) was to many readers a blasphemy and an outrage. Coningsby Dawson, author of *The Glory of the Trenches*, wrote in the New York *Times*: "The story is told brutally, with calculated sordidness and a blind whirlwind of rage which respects neither the reticences of art nor the restraints of decency." But the book was praised by Heywood Broun, Francis Hackett, Sidney Howard, and others, and eagerly welcomed by the young hopefuls of literature.

"All my life I've struggled for my own liberty in my small way," says Martin Howe, the hero of *One Man's Initiation*. "Now I hardly know if the thing exists." That, of course, was the lesson of the war. Like young Howe, Dos Passos had fought against "all the conventional ties, the worship of success and the respectabilities that is drummed into you when you're young." And the battle had not gone too badly; one could even write in the *Harvard Monthly* that industrialism was a mistake and civilization was on the wrong road. But he had underestimated the strength of the enemy. The enemy could pick you up and put you into uniform, wipe out your individuality, make you part of the machine.

Yet *Three Soldiers*, for all its bitterness, is essentially a hopeful book, as Dos Passos remembered when, in 1932, he wrote an introduction for the Modern Library edition: "Any spring is a time of overturn, but then [1919] Lenin was alive, the Seattle general strike had seemed the beginning of the flood instead of the beginning of the ebb, Americans in Paris were groggy with theatre and painting and music; Picasso was to rebuild the eye, Stravinski was cramming the Russian steppes into our ears, currents of energy seemed breaking out everywhere as young guys climbed out of their uniforms, imperial America was all shiny with the new idea of Ritz, in every direction the countries of the world stretched out starving and angry, ready for anything turbulent and new, whenever you went to the movies you saw Charlie Chaplin." The sufferings and defeats he depicted in *Three Soldiers* were made doubly black because they were silhouetted against the flaming hopes of the spring of 1919.

Chrisfield, one of the three soldiers, asks Andrews out of his desperation if it would be possible to overthrow the government. Andrews, who stands closest to the author, answers, "They did in Russia. We'll see." If, on the one hand, the war had shown Dos Passos the sheer repressive strength of organized society, it had, on the other, revealed the existence of unsuspected and powerful movements of revolt. *One Man's Initiation* is full of the heady talk of French anarchists and socialists, and if *Three Soldiers* portrays the failure of individual revolt, it holds out, however cryptically, the hope of collective revolution.

It took Dos Passos a long time to come to terms with his war experiences, five or six years. He wrote a book of verse and a bad novel, and he traveled. Always, when he has been unsure of himself, he has traveled. In Spain and the Near East he noted with discouragement the progress of "Henry Ford's gospel of multiple production and interchangeable parts," bringing the whole world to "the same level of nickel-plated dullness." He had fun from time to time, but wherever he went and whatever he was doing, he kept his mind on the problem he had made his own, the problem of living in an industrialized world. He was a serious-minded, conscientious fellow, not much like Ernest Hemingway, who could forget *his* preoccupations in drinking or hunting or skiing or watching a bullfight. He thought he wanted to escape, but he couldn't. And perhaps he didn't really want to. There is a passage in *Orient Express* that comes up suddenly and hits you in the eye. Dos Passos is in his hotel room in Kasvin, Persia, and he is bored. "It is in the West," he thinks abruptly, "that blood flows hot and that the world is disorderly, romantic, that fantastic unexpected things happen. Here everything has been tried, experienced, worn out." He wishes himself—where? At Broadway and 42nd Street.

And that is where, in a manner of speaking, we next see him, when his *Wanderjahre* are over and he is settling down to write *Manhattan Transfer*. If he had always hated industrial, urban civilization, he had also been fascinated by it, and now he admits its fascination. *Manhattan Transfer* is a poem of hate-and-love. The hatred is underlined on every page: for the ruthlessness, the fraudulence, the sycophancy, and the treachery that mark the struggle for success; for the emptiness and the inhumanity of the successful; for the folly and ineffectualness of those who fail in an unworthy cause. But the world Dos Passos portrays is disorderly and romantic, and the things that happen are fantastic, unexpected, and fun to write about. "Why," asks Jimmy Herf, the deracinated intellectual who is as central a character as this deliberately amorphous novel can be expected to have, "why do I go on dragging out a miserable existence in this crazy epileptic town?" But he does, for many pages after the question has been asked, and his ultimate departure is made to seem as hazardous and portentous as the escape from an enchanted castle in a fairy story.

There is not much politics in *Manhattan Transfer*; the book is directed against a way of life, not a political or economic system—against greed and conformity and pretentiousness. It is not, however, calculated to inculcate respect for the qualities that bring success under capitalism, and no reader could suppose that Dos Passos had been reconciled to the capitalist system. In fact, he was affiliating himself with the avowed enemies of capitalism. In 1926, the year after *Manhattan Transfer* was published, he became a member of the executive board of the *New Masses*, which was launched with the aid of a subsidy from the Garland Fund. Although the venture received the support of many of the individualistic rebels who had contributed to the old *Masses*, the communists, as Dos Passos must have known, were running the show.

Dos Passos contributed many short articles and book reviews to early issues of the *New Masses*, but the most interesting of his contributions, and the one that shows how far he was in 1926 from communist or any other kind of orthodoxy, was a debate with Mike Gold on the subject of the magazine itself. He begins, in characteristic fashion, by discussing the special limitations of the writing business. The writer, he says, "takes on the mind and functional deformities of his trade," no matter what his ideas and aims. "The word-slinging organism is the same whether it sucks its blood from Park Avenue or from Flatbush." The magazine will succeed only if it keeps clear of dogmas, imported or domestic. "The terrible danger to explorers," he goes on, "is that they always find what they are looking for. The *American Mercury* explores very ably the American field only to find the face of Mr. Mencken mirrored in every prairie pool." What he would like to see is "a magazine full of introspection and doubt that would be like a piece of litmus paper to test things by."

Mike Gold, a loyal communist and in those days a conspicuous one, was horrified by such heresies. "Dos Passos," he wrote, "must read history, psychology and economics and plunge himself into the labor movement. He must ally himself definitely with the radical army, for in this struggle is the only true escape from middle-class bewilderment today." Dos Passos did not precisely follow Gold's advice, but we do find him writing on the Passaic strike, discussing the economic causes of war, and describing with ardent approval the revolutionary art of Mexico.

Dos Passos, however, was bound to find his own battles and fight them his own way. The ordeal of Sacco and Vanzetti was nearing its tragic climax, and Dos Passos devoted more and more of his time to work for the release of the two Italian anarchists. The pamphlet he wrote for the Sacco-Vanzetti Defense Committee, "Facing the Chair," is factual and calm, but Dos Passos himself was moved as he had not been in many years. He went to Boston the week of the execution, picketed in company with Mike Gold, Dorothy Parker, Edna St. Vincent Millay, and many others, and spent a night in jail. What he felt he put into words nearly ten years later, when some of his political theories had changed but the emotion remained sharp and unaltered in his memory. It is in *The Big Money:* "they have clubbed us off the streets   they are stronger   they are rich. . . . America our nation has been beaten by strangers who have turned our language inside out who have taken the clean words our fathers spoke and made them slimy and foul." He sums up: "all right we are two nations."

The electrocution of Sacco and Vanzetti was another of Dos Passos' traumatic experiences. Like so many idealists, he had not believed that it could happen, had been convinced to the end that justice and decency had to prevail. He was not being literary—and certainly not chauvinistic—when he talked about strangers. That was the way it seemed to him; the people who had "bought the laws and fenced off the meadows and cut down the woods for pulp and turned our pleasant cities into slums and sweated the wealth out of our people" were spiritual aliens, nurtured in a different tradition from that on which America was built. They were interlopers, usurpers, bandits, and they must be driven out. In a confused and crowded play that he wrote just after the death of Sacco and Vanzetti, *Airways, Inc.*, he examined for the first time the dialectics of fighting fire with fire.

Dos Passos visited Russia in the autumn of 1928, and his impressions, though considerably short of rapture, were favorable enough to be published in the *New Masses.* Anyone might have known, however, that he could come to communism only by an American route, and his observations in the Soviet Union seem to have

had little influence, one way or the other, on his thinking. When, shortly after his return from Russia, he sat
down to begin *The 42nd Parallel,* first volume of the
trilogy *U.S.A.,* he accepted the basic Marxist conception
of the class struggle, but it was not an idea he had picked
up in the USSR or, for that matter, acquired from the
reading of Marx. His observations, especially in the matter of Sacco and Vanzetti, had taught him what he knew
about the two nations.

Sooner than most Americans, including the orthodox
communists, Dos Passos saw the implications of the
depression that began in 1929. The class war, he realized, had actually begun, and he wrote articles, both
in the *New Republic* and the *New Masses,* urging
middle-class liberals to make sure that the struggle was
conducted "under the most humane conditions possible." This was a novel suggestion to come from a
fellow-traveler, and the suspicious communists promptly
denounced it as wishy-washy liberalism. In time, however, they perceived that Dos Passos, whatever his
motives, was tactically sound, and the "neutralizing" of
the middle class became a major communist aim.

What Dos Passos was seeking was a compromise
between his liberal, humanitarian traditions and his
communist sympathies, but, in spite of his intellectual
reservations, his practical activity was directed into communist channels. He helped to organize the Emergency
Committee for Southern Prisoners, and later was chairman of the National Committee to Aid Striking Miners
Fighting Starvation. In the autumn of 1931 he and
Theodore Dreiser and half a dozen other writers went to
Harlan County, Kentucky, to call attention to the viola-
tion of civil rights in a communist-led strike. He was
one of the founders and for several years the treasurer
of the National Committee for the Defense of Political
Prisoners, and he was active in the Scottsboro case and
in other cases in which the communists took an acutely
political interest. As had been noted, he was one of
fifty-two writers and artists who signed a statement in

support of the communist candidates in the 1932 election.

In that summer of 1932, V. F. Calverton, editor of the *Modern Monthly,* asked various literary figures some tendentious questions, among them, "Should a writer join the Communist Party?" Dos Passos replied: "It's his own goddam business. Some people are naturally party men and others are natural scavengers and camp-followers. Matter of temperament. I personally belong to the scavenger and campfollower section." This was obviously true, and yet Dos Passos was rendering a more valuable service to the Communist Party at just that time than most of its members, for his prestige was great and his sincerity unchallenged. No one had more influence on the leftward swing of the intellectuals in the early '30's.

His growing militancy naturally affected his writing, and *1919,* second volume of his trilogy, gave a sharper sense of revolutionary crisis than *The 42nd Parallel.* What Dos Passos was feeling appeared most strikingly in the biographies: the sympathetic portrayals of the radicals, Jack Reed, Randolph Bourne, Paxton Hibben, Joe Hill, and Wesley Everest; the mordant accounts of Theodore Roosevelt, Woodrow Wilson, and Pierpont Morgan; the indignant, touching poem about the Unknown Soldier. As for the characters of the story, most of them—Eveline Hutchins, Eleanor Stoddard, Ward Moorehouse, Dick Savage, Jerry Burnham, and so on— illustrate the disintegration and emptiness of the middle class. The one worker, Joe Williams, is not romanticized, but he is handled respectfully, and in the latter part of the book we have a bona fide revolutionary, also treated with respect, Ben Compton. Most of the leftwing reviewers observed, with varying degrees of leftwing snobbishness, that Dos Passos was scarcely a bona fide revolutionary, but they felt that he was on the way.

Dos Passos in 1932 was closer to communism than he had ever been—and as close as he was going to get. In his parabolic orbit, though he did not know it, he had reached perihelion. For a time nothing much happened. Although he was less active in 1933 than he had been in 1931 and 1932, he continued to belong to a lot of communist fronts, and when the New Masses became a weekly at the beginning of 1934, he was advertised as one of its principal contributors. He did contribute a couple of articles, but the alliance lasted only a few weeks. In February, the Socialist Party held a rally in Madison Square Garden to protest against the suppression of the socialist workers of Vienna. In the name of the united front, communists invaded the meeting, which ended in a first-class riot, with a blow-by-blow account going out on the radio. A letter criticizing the behavior of the Communist Party on this occasion was sent to the New Masses, signed by Dos Passos and twenty-four others. ("We who write this letter watch with sympathy the struggles of militant labor and aid such struggles.") The New Masses answered with a letter addressed to Dos Passos, which weakly defended communist actions at the Garden and strongly attacked the signers of the letter. Some of the signers, the New Masses said, were well-known Trotskyite troublemakers, and others had given little evidence of their sympathy with militant labor. In a fervent peroration the editors objected to being addressed as "Dear Comrades" by such renegades and stoolpigeons. "You," the editorial concluded, "are different. To us, you have been, and, we hope, still are, Dos Passos the revolutionary writer, the comrade."

If Dos Passos had not already had some doubts about communist tactics, the Garden riot could not have hit him so hard, but it was a peculiarly flagrant example of the brutal literalness with which the party line could be applied. The same tactics had betrayed the striking miners in Kentucky and split the anti-fascist movement in Germany. Dos Passos had seen enough. He did not contribute to the New Masses again, and he ceased to work with communist fronts. For the time being, he issued no denunciations of communism, but his disillusionment was great and it grew rapidly.

Out of his dual disillusionment, the old quarrel with capitalism and the new distrust of communism, he wrote *The Big Money*, and thus completed his trilogy. Again the key is in the biographies: Frederick W. Taylor, Henry Ford, Thorstein Veblen, Isadora Duncan, Rudolph Valentino, the Wright brothers, Frank Lloyd Wright, William Randolph Hearst, and Samuel Insull. It is all a Veblenian world: "the sabotage of production by business, the sabotage of life by blind need for money profits." The Veblenian moral is driven home by the story of Charley Anderson, which occupies the greater part of the novel. "If you're working with us, you're workin' with us," says Old Bledsoe, who is in charge of production in the Detroit airplane factory for which Charley goes to work, "and if you're not you'd better stick around your broker's office where you belong." Charley means well, but "the blind need for money profits" takes him to his broker's office and eventually to his death. Everyone, indeed, ends badly in *The Big Money*—the revolutionaries as well as the capitalists and their hangers-on. There is no optimism, no militancy, and, for that matter, no tragedy—just the sour taste of frustration and futility.

The Big Money was published in 1936. That summer General Franco and his fascists began their revolt against the republican government of Spain, and in America radical and liberal opinion was solidly on the side of the Loyalists. Dos Passos had been in Spain in 1916, 1920, and 1933, and in 1937 he went again, one of his purposes being to collaborate with the cameraman Joris Ivens in the filming of a pro-Loyalist picture called *Spanish Earth*. Dos Passos' sympathy for the Loyalist cause came out clearly enough in what he wrote about the civil war, but his articles didn't quite have the fervor to be found in reports by Ernest Hemingway and others. In Stalinist circles in America, the word went round that Dos had fallen under the spell of anarchists and Trotskyites. Only later was it learned that a friend of his, a Spaniard who had taught at Johns Hopkins University and had been an officer in the Loyalist army, had been arrested by secret police and mysteriously executed.

Dos Passos could speak two years later of the death of José Robles Pazos as "only one story among thousands in the vast butchery that was the Spanish civil war," but it seems to have been at the time another of his traumatic experiences. In *Adventures of a Young Man,* the hero, a disillusioned communist, goes to fight in Spain out of a conviction that here is the final conflict, the real fight against reaction, transcending all sectarian feuds. But this young man, Glenn Spotswood, is arrested by a GPU agent, accused of Trotskyism, and sent to his death. In Spain Dos Passos had concluded the communism was not merely something he could not support; it was as much the enemy as fascism or any other brand of reaction.

Even in 1937, there were plenty of ex-fellow-travelers to agree with Dos Passos, though more of them had been disillusioned by the trials of the Old Bolsheviks than by events in Spain. And there were plenty more by the end of 1939, after the Soviet-Nazi pact and the liquidation of the democratic front. Although the erstwhile communists and communist-sympathizers were well distributed over the political map, as has been said, the majority of them were concentrated in support of the New Deal, and that was where Dos Passos seemed to be taking his stand. Both in *Adventures of a Young Man* and in an article he published in 1941, "To a Liberal in Office," he admitted that he had been wrong in his earlier, leftwing criticisms of the New Deal, which, he said, "in spite of many wrong roads taken," has been "productive of real living good in the national life." *The Ground We Stand On,* a study of some of the founders of American democracy, has a New Deal-ish air, and the second volume of the Spotswood trilogy, *Number One,* a novel about someone like Huey Long, also seemed to belong in the New Deal tradition.

In an interview he gave in the winter of 1949, after *The Grand Design* had been published, Dos Passos said he was surprised that reviewers had regarded the book as an all-out attack on the New Deal; "It was Mr. Roosevelt's foreign—not domestic—policy that disappointed him." As anyone who has read the novel knows, the reviewers could scarcely be blamed, and yet it was true that Dos Passos had not quarreled with the New Deal in the years before Pearl Harbor. What is even more surprising, he appeared to support Roosevelt's foreign policy between 1941 and 1945. At any rate, *State of the Nation*, a collection of magazine pieces published in 1944, is critical only of details, not of general policies, and so sharp-eyed a critic as Edmund Wilson concluded from it that Dos Passos, however reluctantly, favored the prosecution of the war.

But Dos Passos could not have supported either the New Deal or the war without serious misgivings. Nothing is deeper in the man than his fear of power. To begin with, he feared the power of the military, as he had experienced it in the first World War, and the power of men of wealth. The hatred of war and exploitation grew so acute that he accepted for a time the tempting radical doctrine that only power can destroy power. But what he saw of communism in Russia, in Spain, and at home convinced him that the destroying power could be more dangerous than the power it overcame. The New Deal, whatever its accomplishments, represented a great concentration of power, and he must always have been uneasy about it. As for war, Dos Passos hated it in and for itself and because it inevitably resulted in the piling of power upon power.

The misgivings do not figure much in *State of the Nation* or the first part of *Tour of Duty*. (Dos Passos has always been a first-rate reporter, and from these books, less ballyhooed than many of the wartime quickies and as promptly forgotten, future historians will learn things they cannot find elsewhere.) But his uneasiness was preparing the way for a sudden reversal, and it came, as Part III of *Tour of Duty* shows, when he visited Austria and Germany in the autumn of 1945.

"In the Year of Our Defeat" he called this section, arguing that we had been defeated in two ways: we had callously surrendered the peoples of eastern Europe to Russian despotism, and we had no intelligent, humane plan for the reconstruction of the occupied countries. The destruction America had wrought was before his eyes, and its apparent futility stabbed his tender conscience.

Something, he saw, had gone wrong, and his conscience said, "I told you so." He should always have known that no good could come of war, should have seen from the first that no man could exercise the power that had been entrusted to Franklin D. Roosevelt without abusing it. Dos Passos looked at the postwar world and was afraid, more afraid than he had ever been in his life.

Out of his fear he wrote *The Grand Design*. He did not intend it to be a diatribe against the New Deal, but that is what it became. There are "good" New Dealers in the book, but they are defeated by the charlatans and demagogues, by the ineffable Walker Watson, who combines the worst traits of Henry Wallace and Harry Hopkins, by Jerry Evans, the insatiable millionaire from the South, and by the "indispensable" man in the White House. "By the modulations of his voice on the microphone he played on the American people. We danced to his tune. Third Term. Fourth Term. Indispensable. War is a time of Caesars."

The moral of the book is given in one of the quasi-poetic passages with which it is sprinkled:

> We learned. There were things we learned to do but we have not learned, in spite of the Constitution and the Declaration of Independence and the great debates at Richmond and Philadelphia how to put power over the lives of men into the hands of one man and to make him use it wisely.

This is as true as anything can be, but it is also true that we have not learned how to get along at this stage of the development of Western Civilization without putting power over the lives of men into the hands of one man. The dangers are great, and Dos Passos is not the only one who sees them. At the end of *Roosevelt and Hopkins*, Robert Sherwood expresses the hope that the nation will never again find it necessary to place "so much reliance on the imagination and the courage and the durability of one mortal man." But unfortunately the perception of a danger does not automatically provide a way of avoiding it.

"Socialism is not the answer to the too great concentration of power that is the curse of capitalism. We've got to do better than that." So Dos Passos wrote in "The Failure of Marxism," published in *Life* Magazine in early 1948. But the article, instead of being concerned with the "better than that," complains peevishly that such phrases as "public ownership" and "planned economy" have acquired a favorable connotation, apparently through the operations of some sinister conspiracy, and proceeds to run through the stock objections to socialization with as little originality as a National Association of Manufacturers' leaflet. Dos Passos' horrible examples include not only Russian tyranny but also British Labor bureaucracy. He sees the British government's "direction of labor" measure not as a temporary expedient nor even as a mistake that can be corrected through the democratic procedures that do, after all, survive in England, but as a step that will inevitably lead to totalitarianism. The evils of capitalism, though they are occasionally mentioned, seem scarcely worth bothering with.

Dos Passos is not, of course, a defender of vested interests. On the contrary, his sympathies are wholly with the people who get pushed around, whether it is Big Business or Big Government that does the pushing. His trouble is simply that he has not found the "better than that," the alternative to both bignesses, and hence his growing fear of government can only be accompanied by a growing toleration of business. ("The untrammeled power of the ruling class in the Soviet Union makes you wonder whether the profit motive is as bad as it has been painted.")

The "Anarchism" of John Dos Passos

DAVID   SANDERS

John Dos Passos no longer surprises his old readers when he publishes something like his recent foreword to William Buckley's *Up From Liberalism* (McDowell, Obolensky, 1959). This most passionate defender of Sacco and Vanzetti has long been one of the older voices of American conservatism. The *District of Columbia* trilogy, which seems to contrast so sharply with *U.S.A.*, was begun over twenty years ago, and his key historical study, *The Ground We Stand On*, was published in 1941. Still, his present position seems curious for the novelist who once idealized American radicalism so compellingly, and the reasons for the change are too often reduced to the mere label of anti-communism, an easy simplification since much of Dos Passos' writing suggests it very bluntly. However, the man's thought has been too complex and his study much too extensive for him to be characterized merely as a reformed Greenwich Village radical. From the very beginning of his career, he has been concerned with the idea of self-government beyond all other ideas. Even as he inquired sympathetically into the nature of the Soviet experiment, he wrote of individuals fighting systems. Dos Passos has been driven to his present conservative alignment by an anarchistic philosophy which has made him a conservative because he now identifies liberalism with big government and the submergence of the individual.

From *South Atlantic Quarterly*, 60 (Winter 1961), 44–55. Reprinted by permission of the author and publisher.

Without defending Dos Passos' politics, it must be said that hostile reviews of his work in the late thirties have been too readily accepted by literary historians ever since. What is called "development" in many writers has usually been termed "inconsistency" or "deterioration" in John Dos Passos. Once, the conventional outline goes, Dos Passos was on the editorial board of *New Masses*, and decades later he completed his second trilogy with the Soviets figuring as archvillains of the twentieth century; in this, as in most oppositions of an early and a late Dos Passos, a polarity emerges which seems to explain why the writer has "fallen off" (artistically as well as politically), or why he personifies the vitiated energy of surviving writers from the twenties, or why he represents some other patent hypothesis of literary decline.[1]

Of course, *The Great Days* (1958) is not as good a novel as *1919*, and Dos Passos has, very strictly speaking, swung from left to right—insofar as these directions remain workable political labels. (Are there now any authentic active leftists in the United States? Is there one who can be put clearly outside the huge Center?) Left or right, however, Dos Passos is a man with a single lifelong political obsession, first made explicit in his neglected travel book of the early twenties, *Rosinante to the Road Again* (1922). Here, certain chapters introduce Dos Passos' own "anarchism," [2] the direct antecedent of his present day conservatism, and a viewpoint which appears, to greater or lesser degree, in everything that he has written. It is the viewpoint from which he dissects American materialism in *Manhattan Transfer* and *U.S.A.*, just as it limits whatever sympathy he may have shown toward the Communists in those times. It is amplified by his rediscovery of historical American liberalism in *The Ground We Stand On*, and it wholly informs the positions of those characters in the *District of Columbia* trilogy who oppose the major forces of social, political, and economic organization which began to accelerate in 1933.

Rosinante to the Road Again contains essays on Spanish life and culture upon a narrative framework of the travels of its two heroes, sensitive young Americans remarkably like Martin Howe in *One Man's Initiation* and John Andrews in *Three Soldiers*. They aren't burdened by a social conscience as they take to the road, responding instead to "maroon and purple cadences" which evoke the "gesture of Spain." With John Andrews they cherish the artist's isolation, learning as they proceed that the artist is inescapably a political individual. They do not shout that "art is a weapon," but they come to believe that the brotherhood of man is a meaningful term if it can stand for the latent sympathies that must arise between embattled individuals.

" 'Ca en America no se divierte," a Spanish drover informs them as they leave Madrid in search of the "gesture." In America one cannot have fun. While they agree mostly because of their holiday mood, even at this point they suspect that America is so thoroughly joyless because it is regimented. " 'Ca en America no se hase na'a que trabahar y de'cansar." (As Dos Passos notes, the drover speaks "an aspirated Andalusian that sounded like Arabic.") Americans merely work and rest from work, so many interchangeable parts on the long national line. *Rosinante to the Road Again* is pitted with these simplifications in the early pages of fairly conventional travels and thoroughly predictable travelers' responses until the reader is brought suddenly to the book's most extraordinary chapter, "The Baker of Almorox," where within the limits of an essay there is a description of Spain (and the center of Dos Passos' political principles), whose incisiveness falls short only of the developed study of the United States which appears in *U.S.A.*

Almorox is a village not far from Madrid, figuring at first as an excursion point where the young travelers may absorb Spanish rural life. While this touristic consciousness does not fade entirely, the village's deeper significance becomes quickly apparent. Years before he would write *The Villages Are the Heart of Spain*,[3] Dos Passos had discovered that pamphlet's thesis at Almorox.

The baker, interrupted in his work, hospitably guides the travelers to a summit overlooking his village and all of the neighboring terrain. Pride overcomes the natural deference he feels in speaking to strangers from the city, and from his simple words there emerges a concept which startles the narrator. For this baker there is an absolute division between Almorox and what is not Almorox—a simple enough creed, but one which can become the innate ethos of any man, the recognition of himself threatened by the ligatures of industrial, centralizing modernity.

> In him I seemed to see the generations wax and wane, like the years, strung on the thread of labor, of unending sweat and strain of muscles against the earth. It was all so mellow, so strangely aloof from the world of feverish change, this life of the peasants of Almorox. Everywhere roots striking into the infinite past. . . . But always remained the love for the place, the strong anarchistic reliance on the individual man, the walking, consciously or not, of the way beaten by generations of men who had tilled and loved and lain in the cherishing sun with no feeling of reality outside of themselves, outside of the bare encompassing hills of their commune, except the God which was the synthesis of their souls and of their lives.
>
> Here lies the strength and the weakness of Spain. This intense individualism, born of a history whose fundamentals lie in isolated village communities . . . over the changeless face of which, like grass over a field, events spring and mature and die, is the basic fact of Spanish life.

Individualism like this, anarchistic in its opposition to distant laws, yet firm in its basic loyalties, could be found in Spain and clearly not in joyless America. Superficially, this lesson at Almorox differs little from many personal discoveries made by American expatriate writers, but Dos Passos proceeded shortly afterward to the Soviet Union and to yet another jarring contrast with the world of his early education. He had, therefore, among American writers who would be concerned with the world's political condition between the Sacco-Vanzetti executions and the outbreak of World War II, a singular background. Even within *Rosinante* the baker's creed does not remain simply a rationale for Dos Passos' complaints against regimentation, because to this sensitive observer it suggested a past individualism in Western Europe and the nations of Western Europeans across the Atlantic, where it had been wholly swept away by materialism and urbanization. What remained of it in Spain in the early twenties had to contend with the forces of governmental centralization which sought to destroy it. Dos Passos concludes this chapter by specifically drawing Spanish anarchism from the baker's individualism:

> The problem of our day is whether Spaniards evolving locally, anarchically, without centralization in anything but repression, will work out a new way for themselves, or whether they will be drawn into the festering tumult of a Europe where the system that is dying is only strong enough to kill in its death-throes all new growth in which there was hope for the future.

Clearly, what he has described in this chapter is the struggle which would become the dominant theme in his fiction, at least in all of the novels from *Manhattan Transfer* to *The Grand Design.*

Still another baker contributes to Dos Passos' "anarchism," when in a later chapter Pío Baroja's revolutionary quality as a novelist is established as anarchistic. Dos Passos stresses first the individualism in Baroja's Basque background, then hails a thematic opposition between the individual and society emerging from the writer's operation of a Madrid bakery. The sheer competence with which Baroja turned out sweet loaves of bread left him that much freer to analyze Spanish society. While no comparable business would so serve Dos Passos, the resulting attitudes influenced both his political thought and his aesthetics. The social novelist's function, he concludes from Baroja's example, is inevitably *destructive*—or anarchistic. Dos Passos is careful to show how Baroja differs from bomb-throwing compatriots.

> The anarchism of Pío Baroja is of another sort. He says in one of his books that the only part a man of the middle classes can play in the reorganization of society is destructive. He has not undergone the discipline, which can only come from common slavery in the industrial machine, necessary for a builder. His slavery has been an isolated slavery which has unfitted him forever from becoming truly part of a community. He can use the vast power of knowledge which training has given him in only one way. His great mission is to put the acid test to existing institutions, and to strip the veils off them.

Of course, this describes the subsequent Dos Passos much better than it does Baroja at any time. (*The Struggle for Life* trilogy, closest of Baroja's works to these standards, has less anarchistic commitment than *Manhattan Transfer*, its characters stealing and starving and engaging social institutions in guerilla raids at most.) Here also is the most useful early reference for those who too willingly claim that Dos Passos "vacillated" in his political commitments. Here is really his own "anarchism" as a writer, that point of view from which he has documented Charley Anderson's decay, Mary French's martyrdom, and the public careers of "Meester Veelson" and Mr. Roosevelt.

To conclude with *Rosinante*, we must notice briefly Dos Passos' attention to Unamuno, whose outlook was largely repugnant to the young American. "Instead of the rationalists and humanists of the North, Unamuno's idols are the mystics and saints and sensualists of Castile, hard stalwart men who walked with God, Loyola, Torquemada, Pizarro, Narváez, who governed with whips and thumbscrews and drank death down greedily like heady wine." Yet, in reading *Vida de Don Quijote y Sancho* and *Del Sentimiento trágico de la Vida*, Dos Passos selects a call to action which complements the critically destructive position he had gained from Baroja and which goes a long way toward explaining the motivation of so many of his fictional heroes. Dos Passos' own translation from *Del Sentimiento trágico de la Vida* follows:

> What is, then, the new mission of Don Quixote to this world? To cry, cry in the wilderness. For the wilderness hears although men do not hear, and one day will turn into a sonorous wood, and that solitary voice that spreads in the desert like seed will sprout into a gigantic cedar that will sing with a hundred thousand tongues an eternal hosanna to the Lord of life and death.

The connection between such a mission and the itinerant struggle of Fenian McCreary in *The 42nd Parallel* may seem very tenuous, yet there is no earlier account of such militancy within the essays and novels of John Dos Passos. Martin Howe, of *One Man's Initiation*, meets French soldiers who speak wildly of a postwar world regenerated by a popular revolution or a universal church; John Andrews, of *Three Soldiers*, is grateful to an anarchist captain of a fishing boat who pulls him out of the Seine. But these are incidents in which merely casual sympathy is extended to aesthetes who are having a bad time of it. Howe and Andrews proceeded to no sort of action—let alone anarchism. They withdrew even further than most their contemporaries with shattered sensibilities. The epigraph to *Three Soldiers*, taken from Stendhal, makes this quite clear: "Les contemporains qui souffrent de certains choses ne peuvent s'en souvenir qu'avec une horreur qui paralyse tout autre plaisir, même celui de lire une conte."

From Unamuno, then, came the lesson of a lonely

struggle which must ignore such appealing distractions as reasonableness and the world's material progress. From Baroja, the destructive view of society—totally destructive insofar as it acknowledges even the failure of man's social impulses. From the baker of Almorox, man's allegiance only to that which is really his: village, land, hearth, family. These discoveries form Dos Passos' "anarchism," presented first in *Rosinante to the Road Again.*

While proof of his "anarchism" rests in an extended study of Dos Passos' political development, its outlines may be taken from the works which follow *Rosinante.*

There is a bare beginning in *Manhattan Transfer,* in which the declared anarchists (Congo and Marco) are little more than caricatures, and the actual hero, Jimmy Herf, is a pathetic misfit rather than a political actor. The *system* pervades *Manhattan Transfer,* a colossus which admits only prostitutes and compromising politicians; individualists of any variety are snuffed out quickly. The real American confirmation of his Spanish discovery came first in the Sacco and Vanzetti case, where Dos Passos' anarchist sympathies were engaged at once. He saw the men as anarchists and believed this to be the real basis of their persecution. His report, "The Pit and the Pendulum," [4] traces an elaborate sociological structure of New England to demonstrate that Sacco and Vanzetti were farther from its center than anyone else. Evidence brought against them had been circumstantial, and Dos Passos suggests that even more damning were the unspoken circumstances of their foreign birth, their draft evasions, and their political activity. They were anarchists and so persecuted by those who were not. Sacco and Vanzetti were "wops, aliens, men who spoke broken English, anarchists, believing neither in the congregationalist nor the Catholic god, slackers who had escaped the draft." To the people of Massachusetts, they were "an object, a focus for the bitterness of their hatred of the new young vigorous unfamiliar forces that are relentlessly sweeping them off the shelf." More than anarchism may enter Dos Passos' political sensibilities at this point, but it is this sympathy for Sacco and Vanzetti and *their* anarchism which committed him to political action, all the while governing that action severely. As his subsequent writings prove beyond dispute, Dos Passos' tolerance of Communism in the United States stretched only until the Communists were revealed to him as more hostile to individual action than even the 1927 Commonwealth of Massachusetts.

"Anarchism" determines the organization of the novels in *U.S.A.* In each of them, one figure is opposed to many: *only* one figure facing the entire line-up of existing institutions. Fenian McCreary rambles through *The 42nd Parallel*, a wobbly, a rootless embodiment of American radical protest before World War I. Against him is arrayed all of the dominant society, whether represented by the public relations pioneer, J. Ward Moorehouse, or the fraudulent labor leader, G. H. Barrow. In 1919, the lonely figure is Ben Compton, East-Side intellectual and radical agitator, who confronts the monolith of the United States at war. Every other character to whom sections are devoted loses his identity, usually through some compromise with the system: Moorehouse again, Richard Ellsworth Savage (a compromised intellectual), Daughter, Joe Williams and his sister Janey, and, however distant from these fictional characters, the most bitterly drawn example of traduced idealism, "Meester Veelson." With these successive annihilations of the individual in *The 42nd Parallel* and *1919*, a monstrous system inflates in *The Big Money* to a point where it all but obscures the extinction of Mary French, the last embattled individual in this trilogy. Yet she emerges a most revealing Dos Passos "anarchist." She does not merely reject the Veblenesque monster of boomtime American society; she learns, as well, that there is no place for individual protest within the Communist party. Communist involvement in the Sacco and Vanzetti demonstrations, or in the Passaic strike, is clearly revealed to her as a piecemeal operation of Soviet foreign policy. Contemporary readers who understood Mary French's experience had no reason to be shocked when they were presented with the political career of Glenn Spotswood in *Adventures of a Young Man*.

Glenn Spotswood is a novel-length presentation of the type which had appeared fragmentarily in *U.S.A.* His "adventures" are the trials through which he comes to learn that a man must strike out alone against social evil. The Communist party in America, of course, rejects him for his individuality, because he is, from their point of view, a classic "deviationist." (While this may not be the place to comment on the adverse critical reception to this novel, the reader would find the *New Masses* reviews of this novel and *The Big Money* unusually interesting. Alarms over the portraiture of Communists in *The Big Money* are followed by thundering accusations of "Trotskyist agit-prop" in the reviews of *Adventures of a Young Man*.[5] This sectarian criticism is unfortunately the starting point for the more general downgrading of Dos Passos' work and the widely echoed thesis that artistic decline followed upon political disillusion.)

Glenn Spotswood is a characteristic Dos Passos hero. Although an intellectual (Columbia, *cum laude*), he is first distracted from the end goal of Communism by his compassion for striking miners. He works on splinter-group publications in New York because his voice must cry out in the left-wing wilderness of the thirties. He deplores Communist action in breaking up a Socialist meeting at Madison Square Garden, yet does not approach the latter group. Entirely on his own initiative, he goes to Spain—Telemachus fighting for the Loyalists— and he would have fought for them if the Party police had not imprisoned him first. The novel's concluding scene is a devastating illustration of Dos Passos' "anarchism." Glenn, in a jail cell awaiting a death sentence, scrawls on the wall: "I, Glenn Spotswood, being of sound mind and imprisoned body, do bequeath to the international working class my hope of a better world." But, the novel follows, "he suddenly felt ashamed and rubbed it all out with the palm of his hand." "International working class" becomes a thin slogan to the prisoner and "better world" a foolish chimera, both of them phrases twisted beyond meaning by his captors.

Number One, second novel of the *District of Columbia* trilogy and a study in native American demagogy, might appear to lack a further representative of Dos Passos' embattled individuals. Its central figure, Tyler Spotswood, is a study in alcoholism rather than in political protest. No fictional character emerges as the antagonist to Chuck Crawford, Dos Passos' Huey Long. Yet this novel closely approaches some of the ideas of twenty years before in *Rosinante to the Road Again* when in the prose-poetry of the interchapters the novelist identifies "number one." The American people must be Crawford's final opposition, but this should not be mistaken for any kind of collective effort. "People" are emphatically considered as individuals quite as devoted to their local and familial concerns as was the baker of Almorox.

when you try to find the people, myriadfigured pyramid precariously balanced on every one
alone:
. . . the people is everybody
and one man alone;
weak as the weakest, strong as the strongest,
the people are the republic,
the people are you.

The final novel in the trilogy, *The Grand Design*, opposes the individual to New Deal statism. Conventionally, and especially for the public personage of Dos Passos as an ex-radical, this is an ironic opposition, and this irony is actually the governing attitude of the novel. The atmosphere of the opening pages is one of hope, in which such radicals and reformers as those who were defeated in *U.S.A.* may feel reconciled with their country in the advent of the Roosevelt administration. At least it seems this way to Millard Carroll, who drops a family business in Texarkola to go to Washington; and certainly it is the prospect that Paul Graves believes to be at hand as he returns to the Department of Agriculture. "To make America over" is the sweeping theme of these early pages, a refrain in the interchapters. But even as such dedication is uttered, there are the disquieting presences of fixers, men in the know, and abstract theorists. Washington is to be a far different pyramid from one which might rest on an individual American, "weak as the weakest, strong as the strongest." Bureaucracy is to congeal the "rendezvous with destiny," and if there is to be "one man alone," it can only be Franklin Roosevelt, who assumes symbolic proportions beyond those Dos Passos implied for "Meester Veelson" in 1919. Graves and Carroll are deployed against all of this. Carroll, the cabinet member, is less dramatically posed, for he is at his desk long after his illusions have been crushed. Paul Graves more precisely represents the anarchist pattern as he fights for the family-sized farm. If the New Deal would accomplish just that much, Graves believes, it could re-establish the basis, the old Jeffersonian basis, of the Republic. He knows eventually that of course it will not do this. A world war intervenes and at the apex of the pyramid:

> The President of the United States
> was a man of great personal courage and supreme confidence in his powers of persuasion. He never spared himself a moment, flew to Brazil and Casablanca, Cairo
> to negotiate at the level of the leaders;
> at Teheran the triumvirate
> without asking anybody's leave got to meddling with history; without consulting their constituents revamped geography,
> divided up the bloody globe and left the freedoms out.

And the American people were supposed to say
thank you for the Century of the Common Man
turned over for relocation behind barbed wire so help
him God.

We learned. There were things we learned to do,
but have not learned, in spite of the Constitution
and the Declaration of Independence and the great
debates of Richmond and Philadelphia
how to put power over the lives of men into the
hands of one man
and to make him use it wisely.

Repossessing the rhetorical force of his *U.S.A.* portraits,
Dos Passos restates his old theme. To be sure, it is somewhat modified by the studies which formed his historical inquiry, *The Ground We Stand On,* but these
studies—of Joel Barlow, Roger Williams, and Thomas
Jefferson—proceed indisputably from that early discovery
of "anarchism" in Spain. The thesis of *The Ground We
Stand On* and the Spotswood novels is that individual
self-government should be the essential principle in
American political behavior. Parallels become overwhelming. Dos Passos in 1922 decried the Europeanization of Spain. In 1939, he warned against another sort
of Europeanization menacing the United States. At both
times he was explicit about the threat of forces of
organization to the individual. The following statements
from *The Ground We Stand On* offer possibly the surest
evidence:

Even if it means reversing the trend of our whole
society in order to make it continually more self-governing instead of less, the trend will have to be reversed. The alternative is destruction.

If we can keep the fabric of a self-governing republic
unbroken at home, we are in no danger from the attacks of the slave states of Europe and Asia; if we
cannot, everything we as Americans have stood for
from the beginning will have been in vain.

Through a novel, two trilogies, and volumes of "reportage," Dos Passos' thought is remarkably continuous—so much so that his "anarchism" can be identified with the ideal of self-government. Dos Passos, as a conservative in the sixties, is little less an "anarchist" than he was in Spain forty years ago.

Dos Passos and the New Liberalism

CHESTER E. EISINGER

The need for the new liberalism arose out of the betrayal of the Soviet Union and the horror of Fascist dictatorship. Men discovered that old ways of thinking and acting were not relevant in meeting the challenges issued by these two forces—challenges about the nature of man, the nature of political power, the structure of economic life. As they cast about for a new stance, one that would not force them to abdicate every belief they had cherished in order to meet these challenges, some men came to the new liberalism. Its prophet in England was George Orwell, in Italy, Silone. In America, no single commanding figure emerged, but the movement found spokesmen from the field of political history in Arthur Schlesinger, Jr., and Granville Hicks, and from the field of literature in Hicks, John Dos Passos, Mary McCarthy, and, above all, Lionel Trilling. All these people were engaged in what Schlesinger has called, in *The Vital Center*, "the fundamental enterprise of re-examination and self-criticism which liberalism has undergone" during the forties.

In reshaping the liberal mind, neither rationalism nor a naturalistic bias was sacrificed, but the limitations of reason were recognized. It was now understood that reason could not be counted upon to solve all problems, and that, indeed, not all problems were soluble.

From Chester E. Eisinger, *Fiction of the Forties* (Chicago: University of Chicago Press, 1963), pp. 118–25. Copyright, 1963, University of Chicago Press. Reprinted by permission of the publisher.

This recognition constituted a retreat from the naïve optimism of an earlier day. It also meant that reason could not be trusted to contrive political or economic systems which would meet all exigencies and guarantee a good life. In short it was now necessary to reject total planning. Ideology—conceived as a dogmatic intellectual construct of given propositions—fell into disrepute, and the idea of utopia as a closed and closely organized system of social beliefs came under suspicion. In place of total solutions, the new liberalism returned to the American tradition of improvisation and experimentalism, of exploration and tentative progression. It accepted the possibilities of what Karl Popper has called, in *The Open Society and Its Enemies*, piecemeal social engineering. In every sphere of human activity it narrowed its optimistic conceptions; from seeing the world as open possibility it came to see it as limitation. A deepening knowledge of man led it to view the human being as the prey of alienation and as a fallible, uncertain creature. Starting now from this dark view of man, it expected less of him than before, while urging him with tempered insistence to fight his self-division and his estrangement from society. The tough-minded sobriety of the new liberalism rejected the bleeding-heart attitudes that had moved earlier liberals to action. There was no room now for sentimentality about man, especially mass-man or the proletariat who, it was discovered, was not a particularly attractive fellow. Nor could there be any sentimentality about the dangerous potential in centralized power. The new liberalism tried to be clear-eyed in its vision and slow, almost tentative, in its commitments. It tried to be disciplined and responsible. In the forties it was the best guardian of the liberal idea in America.

John Dos Passos' relationship to the new liberalism lies more in what he has rejected than in what he has embraced. Communism, native fascism, and centralized bureaucracy are all unacceptable to him, for he sought in the American past, during the forties, a definition of individualism that would be viable in the present. The theme of all the writing he did between 1939 and 1951, including the history and reportage as well as the novels, has been the imperative need to guarantee the survival of the individual in the modern state and to protect his personal liberties. In seizing upon this issue, he acted to meet the crisis of modern, secular man, the crisis of man and society in an age of reconstruction, as Karl Mannheim has called it. That crisis arose as the result of the breakdown, in the long view, of nineteenth-century democracy and freedom. In the more recent past it is the product of totalitarianism, with its corrupting power, its planless regulation, and its abrogation of democratic culture. It is the result, in this country, of a failure in democratic planning, represented by the New Deal, which threatened the survival of human responsibility and individualism. In the spirit of the new liberalism Dos Passos turned from the left, away from the centralized, social-service state and the planned society. In the spirit of a new Americanism he turned toward a Jeffersonian conception of individualism, seeking in the past his solutions to that crisis. His nostalgic and sometimes sentimental effort to revivify the American heritage in the twentieth century, drawing upon the Jeffersonian conception of power and equality and the mystical Transcendental faith in the people, separates him from the new liberalism; but his sense of quest for individual and political fulfilment identifies him with it.

Dos Passos' nonfiction reveals a series of disengagements from contemporary power structures and ideologies. Once close to communism, although probably never a Marxist, Dos Passos said in *Tour of Duty* in 1946 that in the past the Soviet Union had been a dream but is now an ugly reality. It has failed to build a free society; it does not permit the individual to talk back to his government; it has given absolute power to one man. Uncritical liberals, he wrote in *The Prospect Before Us*, have been the victims of their own honorific abstractions. They cannot make an honest analysis of world socialism because they are blinded to the harsh reality by a terminology they are conditioned to accept. The "curse of capitalism" in our world is, like that of socialism, "the too great concentration of power." It creates a society in which freedom is denied to many people. Dos Passos then rejected all aspects of corporate society—Marxist, Socialist, and capitalist—finding each one a mode of regimentation corrupted by the dirty itch for power.

Having surveyed the contemporary scene and found it a wasteland, Dos Passos concluded that his only recourse was to lay a claim against the American past as a source of solutions to man's problems in the present time of troubles. Investigating the past in *The Ground We Stand On* and *The Head and Heart of Thomas Jefferson*, he found that the spirit of the Commonwealth had taken root in America. It had helped to make the early heroes of American history Protestant, dissident, individualistic, rational, and unhappy with the status quo. He found that the habits of a society determine its character and destiny. He admired the Founding Fathers who, understanding human behavior, had limited the power of the governors in order to protect the liberties of the governed. All his beliefs were summed up in Jefferson, who understood that the conflict between authority and self-government is never quite resolved, but that government must protect each man's freedom of action under a system of law. These American affirmations—self-government, individual freedom, limited state power—are the means Dos Passos would use to fertilize the contemporary wasteland. More than this, the excursion into the past, like Jack Burden's in *All the King's Men* and like that of so many of the heroes of Wright Morris' novels, becomes Dos Passos' quest for his own identity.

Dos Passos' nonfiction bears a symbiotic relationship

to the four novels he published in this period. The *District of Columbia* trilogy deals with three varieties of political experience. *Adventures of a Young Man* (1939), the first volume, is an examination of the relation of the individual to the Communist Party; *Number One* (1943), the second, is the story of a dictator's rise in a democracy; and *The Grand Design* (1949), the last, examines the relation of the individual to the "democratic" bureaucracy. In these novels Dos Passos rejects the party, the dictator, and the centralized bureaucracy, all of them forms of concentrated power in the hands of the all-engrossing state. The individual or the people—i.e., the common man—in these novels, however, are triumphant or at least defiant. *Chosen Country* (1951) is a hymn to America as Dos Passos accepts his native land, for good or for bad, with all her inconsistencies.

The governing imaginative principle in the novels of the trilogy is the shocking disparity between appearance and reality, a view of experience eminently appropriate to the sceptical tone of these works. The appearance-reality dichotomy reveals the gap between Communist profession and performance in *Adventures of a Young Man,* between the would-be dictator's promise and what he is and does in *Number One,* between the New Deal's aspirations for the people and the way it humiliates them in *The Grand Design.*

The hero of *Adventures of a Young Man* is Glenn Spotswood, a naïve idealist who is unfitted by his liberal heritage to cope with the party or with American capitalism. Dos Passos' problem is to endow this character with will and personality in order to make him a free and responsible human being, even while accounting for many of his actions as the result of his environment and parentage. It is a problem he does not fully resolve, and his failure weakens his statement of theme in the novel, which is that the party destroys the individual as a free man aware of his own identity. One of the Communist leaders says, "We are not interested in the fates of individuals." Both Glenn and his scientist friend Paul Graves rebel against this indifference toward man. Paul has the pragmatic, experimental, and inductive qualities of mind that mark the scientist and the democratic American. He goes to Russia in the spirit of inquiry, but leaves because there both social and scientific experimentation are frustrated by political dogma and the prevalence of terror. Glenn, who moves from the single tax to radical syndicalism, then to the party, and finally to lonely, unilateral dissent, dies in the Spanish Civil War through the treachery of the Communists. His quest for political salvation has been his education. What he learns proves fatal. The moral indignation and love of mankind that fired him do not save him. The last resort of idealism is martyrdom to an organization of power that will not tolerate decent human behavior. Yet Glenn's dedication to principle does demonstrate the authority of individual integrity.

Number One is Dos Passos' grim analysis of the native Fascist. The would-be dictator presents a public face composed of egalitarian features: spontaneous good fellowship; an economics—"Every Man a Millionaire" is his slogan—based on the communal sanctions in the Bible and on hostility to the corporations; identification with the common man. Beneath this mask Chuck Crawford is a rock-hard manipulator of men and money, an adulterer, a hypocrite, a careful politician whose spontaneity comes out of a card file. Frightening as this portrait is in the dangerous difference it reveals between appearance and reality, it is still a stereotype. Crawford simply mushrooms ineluctably under Dos Passos's hand, filling every crease in the face of the idealized version of the dictator. He has no hesitations, no moral ideas, and no moral conflicts. He moves on the straight string of violent inevitability. As a Fascist he is chilling, but as a character he is a convincing demonstration of Dos Passos' tendency to run to types.

Yet Dos Passos does create moral conflict in this novel. Tyler Spotswood, Glenn's brother, works for

Chuck. He is caught between his own moral idealism and Chuck's total immorality, a conflict Dos Passos does not make particularly believable. The climax of the novel comes when Tyler must make a choice between accepting the punishment he deserves or making a dirty political deal that might lead to his exoneration. He chooses the former because his brother Glenn has exhorted him in a posthumous letter from Spain not to sell out. To save the nation and the people, Tyler knows, we must begin by saving ourselves. Tyler frees his will for a moral act whereby he destroys his life that he may gain it.

It is not clear that "the people" will profit from Tyler's act, but of Dos Passos' emotional attachment to this abstraction called "the people" there can be no doubt. Each chapter of this novel is preceded by a forechapter which begins, "When you try to find the people . . ." Like Whitman, Dos Passos finds and identifies with many different kinds of people, until he discovers that when you try to find the people you find that the people are everybody, the people are the Republic. Dos Passos believes in both the one and the many, in the individual and the mass. It is a Transcendental problem in reconciliation that Whitman also had to face. Both writers celebrate the co-equal sovereignty of the self-conscious, self-willed individual and of the mass who make the nation. Thus we can say that *Number One* is a rejection of dictatorship on moral grounds by a revitalized individual acting in the name of the people who "rise at once against the never-ending audacity of elected persons."

The Grand Design is based on a pattern of rejection-affirmation. Dos Passos turns away from the New Deal as an example of bureaucracy in the corporate state, from the Communist party once again, and from the city of Washington, the symbol of government as Leviathan. He turns toward, or back to, Jeffersonian individualism and agrarianism and the Whitmanian mystique as regards the people. It is these roots in the past which enable his characters to survive. The first extra-narrative section in the novel gives us the mood and method of Whitman: a ubiquitous consciousness, identifying with people on the farm and in Wall Street, participating with boundless compassion in their lives. The principal characters in *The Grand Design* are attached to the Department of Agriculture, among them Paul Graves, whose great objective is to save the small, family-owned farm. In *State of the Nation*, which is the source book for this novel, Dos Passos had said that the independent farmer was the balance wheel of popular self-government. In the novel, Paul tries to give flesh to the Jeffersonian dream of agrarian democracy by settling people on the land and making them independent.

The frustration of the Jeffersonian and Whitmanian ideal is the heart of Dos Passos' criticism of the New Deal. Paul discovers that the corporate state in reality humiliates people while professing to help them. It lowers their consequence. Furthermore Dos Passos claims that big government means the concentration of power in the hands of one man, although no man is good enough to be trusted with more than limited power. The book ends with the bitter charge that the President, the only one who has power, has misused his power in redesigning a world in which men's freedoms are left out. Finally, Dos Passos sees the decline of the New Deal when politics interferes with the performance of the bureaucrats and crisis pushes it from experimentalism to conservatism. The point is made in the almost vicious portraits of characters who resemble Henry Wallace, Harry Hopkins, and Jesse Jones.

In 1951 *Chosen Country* appeared, the story of the making of an American. It is the love story of Jay Pignatelli and Lulie Harrington, of John Dos Passos and the United States. The time of rejection has passed. Jay, in a position to make a conscious choice, since he is as much European as American, deliberately chooses to be an American and live in America. But not until he has made his journey of self-discovery which has led also to the discovery of America, his new-found land. It is a sober but exhilarating assessment of the American experience. The horror of war, the assassination of a radical labor leader, the judicial tragedy of what is called the Sabatini case, the bourgeois persecution of the creative mind are all here. These are the experiences that had broken the heart and pierced the faith of earlier Dos Passos heroes, and of Dos Passos himself, but here they are assimilated in the love and understanding of a country where the frustration of the present is mitigated by the "feeling of anticipation of a dazzling future," where everything is new and unformed, and where freedom's scaffolding, the institutions that are the Republic's framework, is renewed daily. American society, with all its opportunities and defects, gives the young man the freedom to find happiness. The testament to America is palpably Dos Passos' conviction, for Jay Pignatelli is Dos Passos. The shy autobiographical intimations of the Camera Eye in *U.S.A.* are superseded here by thinly veiled personal experience: the "real" experience of Harvard, the war, the Sacco-Vanzetti case, and the spiritual experience of the diffident spectator, always a little alien, accepting at last his identity as an American.

Dos Passos has in this novel expressed a more buoyant confidence than the new liberalism, in its chastened and cautious temper, might reveal and has accepted more than it might be willing to endorse. In fact, a certain ambiguity of allegiance appears in the total process of self-criticism and in the enterprise of rethinking his political position that he undertook in the forties. His rejection of old-fashioned liberalism was not a rejection of traditional liberalism. He saw his task as the restoration of Jeffersonian principles, as the need to save them from those in the twentieth century who had corrupted them. Dos Passos found he could not savor the historical irony that had made Jefferson the patron saint of the liberals who, in the thirties, sanctioned the growth of the corporate state. As a consequence, his attack upon those liberals and his reliance upon tradition brought him into an apparently sympathetic relationship with the reinvigorated right in American life, especially that segment of the right that found its conservatism in preserving, paradoxically, our tradition of liberalism. Yet finally I should say that Dos Passos belongs in the company of the new liberalism because he has expiated the guilt and failure of American liberalism in the two preceding decades. In the end, it can be said that he spoke up more for traditional liberalism than for tradition.

John Dos Passos
Liberty and the Father-Image

MARTIN KALLICH

In an article appearing in the November, 1948, issue of *Fortune*, John Chamberlain pressed American writers to explore the realities about business and to write of businessmen with good will and common sense. Chamberlain is convinced that their protest against business values is but the manifestation of an unconscious and irrational neurosis, the Oedipus Complex, the roots of which are deep in childhood:

> they seem bent on pursuing a Freudian quarrel with their father, most of whom happen to be businessmen. Thus maturity (which consists of making peace with your antecedents and going ahead with your own work) is denied the modern litterateur.

The Freudian psychology suggested in this diagnosis is worth documenting in Chamberlain's friend John Dos Passos, for not only do the works of Dos Passos indicate the kind of neurosis that Chamberlain describes, but, even more important, this neurosis is of crucial importance in any attempt to understand the flux of this writer's social philosophy from youth to middle age—rebellion in his teens and twenties, radicalism in his thirties, and, perhaps finally, conservatism in his forties and thereafter.

However, in Dos Passos' life the full implications of

From *Antioch Review*, 10 (March 1950), 100–105. Reprinted by permission of the *Antioch Review*.

this complex can be understood only when examined within the context of freedom, a theme that underlies all others in Dos Passos' works. From its constant repetition in his fiction and nonfiction, we can infer that the necessity of freedom is the central fact in Dos Passos' life and thought, a kind of unchanging monomania lending unity to all his creative work. No characters in Dos Passos' novels and plays are treated with the sympathy, respect, and understanding comparable to the treatment accorded the lovers of liberty. Martin Howe of *One Man's Initiation* (1920), John Andrews of *Three Soldiers* (1921), Tom of *The Garbage Man* (written 1923), Wendell of *Streets of Night* (1923), Jimmy Herf of *Manhattan Transfer* (1925), Morry Norton of *Fortune Heights* (1934), and Glenn Spotswood of *Adventures of a Young Man* (1938)—all these major characters in Dos Passos' early and late works unconsciously betray Dos Passos' intense narcissism as they make articulate his obsession with liberty. If these characters are Dos Passos' serious imaginative projections, then freedom can very well be the secret key to an understanding of his shift from dissent to consent.

Dos Passos' libertarianism is generally anarchist in character. That is to say, Dos Passos believes in absolute or primitive liberty, the supreme good of the anarchist creed. With Lord Acton, he believes that power always corrupts because by its very nature it exercises restraints. All social wrongs are therefore rooted in family, government, or state authority; and the remedy lies in the curbing of this oppressive power. Each individual must live as he wishes and must not permit anyone to rule over his fellows, for each is a sovereign power. However, co-operation with others in a group or association is possible, but it must be voluntary. Only by means of the individual's given consent can society function freely, harmoniously, and to the advantage of all.

Three general stages in Dos Passos' libertarianism can be traced, corresponding roughly to the three stages of his life and his published work. In the early stage, Dos Passos, like a typical child and adolescent, sought freedom only from his immediate family, from the authority of his parents and the restrictive institutions, such as school, supported by them. Just this desire for freedom, first nurtured in childhood, is responsible for a rebellious streak which has been, until his middle age, basic to Dos Passos' anarcho-individualism.

For example, John Andrews, who detests military regimentation, has from his private-school days (it is not clear in *Three Soldiers* whether Andrews' school is Dos Passos' prep school, Choate) hated confinement and discipline and so "used to go from the station to school by the longest road, taking frantic account of every moment of liberty left him." Martin Howe breathes freely for the first time in his life only when he escapes his dominating parents. He is thrilled at the discovery of individual and uninhibited freedom, when his parents (like Dos Passos' in 1916–17) died and so offered him release and a rare opportunity for self-expression:

> He has never been so happy in his life. The future is nothing to him, the past is nothing to him. All his life is effaced in the grey languor of the sea. . . . As through infinite mists of greyness he looks back on the sharp hatred and wringing desires of his life. Now a leaf seems to have been turned and a new white page spread before him, clean and unwritten on. At last things have come to pass.

Elsewhere in the novel, young Howe makes explicit his desire for a clean break with his past, his family and its restrictive conventions:

> All my life, I've struggled for my own liberty in my small way. . . . I used to think that it was my family that I must escape from to be free; I mean all the conventional ties, the worship of success and the respectabilities that is drummed into you when you're young.

Tom demands free love, a give-and-take relationship that lies outside the marriage institution and the conventional family; Wendell, and Fanshaw as well, of *Streets of Night*, must both break the stranglehold of mother and father in order to feel free.

Nor can we forget an autobiographical short story "The Shepherd," in *The Harvard Magazine* (1916), in which Dos Passos complains of "the overlordship of his parents" and confesses to an exaggerated "desire to experience, to wander free and unconfined through all the glittering highroads of the earth, [which] racked him with actual physical pain." The mother-censor that in "The Shepherd" obviously blurs the young Dos Passos' "dazzling vision of freedom" appears with such frequency in *Rosinante to the Road Again* as to amount to an obsession. Indeed, all the inhibitions of Telemachus, the name that Dos Passos assumes in *Rosinante*, seem to be caused by his mother.[1] Moreover, the impression of domestic frustration is again confirmed in the character of Andrews, who remembers no one of his family but his vigilant and careful mother and her great importance in his life, just as Dos Passos, himself an extremely sensitive child, felt he was dominated by an anxious and doting mother who, because of their unusual disparity in years (at the age of forty-eight she bore her son John), could scarcely understand her own offspring.

Lastly, Camera Eye (25) of *U.S.A.* tells us of Dos Passos' reactions (in retrospect, of course) to his Harvard years. Harvard seems to have been a detestable vacuum that removed him from life:

> can't sleep   haven't got the nerve to break out of the bell-glass four years under the ethercone breathe deep gently now   that's the way to be a good boy one two three four five six   get A's in some courses but don't be a grind be interested in literature but remain a gentleman don't be seen with Jews or socialists.

The bellglass is the sheltering cover that effectively confines and stifles him. Nor does Dos Passos appear to relish the new business atmosphere in college ("all

the pleasant contacts that will be useful in Later Life"),
for at the time of the first World War the liberal arts had
already succumbed to the business influence, and a new
College of Business Administration was instituted at
Harvard. The college boy rebelled not only against the
complacency of a cold culture but also against the
invasion of business values. However, he did not have
the courage to make a clean break:

> four years I didn't know you could do what you
> Michaelangelo wanted say Marx to all the professors
> . . . and I hadn't the nerve to jump up and walk out
> of doors and tell them all to go take a flying Rimbaud
> at the moon.

Dos Passos' many youthful frustrations, beginning
with those at home, have surely laid the psychological
foundation of such early works as *Three Soldiers* and
The Garbage Man and *Streets of Night* and inspired
whatever passionate revolt against all individual inhibitions is to be found in them.

This early romantic desire for freedom is associated
with a development of the Oedipus Complex in Dos
Passos' unconscious and an almost complete suppression
of his father-image in his creative works. As in the case
of Emma Goldman, the audacious anarchist, Dos Passos' childhood hatred or fear of his father may have contributed to his distrust of all forms of authority that can
possibly invade the individual's rights. Whether this
statement is believed or not, the evidence of the psychological pressure of this complex on Dos Passos' unconscious is unmistakable.

John Andrews has no mental image of his father;
Jimmy Herf never mentions his father, having early lost
him; Tom has no parents at all; Wendell positively rebels
against the persecution of his father, and finding it impossible to be fatherless and free, he attempts to destroy
the image of his father by suicide ("Now in me my
father'll be dead"); while Fanshaw has no father; Richard Ellsworth Savage of *Nineteen Nineteen,* who in his

early life closely resembles Dos Passos, is ashamed of his father and has only a shadowy glimpse of him in the poorly lit basement of his aunt's boarding house; and even Glenn and Tyler Spotswood, in *Adventures of a Young Man,* show very little affection for their idealistic father. In *Rosinante,* Dos Passos' search for the father is mentioned but once; however, as we have said, the influence of the mother appears innumerable times, suggesting again the suppression of the father-image. Even some of the early Camera Eye confessions in *The Forty-Second Parallel* disclose that the relationship between father and son was generally cold, affection being notably absent. "I wished I was home," the young Dos Passos, in an English boarding school, unhappily whines in Camera Eye (18), "but I hadn't any home." This domestic trait—the absence of a true home—is common to all of Dos Passos' male characters and is perhaps the cause for Dos Passos' inability to write with understanding of a normal American family up through *U.S.A.* in 1936.

From this evidence, we may infer that Dos Passos' youthful revolt in the teens and twenties is undoubtedly a form of psychological compensation for oppressive parental authority, *however real or imagined,* certainly not poverty or economic exploitation. His revolt could scarcely have been the result of economic insecurity, for his father John Randolph Dos Passos, described by his writer son as a "self-made literate," was a very successful New York corporation lawyer, a senior partner in the firm of Dos Passos Brothers and Mitchell, author of many books on the law, and active in forming several large trusts, among them the Sugar Trust. Therefore, in this primary stage of his literary career, from *One Man's Initiation* (1920) to *Manhattan Transfer* (1925), John Dos Passos is not a class-conscious proletarian but a neurotic and romantic anarchist, believing in the complete *laissez-faire* of the individual. Thus, in his early works, all solutions are individual solutions; all failures and tragedies, individual failures and tragedies.

Such individual liberty has not been emotionally satis-

fying, as Dos Passos' restlessness during these years indicates. His maladjustment manifests itself in a mental
and physical rootlessness which he describes in the
Camera Eye and often symbolizes by the figure of the
"vag," in *The Garbage Man, Manhattan Transfer, Fortune Heights,* and *U.S.A.* The tramp is simply the literary migrant Dos Passos, who wanders from place to
place in the no man's land between social and economic
classes in quest of the certainty he unconsciously for-
swore when he turned against his father and the middle
class of his origin. The travel-book *Rosinante to the
Road Again* represents Dos Passos' first quest for the
father as a guarantee of certainty, purpose, and emotional security. The very first remark in this book pro-
claims the conceptual and emotional confusion in Dos
Passos as a direct result of the suppression of the father-
image: "Telemachus [Dos Passos] had wandered so far
in search of his father he had quite forgotten what he
was looking for. . . . 'I wonder why I'm here.'" There
are similar symptoms of undirected hunger, confusion,
wavering, and doubt in some of Dos Passos' notes of his
journeys in the Near East:

> Does anything ever come of this constant dragging of
> a ruptured suit-case from dock to railway station and
> railway station to dock? All the sages say it's non-
> sense. . . . They may be right, but most likely this
> craze for transportation, steamboats, trains, motor-
> buses, mules, camels, is only a vicious and intricate
> form of kif, a bad habit contracted in infancy, fit only
> to delight a psychoanalyst cataloguing manias. Like
> all drugs, you have to constantly increase the dose.

Such intellectual bewilderment, expressed in *Orient Express,* is projected into Jimmy Herf and further illuminated by the internal conflict that Dos Passos describes
in Camera Eye (46) – "make money?" – a conflict that
is not resolved until Dos Passos begins to help Sacco
and Vanzetti in 1926.[2]
Wedded to the desire to be free from family restric-

tions is the desire to be free from society, especially the money economy and the state that supports it. Andrews, for example, rebels against the regimentation of the state's army; and Tom objects to the economic treadmill and for a time escapes by tramping around the world; Herf also learns to detest the materialist grind of city existence and, like Tom, romantically demonstrates his need for psychological safety and certainty by deserting society and becoming a vagabond. Dos Passos himself defends the persecuted anarchists Sacco and Vanzetti and vehemently protests against the oppression of the state and the ruling class. Finally, moving closer and closer to uncompromising radicalism, he writes the trilogy *U.S.A.* (1930–36) as a satire of a nation dominated by money values.

In this period of intense social consciousness, when most of *U.S.A.* was being written, Dos Passos fights against economic oppression and for the economic liberty of the underdog, as articles in *The New Masses* and *The New Republic* and his activities reveal. It is in this second stage that he is often the stern radical anarchist, at times showing positive signs of proletarian class consciousness. Thus, for a short time, especially between 1930 and 1932, the years when *Nineteen Nineteen*, the most radical and Marxist volume of the trilogy was composed, Dos Passos has succeeded in finding a substitute for the father-figure in an authoritative complex of ideas associated with socialism. In these years, Dos Passos more and more firmly anchors his hopes in the proletariat, so that in the latter part of this period he becomes, as is well known, a "fellow-traveler" of the communists.

But submission to the collectivist socialist discipline is alien to Dos Passos' basically individualist and middle-class temperament. The psychological strain must have been unendurable beginning in 1934–35, even when *The Big Money* was being written, for the middle-aged Dos Passos has repudiated his radical and rebellious past and has become a Tory anarchist, a rugged individualist.[5] Although liberty is still at the core of his thought and action, as the preface to *First Encounter* (1945) and the article "There Is Only One Freedom," in the April issue of '47, make absolutely clear, the concept is that of the conservative, unsocial, free-enterprise farmer and businessman who desire only the barest minimum of government interference and who are profoundly suspicious of a militant and progressive labor movement. Liberty, in reverse, has carried him from the class of the weak underdog to that of the strong topdog. And so, in the third stage, Dos Passos has returned to his father and to his father's class which he had so vigorously, if unconsciously, renounced for about twenty years. The search for the father as a guarantee for safety and certainty has ended, and Dos Passos' symptomatic doubts no longer appear: the "vag" has died and Dos Passos chooses his side without hesitation. The result of this development in Dos Passos' psychological constitution is the character of Millard Carroll in his latest fiction, *The Grand Design* (1949). Carroll is a businessman who, as Dos Passos portrays him, sacrifices his profitable enterprise and more than comfortable income for the hazards and poor rewards of public administration in the days of the New Deal. He is betrayed by the "idealists" who seek their own selfish interests in Washington. Carroll is Dos Passos' first flattering portrait of a businessman, the product of a mellow Tory imagination. He is Dos Passos' answer to the request made by John Chamberlain, mentioned at the beginning of this essay.

Perhaps, however, because Carroll is so self-sacrificing in a "socialist" program at which business so often sniped, he is too ideally drawn to be entirely credible. And in view of Dos Passos' interpretation of life in *U.S.A.*, it is certainly great irony to observe in *The Grand Design* how a businessman can be destroyed by the dirty politics of reformers. Dos Passos, it seems, is at this stage of his life uttering the cant of business, much as before he expounded the cant of rebels. *The*

Grand Design has only shown that he has substituted one neurotic obsession for another. It is therefore doubtful, Chamberlain's remark to the contrary, whether Dos Passos has achieved balance and maturity in returning to his father.

Of course, liberty is not the only idea that can be found in Dos Passos' works, nor are childhood and adolescent frustrations the only determining factors in his life. But the three types of libertarian anarchism — individualist, socialist (or syndicalist), and conservative — are fundamental to a consideration of Dos Passos' social thought. Such libertarianism is the chief message of Dos Passos' life and work, and it is unmistakably accompanied, and in part conditioned, by an Oedipus Complex.

The Search for Identity in the Novels of John Dos Passos

BLANCHE H. GELFANT

Literature reflects a fascination with the enigma of man's identity. Who am I? What am I doing? Where am I going?—these questions recur, are answered, and yet require always reasking and new illumination. Contemporary fiction projects man's quest for identity against the background of a fragmented and confusing world where the need for self-definition grows urgent because the social supports of the past are weakened and the opportunities for new and strange definitions in the present are enlarged. In a world that exhibits instability as a norm and social fluidity as an ideal, no clearcut self-image can emerge and receive assuring consent. The search for identity in modern literature takes on the form of a pursuit—a curious pursuit, because the object is often undefined and unvisualized. Joyce's Bloom wandering the maze of Dublin streets, Camus' Meursault arrested in the blaze of Algerian sun, Saul Bellow's Henderson invading untrampled African jungle, crying "I want, I want," but unable to articulate a predicate—these characters are impelled by a sense of inner void to pursue their identity as whole and self-conscious beings. Undefined to themselves they are all "strangers" seeking the touchstone of some objective reality that can validate their existence or of some assertive self-knowledge that can acquaint and unite them with themselves. The

From *PMLA*, 74 (March 1961), 133–49. Reprinted by permission of the Modern Language Association.

image of man as divided and a stranger recurs in the looming novels of the century, in the works of Proust, Kafka, Camus, Joyce, and Virginia Woolf; it is beautifully crystallized in the recognition scene at the end of Proust's *Remembrance of Things Past* as the hero's revelatory self-encounter.[1] The failure of Proust's narrator to recognize his image in the mirror, his sense of masquerade and strangeness, the jading of his sensibilities as all seems degraded and lost, and then the unexpected swift revelation which unifies and gives meaning to his life—these have become recurrent experiences in contemporary fiction as it tries to illuminate the jagged course of man's search for identity in the modern world.

In a very special way, John Dos Passos also has dealt throughout his career as novelist with the modern quest for self-identity. His obsessive thematic concern with man's inner dissonances has never been fully recognized or explored, perhaps because his conspicuous skill in creating the outer or objective aspects of his characters' world—the externalities of local scenes, the social mores and talk of the people, the political aura, and the long-range underlying historical drift—capture and hold our critical attention as the brilliant achievement of his art. These multitudinous details of the outer world may be viewed, however, as the formal paraphernalia within the novel for dealing with his characters' personal and often neurotic problems of identity. At the radial point of Dos Passos' art stands a hero obsessed by the elusiveness of his identity, a young man dislocated in his society, self-questioning, uncertain, unnerved, and estranged. When he tries to confront himself he encounters "an unidentified stranger / destination unknown / hat pulled down over the has he any? face."[2] This faceless and perturbed young man is the generic figure in Dos Passos' fiction. He is defined most clearly in the fleeting impressions of the Camera Eye, but he moves also through all the novels as their real protagonist; and all the novels, no matter what their particular subject or setting, dramatize his obsessive search for identity. When this highly subjective element of inner need is seen as the crux of Dos Passos' art, puzzling vacillations in his ideas and retrenchments in his political position fall into pattern as the logical and perhaps utterly necessary objectification of the inner trials and errors inherent in man's search for himself. The innumerable characters of the novels in some way extend and explore various facets of the personality in the Camera Eye: they dramatize possible alternative destinies and represent various social masks he could assume to cover his facelessness. For, the reality that the hero cannot sense from within he tries to impose upon himself from without. This means that he is ready to take on whatever coherent social role is prescribed by his times. Thus the sequential pattern of the novels as they expand, modify, or reject what they have previously resolved is determined by those roles which Dos Passos has seen emerge in his lifetime: the Harvard aesthete in the first decade, the disillusioned soldier of World War I, the radical or revolutionary of the twenties, the proletarian champion of the thirties, the anti-Communist and anti-New Dealer of the forties, and now the stolid organization man in his gray flannel suit.

Certain contradictions as well as changes in viewpoint in the novels take on new perspective against the germinal theme of man's search for identity. This search, for example, leads the pacifistic hero to volunteer eagerly for a role that goes against his principles, in an organization he can only detest; it leads him too to become involved in social conflicts even though he feels himself because of class origins outside of and unimplicated in these conflicts. His social commitments grow out of personal dilemmas, representing as they do his renewed attempts to find a social mask that will serve as a true face. The fitting on of the various masks of his times requires him to describe in his own actions the contemporary pattern of rebellion, but since rebellion carries him further off from the stability he is inwardly impelled to seek, he must eventually repudiate this role and retrace his path. Thus the political themes so germane to Dos Passos' novels are a reflection of the inner life or, more accurately, the lack of inner life of the generic hero as he tries to achieve a sense of reality through objectified political actions. Why these political actions become necessary, why the hero cannot confront himself, why there is this compulsive search for identity and the inner feelings of loneness, dislocation, and estrangement—these questions take us back to the hero's childhood where the failure in identity begins.

"I wished I was home but I hadn't any home." [3] This is the cry uttered by the boy in Camera Eye as he shuttles from one European country to another, from one American locale to another, always on the move, now in Mexico, now in Canada, now in a taxi, train, or boat, always going somewhere but never finding home. These early years of restless and uprooting travel, of change and instability in environment, leave Dos Passos' hero with a traumatic childhood experience of homelessness. Homelessness is the generic hero's emotional starting point; homelessness shapes the pattern of his life into a quest for self-identity, for stability, and roots. The passionate attention he gives to the contemporary social scene reveals his search for some group to which he can belong, and his recurrent interest in the historical past reflects his need for roots. The more he yearns for a home, the more, on the other hand, he seems neurotically driven to wander. In time, movement itself, travel or even vagabondage, becomes his narcotic for the gnawing sense of homelessness; but mere movement inevitably defeats his quest for stability, and the desire to return to a home grows always more imperative.

The Camera Eye offers no clear explanation for the emergence of this peculiar pattern of childhood (though its autobiographical sources are widely recognized), and within the novelistic context perhaps no explanation is necessary: what is important to the novels is the emotional consequences of childhood as they make themselves indelible in the memories and needs of the generic hero. Because the hero as a child has never belonged to a home, a family, or a country, he can never as a young man have an unquestionable and intuitive sense of belonging. His crucial experiences are of dislocation; his early sense of himself is of an alien or stranger. The residue of his childhood experience lies in his lasting feeling of displacement and his sense of the elusiveness of his own identity.[4]

In *Chosen Country*, the stream of childhood memories that flow through young Jay Pignatelli's mind on his return to America coincide scene for scene and mood for mood with those in the Camera Eye. Like the Camera Eye protagonist, he relates his pervasive sense of aloneness and alienation to specific causes—the death of his parents and the years abroad that have separated him from his country. But as in the Camera Eye aloneness and alienation are also the quintessential realities in all his experiences; they create an emotional aura beyond which he cannot project himself. Even though his nearest achievement to a sense of belonging comes from being on a train ("A train's the only place I feel at home he told himself"),[5] he feels himself apart from his fellow travellers whom he can only envy because they fall into family groups. Like the boy in the Camera Eye, Jay distills the essence of his childhood experience in the brooding thought, "We never really had a home" (p. 31). Again like the boy in the Camera Eye he recalls how his attendance at an English boys' school made him a "double foreigner": "An Englishman in America and an American in England" (p. 32). Both boys cry over *The Man Without a Country* as the symbol of their own inchoate destiny of wandering. Jay identifies himself with all the driven wanderers of myth and literature, with Ishmael, Cain, and more happily, Phileas Fogg as he circumscribes the world. The child's romanticizing of the mythical wanderer thus prepares for the recurrent adult identification with the wanderer on the social scene, the Vag, who becomes a hero to the generic hero when he grows up.

In *Manhattan Transfer* the return to a homeland in which the hero has no home is epitomized in Jimmy Herf's arrival in New York, after years of travel abroad, on the Fourth of July. The spectacle of flags and fireworks and holiday celebration excites the boy, though its essential meaning escapes him. What bond can there be between him and his country when it is strange and unknown to him? If he realizes any affinity to the land to which he now returns it is only because he is told, not because he intuitively feels, that it is homeland. "This is where you were born deary," his mother tells him;[6] but his relationship to the place of his birth is merely that of a tourist. Like a holiday tourist, he is shown New York's landmarks, the Statue of Liberty, Brooklyn Bridge, Broadway, the Flatiron Building, and like the tourist he comes at the end of the day to a strange hotel where he lies "hemmed in by tall nudging wardrobes and dressers" in a "tall, unfriendly room" (p. 71). His childhood at the Ritz can be summed up by the phrase Jay later applies to himself: it is "a hotel childhood," and Jimmy Herf is thus set within the generic pattern.

For all the characters who come back to America, the children and later the mustered-out soldiers of World War I, the act of return takes on the symbolic significance of a discovery. They are looking at a country anew, with critical and appraising eyes, and with some wonder. Jay Pignatelli notes this attitude in a letter to his French girlfriend when once back in America he writes her, "Revenant en Amérique I always feel a little of the intoxication of the early discoverers" (*Chosen Country*, p. 394). The generic hero examines his country in the manner of a foreign observer, questioning its values, assessing its habits and mores, and judging its achievements against the perspective of its historic mission as a democracy. But unlike a foreign observer who can maintain an emotional detachment from the scene (because usually he is detached) the generic hero is emotionally involved. He needs a home and he wants to give assent to his country, but he has never acquired the habit of natural or intuitive acceptance; and he is appalled and stopped by the surface discrepancies between social facts and historical ideals. The process of assimilation to his native land is long and difficult. Positive commitment through conscious choice seems as unnatural as the feeling of belonging. The selection of a homeland, which must be made as the hero's considered and deliberate choice, is nonetheless a vital prerequisite for the establishment of a self-identity. The resolution of the hero's ambivalent and conflicting feelings towards his homeland takes place only in a later novel among Dos Passos' works, *Chosen Country*, where the very title reflects the two important emphases that underlie all the novels, the one on choice, and the other on homeland.[7]

Within the pattern of childhood in Dos Passos' novels, the child's only sense of stability comes from a strong attachment to his mother; and this stability is invariably destroyed by death. The early death of the mother leaves the generic hero (Jimmy Herf, Glenn Spotswood, Jay Pignatelli, the Camera Eye) with a lingering ideal of femininity framed in the image of a gracious, fragile woman, ailing but still lovely in a silken teagown with training "legomutton" sleeves. (These sleeves are always in the picture, exerting some compulsive power of recall as the quintessential symbol of the mother's gentility and feminine appeal.) The stereotype of the beautiful ailing woman is etched in the Camera Eye by the parenthetical notation, "She was feeling well for once."[8] This recalls the remark of Jimmy Herf's mother before she is stricken: "Oh, I'm so tired of never really feeling well" (p. 80); and the "wilted smell of colognes and medicines" of the sickroom in *Manhattan Transfer* reiterates the "faint stale smell of cologne and medicines" in *Streets of Night*.[9] After the mother's death in *Adventures of a Young Man*, the father recalls how she had always been delicate since the Caesarean birth of her son.[10] The pattern of early death is repeated yet again in *Chosen Country*, where the sudden collapse of Jay Pignatelli's mother in the hotel restaurant is framed in circumstances similar to those in *Manhattan Transfer* when Jimmy Herf's mother is stricken in their hotel room.[11] (The proletarian children too are bereft of mothers, although theirs die less dramatically, like Fainy's mother, wilted from overwork and succumbing swiftly to death.) Most poignantly written is the beautifully toned Camera Eye memoriam on the deaths that have touched the young man: each death, that of his mother, his father, an unknown girl on a train, marking the end of some phase of his life; and all of them leaving him a cumulative horror over the "rotting death" of war.[12]

In the hero's cycle of life, the death of the mother marks the final dissolution of the home—of its tenuous existence as a sentiment even if not as a physical reality. As Jay Pignatelli aptly remarks in *Chosen Country*, "The only home I ever knew [was] just grief's cramping tedium round Petite Mère's sickbed" (p. 32). The mother's death also throws into relief an estrangement between father and son that weaves through the novels as a returning contrapuntal theme. Regardless of the particular circumstances that surround this estrangement, it exists as the indestructible hard core of the hero's emotional experience. In the geography of his emotions, father and mother represent antipodes of hatred and love. All love is polarized about the mother, while the father receives the dregs of his son's feelings —jealousy, resentment, and hate. As the mother's death destroys the one bond between father and son, the hero's festering filial resentment is finally released and expressed by open repulsion. If the boy's visual image of the mother has the perfection of a delicately traced miniature cameo, his perception of the father is always distorted by a mortifying, magnifying eye that searches each enlarged pore and blemish, each deepening wrinkle and drying flaky area of skin, each broken capillary and straggly hair to consummate a repulsive image of physical ugliness. In one of the more kindly intentioned imagistic fancies, Jay Pignatelli sees his father (after a close observation of the ugly details) as a "pale old whiskered worm" (*Chosen Country*, p. 33). In *Most Likely to Succeed*, Jed Morris, who is always thrown into hysterical tension in his father's presence, concentrates on the old man's "yellow and shriveled face," the "old mouth wrinkled into a distant detached unamused smile," the "long creases" on his cheeks, until all the features seem to become "waxen and green," and the face turns into a death mask.[13] Also focussing upon every epidermal blotch, Glenn Spotswood's disgust with physical ugliness enlarges to contempt for his father's character: "Glenn felt his mouth hardening with dislike as he looked across the table at his father's pale lumpy face with its straggly mustache trimmed a little uneven and the thin nose with the enlarged pores down the sides and the red marks the glasses left on either side of the bridge and a few blond hairs on the flattened end of it, and the big gray eyes bulging out of red rims. He's only thinking of himself, Glenn was thinking" (*Adventures of a Young Man*, p. 27).

The hero dislikes his father because he is ugly; and he appears so ugly because he is viewed with immense dislike. But there are other than aesthetic reasons for the son's antagonism: strictly practical considerations engender a lasting resentment towards a father who cannot fulfill his moral or financial responsibilities. Sooner or later the fathers fail their sons as in one way or another they withdraw their support, if they have ever given it in the first place. Some fathers simply disappear, while others never make even a token appearance. In *Manhattan Transfer* Jimmy Herf enters the scene fatherless—except for one slip of the tongue, he gives no indication that he ever had a father or that he realizes he is missing one. In *Streets of Night*, at least Fanshaw recalls that he once did have a father who had died when the boy was ten. (Both characters are of course emotionally involved with the mother; for Fanshaw the mother is openly the inhibiting force that keeps him from achieving sexual maturity and marriage.) *U.S.A.* for all its multitudinous characters is notoriously delinquent in fathers: they vanish; they lose their money; they beat their children; they disgust them. Charley Anderson's father, for example, inexplicably disappears the day his son is born: "He'd had to go West on account of his weak lungs, couldn't stand the hard winters, was how Mrs. Anderson put it." [14] Dick Savage's father, after having embezzled money and ruined his family, also drops out of the boy's life (into jail) and is expunged from memory: "The years Dick was little he never heard anything about his dad. . . ." [15]—this opening sets Dick into the generic pattern. Joe Williams' father takes an unaccountable dislike to his son and beats him brutally in a senseless contest of wills. As for Ward Moorehouse in the trilogy, he holds a "lasting bitterness" against his father, who has been crippled by a fall and then defrauded by his company.[16] Sudden illness topples Ben Compton's father from position as head of the family, and he too becomes a tolerated ineffectual figure once he can no longer support his son. The fathers show an aptitude for mishandling investments, so that under their guidance the resources of Jay Pignatelli and Jed Morris dwindle conspicuously after the mother's death. The mother's death sometimes precipitates a financial crisis because the annuities from the maternal family to the child then cease. Glenn Spotswood and Jed Morris lose their security this way: indirectly their fathers are responsible for the sons' loss of needed income since the aversion of the maternal family to the father in time implicates the son. (In this respect Jimmy Herf is fortunate, because having no father there is no cessation of his mother's legacy after her death.) All in all, the fathers are some-how squeezed into a position where they must ab-negate their financial obligations to their children, and the alienation between father and son is only intensi-fied by embarrassing interviews or letters which express the parents' inability to support the hero who being now bereft of his mother more than ever needs support.

The extreme to which the son's hatred for the father can drive the hero and the lengths to which he will go in his compelling need to annihilate the parental image are explored in Dos Passos' early novel, *Streets of Night*. Here the father-son relationship is worked into a tight and awful pattern of constriction that frustrates Wenny in every one of his desires: in his desire for sexual ad-venture, for love, and for an unconventional, free, and exciting future. Wenny identifies his self-defeating in-hibitions with his father's early injunctions, so that his conscience now represents unmistakably the internali-zation of his father's commands. But this conscience has also made of him a vacillating Hamlet-like coward who cries out in pain or whimpers and whines but can-not act. Wenny thus identifies his father with the half of himself he hates, and, as if this were not enough, he sees his father as creating and expressing a social milieu which further divides and defeats him. His father sym-bolizes the cultural aridity Wenny faces in Harvard, and the stagnant and stultifying Puritanism he feels in Boston as its prevailing atmosphere. On specific occa-sions also, Wenny is stymied by his father-fixation: he cannot consummate the sexual act because he re-lives his father's experience of impotence as it had been re-counted to him.[17] He cannot insist upon love because of an inbred fear of strong emotion and a kind of moral cowardice. In his drunken despair over his failures to achieve anything "real," he becomes panic-stricken by his dimming image in the mirror: "Panic terror swooped on him all of a sudden; it was not his face. . . . My face, my father's face. . . ." (p. 197). Gradually the identification between himself and his father becomes certain—"That face is my face and my father's voice is my voice. I am my father" (p. 199). From this recognition of a self antithetical to everything he admires he moves inevitably on to death. His failure to achieve self-identity impels him to destroy the false self which has become his social mask. "God damn my father," he thinks frantically, "I'll live him down even if it kills me" (p. 172). And his last thought before he shoots himself is "now in me my father'll be dead" (p. 200). The compulsive need to destroy the father, so clearly stated in *Streets of Night*, is certainly a running theme in Dos Passos' fiction. (At least one character succeeds in killing his father, Bud Korpenning in *Manhattan Transfer*.) The reasons for this theme that exist within Dos Passos' own psychological makeup have been explored in an article entitled, "John Dos Passos: Liberty and the Father-Image," [18] where a clear-cut equation is made between Dos Passos and his heroes. Whatever dangers may lie in making such an equation,[19] despite the strong internal evidence, there can be no doubt of the fictional characters' ambivalence or straightforward aversion towards the father. Their need to repudiate their fathers as a model for themselves leaves them with a strong sense of alienation that drives them to arrive at some affirmative definition of themselves. Yet so strongly are they implicated in their fathers' personalities that they cannot make an ultimate repudiation and still survive. Wenny's attempts to create his self-identity by destroying the paternal elements within him that he detests must later be balanced by Jay Pignatelli's efforts to remake himself finally in his father's image. Thus the search for identity leads ultimately, by a circuitous path, to the acceptance of the total identity of the father as the reality of one's self.

Childhood, with its peculiar ambivalences, plants the divisive self-doubts of a lifetime. Childhood also lays the foundation for the social sympathies that are to sway the hero passionately and unremittingly in the future. The moment that the generic hero achieves his greatest stature—when he cries out in the Camera Eye with anguish and defiance: "all right we are two nations" [20] —this moment traces back to an awareness of inequalities and class divisions that dawns upon the child. The child perceives the social world through a series of images in montage; life unreels before him like a movie, in swiftly changing juxtaposed pictures; and being both participant and observer the child sees himself as within some of the pictures and as forever excluded from others. Just as the Camera Eye protagonist, as observer and commentator, is structurally separated from the mainstream of life in U.S.A., so the little boy is separated from and yet made aware of a contrasting way of life which goes on vigorously, boisterously, productively about him. He moves in taxis, pullmans, yachts, through hotels, restaurants, cathedrals, but he manages to catch glimpses of another world and other actions that both frighten and fascinate him—glimpses of enormous factories ablaze at night, of strange coarsely dressed and remote working people at church, of reckless aggressive children shouting dirty words at play. He hears rumors of struggle and need and violence ("who were the Molly Maguires?").[21] These momentary glimpses of a closed alien world become for the child moments of self-evaluation against a class-conscious perspective, a perspective which he is to grow up with and keep for the rest of his life. It is later to make him derogate the middle class and himself as a middle-class intellectual, just as the child derides himself as a puny poor little rich boy. Knowing himself, the timidities and hatreds and inhibitions that thwart him, the child naturally endows the image of his opposite with all the virtues he longs for and in all honesty knows he does not possess. He formulates an ironic definition of contrast between the "nice" boy like himself who is really cowardly and ineffectual, and the "dirty not-nice" boys like the children who are skating on "the pond next to the silver company's mill," flinging dirty words and loaded snow-balls at each other: *they* are the "muckers . . . [who] put stones in their snowballs write dirty words on walls do dirty things up alleys their folks work in mills [and] we [are the] clean young American rover boys." [22]

In his daydreams the cleancut American rover boy escapes the controlling influence of a pure and virtuous mother, and projects himself into the life of the "mucker." Thus Wenny in *Streets of Night* recalls how "he'd lain awake at night thinking of muckers when he was a kid, making himself stories of fights, things with girls, adventures he'd do if he were a mucker, if he were to run away from Aunt Susan and be a mucker" (p. 115). The actual childhood contacts with the "muckers" are few; but their recurrence in novel after novel points to their importance as a shaping influence, for by introducing the child to his opposite or double they present him with the possibilities of another social role. The generic hero sees first in the mucker and then in the Vag a romanticized and readymade identity that seems whole and wholesome; and he dreams that by putting on the external symbols of the lower class (clothes, speech patterns, habits of work, and vagabondage) he can assume a new identity in place of his own. This seems one possible direction to pursue among the various roads that might lead to self-identity.

In *Streets of Night* the hero's wish to change places with a double is unrealized, and therefore the explorations of the relationship between hero and Vag remains tentative. Nevertheless, Wenny's chance encounter with Whitey the hobo is pivotal to the novel, for it provides a standard of reference for all Wenny's subsequent judgments and decisions. The two come together at a moment when Wenny faces the collapse of his dreams of love, adventure, and "reality"; he has failed to "burst through the stagnant film of dreams" into "headlong adventure" (p. 116); he has been humiliated in his confession of love to Nancibel; he has lost his chance for recognition, personal contact, marriage—his one chance "to live like a human being" (p. 124). At this moment the hobo appears before him as an epiphany: here is a young man who has freed himself from dreams, has run away from his hated father and broken the ties of convention, who has conquered his sexual shame and released his inhibitions, who has broken the tyranny of fear, doubt, and desire, the trio of emotions that overcome and immobilize the hero. By a vapidly straightforward interview, Wenny probes into the hobo's way of life, and when once again he is alone, he mulls over all that he has learned and establishes it as his standard. He wishes to identify himself completely with this young man who resembles him and yet is his opposite. "I must live like that," Wenny concludes; and in his Hamlet-like juggling of possible courses of action, he thinks, "To be or not to be—like Whitey, that was better" (p. 136). So complete would be his empathy, he would even have within his memory the romantic images of towns and places which are the residue of Whitey's travels. Wenny's day-dream of himself as the Vag, and his abortive efforts to ship out and get to wandering, is the grown-up version of his childhood fantasy of running away and becoming a "mucker." The Vag is a romanticized ideal, and indeed, the structure of the novel is based upon certain implicit idealizations—that of the renaissance man (Fanshaw's ideal), of the Vag (Wenny's ideal), and of a virile cavemanlike Italian worker (Nancibel's ideal). The theme of the novel is the failure of each character to embrace his ideal. The real "hero" of *Streets of Night*, as distinct from protagonist, is not Wenny at all, but an abstraction—an idealized hypothetical Italian worker whom Wenny is supposed to resemble temperamentally and physically (he has the "shambling walk of an Italian laborer," the "hands of a ditch-digger," "dirty fingernails," "grime round his collar," and even a passion for spaghetti).[23] After Wenny's death, Fanshaw recognizes this affinity by his maudlin thought: "Wenny would have wanted to be one of them [the workmen] red-faced spitting men . . . who had dug [his] grave" (p. 220). The suggestion of the double is further carried in the love story that parallels the frustrated affair between Nancibel and Wenny, the daring and scandalous elopement between Nan's friend and a handsome Italian waiter, which implies that romance is still possible, but only for the virile man of the masses.

In *Manhattan Transfer* a similar suggestion of duality exists in the relationship between Congo Jake and Jimmy Herf. As in classical tragedy, the wheel of fortune turns fatefully and transforms the poor dirty immigrant Congo Jake into the suave millionaire Armand Duval at the same time that it denudes Jimmy Herf to the level of the Vag wandering without destiny into the night. Thus Jimmy says to Congo Jake: "The difference between you and me is that you're going up in the social scale, Armand, and I'm going down. . . . When you were a messboy on a steamboat I was a horrid little chalkyfaced kid living at the Ritz. My mother and father did all this Vermont marble black walnut grand Babylonian stuff. . . . There's nothing more for me to do about it" (p. 383). Jimmy uses a class-conscious argument; his implicit assumption, the assumption inherent in the intellectual's radical pose of the twenties, is that the lower class has a monopoly of virility, vitality, and drive.[24] Yet despite his attraction to the lower class, Jimmy never succeeds in becoming a full-fledged radical, and the criticism directed against him in the novel (echoed later in a radical review of the book) [25] is that because he has not done so, his actions remain unintegrated and his purposes vague and undefined. Thus when one of the characters refers to him as "a bolshevik pacifist and I.W.W. agitator," his wife replies that "the trouble" with Jimmy is that "[he's] not exactly that. I kind of wish he were. . . ." (p. 341).

In *Adventures of a Young Man*, the transformation of the generic hero is completed as Glenn Spotswood becomes Sandy Crockett, the voice and instrument, and finally, the victim, of the Communist Party. What moves Glenn to abnegate family name, personal hopes, and class loyalties in devotion to Party? His concern for the underdog is genuine, as is his belief that the Communist Party is the underdog's only aggressive champion. But his personal need for recognition, for a sense of belonging, for direction and a goal, are as important as his social sympathies in veering him towards communism.[26] The Party's great attraction lies in an organized and coherent social role not merely offered but imposed on the individual. For individuality is burdensome to Glenn: his attempts to shape his own destiny in response to the need for love, home, and self-realization end like Wenny's attempts, like Jimmy Herf's, in a depressing recognition of ineffectuality. His resolution to serve an impersonal social cause follows upon suicidal thoughts after the rejection of his pleas for love, a plea like Jimmy Herf's to Ellen, and Wenny's to Nan, that without love "I'm not a human being." [27] Convinced that he is to be denied love or any personal emotion, he dedicates himself to the "revolutionary working class" of America:

> Inside his head he was standing on a platform in a great crowded hall hung with red bunting, making himself a speech: Wasn't it about time Glenn Spotswood stopped working himself up about his own private life, his own messy little five-and-ten-cent store pulpmagazine libido. Suppose it had jumped off the Manhattan bridge, a damn fool cum laude grind who'd broken down from overwork and sexfrustration, to hell with it, let it go out on the tide past Sandy Hook with the garbage barges, a good riddance like the upchuck when you've had too much to drink. The *new* Glenn Spotswood who was addressing this great meeting in this great hall was going on, *without any private life*, renouncing the capitalist world and its pomps, the new Glenn Spotswood had come there tonight to offer himself, his brain and his muscle,

everything he had in him, to the revolutionary working class. Hands clapped, throats roared out cheers.
(P. 135)

Like all the generic heroes, Glenn deplores the idling
of his youth in vain dreams and inanition, and he resolves to compensate for "wasted" time by engaging in
"real" activities and serving a "real" cause, which he
supposes must lie outside the white collar class, with the
workers: "Glenn got to talking about how he felt he'd
wasted the last three years . . . all the time what he'd
really wanted to be doing was beat his way around the
country [the Vag motif] living like working people
lived. The white-collar class was all washed up. It was
in the working class that *real* things were happening
nowadays. . . . Of course, some things had been real,
there had been a girl named Gladys. But gosh, it was
hard to keep your life from getting all balled up. What
he'd decided was to hell with your private life. He'd
live for the working class. That was real" (p. 147).
Glenn expresses such views to his friend Paul Graves,
whose intermittent visits come to provide a gauge for
his own progress. Against the fruition of Paul's projects,
Glenn measures his achievements and finds them
meagre. Thus the two characters function in apposition:
Paul is the "double" who illuminates Glenn's course as
generic hero. Paul's appeal to Glenn, unlike that of the
Vag to Wenny, resides in his steadiness and his conformity to a more conventional code of success. Just as
Wenny wished to become footloose and free like the
Vag, so Glenn longs to become stabilized like Paul as
a husband, father, and productive member of society.
Despite his apparent conviction when he speaks of his
dedication to the class struggle Glenn finds his friend's
visits upsetting because they force him to recognize a
basic contradiction in his life—the contradiction between what he most wants, a home, wife, children, and
respectability, and what he has chosen as poorly inadequate substitute goals. These unexpected and illumi-

nating visits leave Glenn increasingly destitute because "he didn't have anything in the world, no wife, no children, he'd even thrown his name overboard" (p. 238). Paul's remark, "I'd rather you'd kept *your* identity" (p. 237), becomes ironic by implying that Glenn had renounced a true identity to become Sandy Crockett when the context of his decision has already shown that he assumed his incognito only to avoid the desperate sense of being nobody.

Adventures of a Young Man is Dos Passos' fullest exploration of the middle-class radical expressed in the terms of his idiomatic hero. It shows that the radical pose demands greater self-effacement than the hero can produce despite his willingness to serve a social cause. In the end, the hero's loyalty to the individual rather than the organization, and his concern over means rather than ends only, destroy his social mask. He is impaled by conflicting demands, those imposed by a stereotyped role and those innate to his sense of decency. The resolution of this conflict is his sad early death. That Glenn was not destined to achieve identity by joining the revolutionary movement might have been surmised from the fate of Ben Compton in *U.S.A.*, whose career as a Party member sets the pattern for Glenn. Dos Passos' depiction of the working man himself also suggests that the faith placed in the lower class (see the ringing words at the end of *First Encounter*) [28] is self-deluding. Someone like Joe Williams in *U.S.A.* remains a victim all his life, lacking the insight, knowledge, and drive to shape his destiny. Mac in *The 42nd Parallel*, who develops into a self-conscious, or class-conscious, workingman, educated to a radical philosophy and aware of his destined historical role in the class struggle, fails at the crucial test. His final surrender to inertia confounds the hopes that the generic hero characteristically expresses in extolling the vigor of the working class. If Mac, who, unlike the hero, has the *right* social origins, the class-conscious philosophy, the education by and participation in the most articulate revolutionary group of the time, fails to carry out the role of the proletariat prescribed by Marxian doctrine, then the prospects for such aliens to the working class as Ben Compton or Glenn Spotswood must be doomed from the start. Glenn might have been illuminated by his early experience with Ben Noe, the itinerant harvest-hand with whom he works while he is still at college. What real courage is there, what hope for change, in this example of drunkenness and dissipation? Glenn is pulled down with his partner, just as earlier in *The 42nd Parallel*, the apprentice Mac in exactly the same way is made penniless and ashamed. Thus, however much sympathy towards the working class man may be expressed in the novels by the characters' explicit statements, the actual portrayal of workers, even under most favorable conditions, reveals them as little more than "muckers" grown up. If this is the real version of this class projected by the novels, then the necessary failure of the hero to play his radical role is already partly explained. The class for whom he sacrifices seems little worth the sacrifice. The Party or radical group through which he makes his sacrifices is a destructively monolithic instrument, demanding his individuality and destroying him when he tries to cling to it. Neither by becoming a worker, nor by joining the Party that professes to exist for the sake of the workers, can the hero achieve identity or purpose. The novels subsequent to *Adventures of a Young Man* reiterate this point so bitterly that any Communist figure is depicted as an incredibly despicable moral monster. Perhaps it is because of such earlier attempts to identify with the revolutionary that the revulsion against him becomes so ugly and overpowering in *The Grand Design* and almost pathological in *Most Likely to Succeed*. It would not be surprising to see a Dos Passos novel someday in which the generic hero has finally taken on the crusading role of anti-Communist (*The Great Days* moves in this direction), for the keen disappointments with the Communist Party in Dos Passos' fictional world stem not only from an apprehension of its terrifying goals and acts but also from a recognition of its profound failure to give the individual personal meaning and social reality in our times.

The story of Glenn Spotswood's search for identity within a prescribed organizational role repeats a pattern of action already set down by John Andrews of *Three Soldiers*. Andrews, like Glenn, is impelled by ennui and the unnerving isolation of his personal life to seek escape within conformity to a standardized public role of the times. Caught in the blare and excitement of the early war atmosphere, he inevitably takes on the uniform of World War I volunteer, just as Glenn, in a later historical period, naturally affects the soft collar shirt and corduroy of the young radical. Behind their apparently different social masks, both characters are motivated by the same intentions and desire the same end. Both choose to place themselves in the hands of an authoritarian organization from which there can be no recourse. Both suffer in their chosen roles the same misgivings and betrayals; and for both the consequences of their choice are disastrous.

Insofar as Andrews represents Dos Passos' fullest exploration of the potentialities for self-identity as a volunteer soldier, he is, like Glenn, a synoptic character who moves through Dos Passos' total implacable pattern of the soldier's emotional history and social awakening. It is a pattern initiated by an apparent contradiction between the hero's pacifist sentiments and his voluntary enlistment, whether in the navy (Joe Williams) or in the ambulance corps or the army, usually both (John Andrews, Charley Anderson, Dick Savage, and Jay Pignatelli). Dick Savage, Charley Anderson, and Joe Williams, drifting imperceptibly into uniform, and John Andrews and Jay Pignatelli, moving decisively and with intention, all express antipathy to America's entrance into the war. They suspect a capitalistic plot to seize power and they discredit ostensibly idealistic war aims. All can disclaim being motivated by sheer patriotism—this much Andrews summarizes for them.[29] Behind their act of joining lies a complex of emotions that constitutes the typical syndrome for Dos Passos' hero: self-recrimination and guilt, boredom, and a desperate desire to be reborn.

" 'I threw myself into the army,' " says Andrews, " 'I was so sick of being free and not getting anywhere' " (p. 349). Not getting anywhere and not doing anything constitutes the generic hero's perennial complaint: "Twenty-three years old and I've done nothing ever," cries Wenny in *Streets of Night* (p. 186); "Eighteen years old, and nothing done," repeats Jay Pignatelli (*Chosen Country*, p. 17). The complaint is not merely that of callow youth, nor does it imply a conventional judgment of success or failure. "Not getting anywhere" has specific reference to a state of being the hero recognizes within himself, a condition of psychological stasis—not getting anywhere towards progressive self-realization. The only solution the hero can think of is movement and change, as though manipulation of external circumstances can alter his inner state. For the generic hero feels that he is not real, that things *outside* him are real, and that he will be getting somewhere when he grasps this elusive external reality. He devolved upon the idea of commitment to a social cause as the bridge to reality, but until he makes the commitment he remains lost in dreams that only further nullify his existence. Shut in a private world, he is detached, isolated, and free. But to him freedom means only egocentricity, a total and undisturbed preoccupation with himself which turns into excruciating boredom. Thus John Andrews recalls his enlistment as an escape from boredom and as a way of contacting reality: "He was so bored with himself. At any cost he must forget himself. Ever since his first year at college he seemed to have done nothing but think about himself, talk about himself. At least at the bottom in the utterest degradation of slavery, [i.e., in the army] he could find forgetfulness and start rebuilding the fabric of his life, out of *real* things this time. . . ." (*Three Soldiers*, p. 28).

The desire to make contact with an outside reality, to find a way of belonging and something to belong to, explains the apparent contradiction between the hero's verbal criticism of war and his voluntary enlistment. The intellectual suspicion of the war as a capitalistic move for power is part of a social pose of the times, while the desire to affiliate with a country, right or wrong, is intrinsic to the need to belong. *What* to belong to is never as clear in the hero's mind as his need. Thus, when the young man in the Camera Eye is most uncertain and disoriented, he characteristically seeks refuge in movement (the Vag theme) and in joining: *"Tonight start out ship somewhere join up sign on the dotted line enlist become one of"* (*The Big Money*, p. 196). For Andrews the particular virtue in joining the army lies in the necessary victory of conformity over individuality. Conformity will make him at last one of *"them"*: "'They [the soldiers] were all so alike, they seemed at moments to be but one organism. This was what he had sought when he had enlisted, he said to himself. It was in this that he would take refuge from the horror of the world that had fallen upon him. He was sick of revolt, of thought, or carrying his individuality like a banner above the turmoil. This was much better. . . ." (*Three Soldiers*, p. 22).

The first reaction to army life is exaltation and relief. The weight of boredom and futility seems momentarily lifted; personal decisions are no longer necessary, and yet action, "real action," ensues. The hero feels he is at last starting anew and achieving his dream of rebirth. The initial reaction of Martin Howe, Dos Passos' first soldier, is that "He has never been so happy in his life. . . . As through infinite mists of greyness he looks back on the sharp hatreds and wringing desires of his life. Now a leaf seems to have been turned and a new white page spread before him, clean and unwritten on.

At last things have come to pass" (*First Encounter*, pp. 13–14). And for Jay Pignatelli too, so early in life haunted by the need to shed his old useless self and become a "new wiry Jay, seasoned and tough, alert to lay hold on life," the first encounter is also thrilling: "It had never occurred to [him] that war was fun" (*Chosen Country*, pp. 159 and 196).

But the exaltation burns for only a brief moment. The individuality which has been burdensome to the hero and which he has tried to erase or sublimate within army life cries out shrillingly for expression as soon as it is methodically suppressed. Instead of becoming subdued, the need for self-realization grows more compulsive, for the inner tyranny of personal dissociation is neither relieved nor dissolved by the external pressures of a group tyranny. John Andrews soon discovers that his painful and confusing (and perhaps utterly human) egocentricity cannot be stamped out by a routinized life, nor can his need for identity be satisfied by a standardized role. Indeed, the suppression of his individuality becomes an ultimate and unendurable tyranny as he realizes that the army has deprived him of—certainly not donated to him—the chance to achieve self-identity. In the end, *Three Soldiers* portrays the search for identity climaxed in the spiritual destruction of the man. This is underscored in the novel not only by the parallel stories of Fuselli and Chrisfield, both destroyed, but also by the recurrent symbol of the human being turned into a machine, used and broken and discarded as trash. Once the generic hero apprehends the army's destructive and tyrannical power, his revolt against inner tyranny gives way to revolt against organized domination. The gesture of revolt is the surreptitious dropping of the discarded uniform into the river—the gesture of Joe Williams, the Camera Eye, Dick Savage, and John Andrews. John Andrews alone comes to realize the full implication of his symbolic act of defiance—that a social role once assumed cannot be summarily rejected. (This is also to be the lesson of Glenn Spotswood

when he cannot extricate himself from the entangle-
ments of his social commitment.) When John Andrews,
like Wenny or the Camera Eye, tries to confront his
real self in the mirror, he finds his personal identity
gone; all that remains of himself is now codified, standardized, and shut within the army's files:

> In those office buildings . . . in index cards and piles
> of typewritten papers, his real self, which they had
> power to kill if they wanted to, was in his name and
> his number, on lists with millions of other names and
> other numbers. This sentient body of his, full of
> possibilities and hopes and desires, was only a pale
> ghost that depended on the other self, that suffered
> and cringed for it. He could not drive out of his head
> the picture of himself, skinny, in an ill-fitting uniform,
> repeated endlessly in the two mirrors of the Major's
> white-painted office. (*Three Soldiers*, p. 378)

If the end of the worker in Dos Passos' novels is inanition, of the young radical is victimization and destruction, and of the uncertain and unnerved intellectual is suicide or purposeless wandering, the end of the
soldier is burial within the steel drawers of a closed
army file cabinet. The generic hero may have thought
that the literal act of wearing a uniform could be trans-
posed into the symbolical act of achieving identity, but
he discovers that externalities cannot confer inner reality. The soldier's olive drab is as ineffectual for him as
a dirty shirt and grimy fingernails were for Wenny in
Streets of Night; and the way to acquire identity remains as elusive as ever to the generic hero. Martin
Howe, after his first exaltation, is left with an imperative need to join still another group, this time in a political role (one which Glenn Spotswood later assumes).
Dick Savage and Jay Pignatelli, both recognizing the
destructive potential of army life when they encounter
the forces of censorship, are left after the war still seeking a place and a purpose. John Andrews suffers most
severely the depersonalization of a discipline which im-

plicitly demands that men be turned into machines. He experiences the violence and insult of imprisonment, the inevitable punishment to the individual in rebellion. His loss is the greatest because it frustrates man's most exalted power, the power to create and by creating to liberate his talents towards a total expression of his being. His loss is the greatest also because punishment follows upon the final revelation (which balances his earlier blind relinquishment of freedom) that "Being free's the only thing that matters" (*Three Soldiers*, p. 427). Thus from the moment that Dos Passos' character volunteers for service to the moment he drops his uniform into the river, an implacable pattern of action evolves: enlistment, momentary exaltation, recoil, rebellion, punishment, and finally perhaps death.[30] It is an ironical pattern, because it explores the possibilities for individualistic expression under a necessarily authoritarian rule; yet it seems to be a compulsive pattern in Dos Passos' novels, doomed always to failure by its inherent and irresolvable contradiction.

The desperation with which Dos Passos' protagonist pursues his search for identity—a desperation expressed in the hysterical tone of *Streets of Night* and Wenny's terrible suicide, in the nightmarish urban fantasies of Jimmy Herf in *Manhattan Transfer*, and his final choice of destitution, in the acceptance of the last suicidal mission of Glenn Spotswood in *Adventures of a Young Man*, in the untimely desertion with its unconsciously destructive submission to doom of John Andrews in *Three Soldiers*, and in the frenetic uncertainties and seekings of the man in the Camera Eye—stems from fear of a role which he thinks he must reject but to which he is nonetheless attracted. This is a role indigenous to his society, the successful young business man. His unwilling attraction to success and material rewards goes far to explain his desperate, almost deliberate, self-propulsion into failure.

The uniform of success is the "white Arrow shirt" which, like the other "uniforms" in Dos Passos' novels, represents to the protagonist a defined social part, a tailormade personality he must decide to assume or reject. The decision he makes, whether to become Vag, soldier, or radical, is countered in his mind by the other possibility of wearing the white Arrow shirt. A conscious juggling of the alternatives of success and failure thus takes place tentatively or by implication in some novels, and without remission in others (*Streets of Night, Manhattan Transfer, U.S.A., Most Likely to Succeed, The Great Days*). Wenny's alternative is a professional future at Harvard; Jimmy Herf's is his uncle's offer of a business post with opportunities; Glenn Spotswood's is the respectable bank-job he gives up; Jay Pignatelli's is Raisen's law firm in New York; and Jed Morris' is a Hollywood contract. Even the Camera Eye protagonist, at the impassioned moment of his radical soap-box speech, visualizes his alternative: "maybe after all maybe top-dog make / money . . . money in New York" (*The Big Money*, p. 150).

His consideration of success as a real possibility seems to the hero parenthetical, to come as in the Camera Eye, in a moment of doubt, and his gestures towards success he views as mere dalliance. So Glenn Spotswood rationalizes his respectable bank-job by saying, "He wasn't a gentleman, he was just a workingman who happened to be working for a bank"; and further, "he was a spy in the camp of the enemy" (*Adventures of a Young Man*, pp. 158 and 169). Jay Pignatelli explains his motives by an elaborate sociological interpretation of the lawyer's function, a rationalization that somehow obfuscates the simple fact that he is joining a prosperous firm. It is psychologically necessary for Dos Passos' protagonist to conceal from himself his inclinations towards material success because of his more overpowering need at the moment for rebellion. Success is the norm he identifies with parental values. Success is what the fathers preach, and the world of material ends is what the fathers have created. It follows then that success is what the sons in aversion to the father must reject. The fathers in the novels (or the uncles acting as surrogates for fathers who may be blotted out, i.e., James Merivale in *Manhattan Transfer* and Uncle Mat in *Adventures*) urge the young men to work their way up the ladder of success by dangling before them security, social position, and acceptance. In becoming the Vag or the radical or in losing himself within the army, the hero externalizes his diametric opposition to all that his parent seems to represent. His rejection of parental authority is further reflected in his visualization of success as an authoritarian code which would submit him to a completely routinized life—being "fed in two endless tapes through the revolving doors" of an implacable office building.[31] His rejection of conventional success is also the hero's assertion of independence and freedom, and ironically, this freedom becomes the burden he tries to escape by losing his personal identity in a public role.

The hero's dissociated state of mind reflected in his inability to define goals and progress towards them relates reciprocally to the rejection of success. For the alternative to success as he sees it set down by the father-uncles is simply failure, and failure offers no orientation. Success channelizes activities, concentrating them towards a goal, but failure merely negates and leads to aimless wandering down a winding road that goes "nowhere." Those characters who most unequivocally renounce the success within their reach seem to give themselves over to purposeless yet inevitable self-destruction. In *Manhattan Transfer*, for example, when Stan Emery cries out, "Why the hell does everyone want to succeed? . . . What can you do with success when you get it? You can't eat it or drink it. . . . [Failure is] the only sublime thing" (p. 175), he is already lost, already committed to dissipation and marked for early death. So too when Jimmy Herf in his drunken reverie sees "one of two unalienable alternatives; go away in a dirty soft shirt or stay in a clean Arrow collar," he already knows that that "there's nowhere in particular he wants to go" (pp. 365 f.). His destination at the end of the novel is "nowhere." The rejection of success is thus more than a rejection of the parental image, of an authoritarian and routinized way of life, and of a social system based on gross materialism: it is the rejection of a "readymade" identity with a "for-somebodyelse-tailored dress suit"—a rejection of a pre-scribed social role which leaves the hero still faceless and alone and still in need of an identity.[32]

Repudiation does not come easily to the poor and lonely protagonist because the attractiveness of modern success is always summarized for him in a particularly compelling image of sexual luxury. The symbol of success is a beautiful woman in a taxicab—the cab gliding down Park Avenue or Fifth Avenue, the woman, per-fumed, in furs, entirely sensuous, sometimes locked in the embrace of a man in a dress suit, in the hero's fantasies, his fortunate self. Thus the young man of the Camera Eye equates success with "money in New York (lipstick kissed off the lips of a girl fashionablydressed fragrant at five o'clock in a taxicab careening down Park Avenue)" (*The Big Money*, p. 150). To a character in *Manhattan Transfer*, the seductive image of the woman in the taxicab is so compelling that he actually tries to force his way through the traffic into her cab—but un-fortunately he is run over on the way (pp. 170 f.). In *U.S.A.* Ward Moorehouse's first big step towards suc-cess is marriage to the rich beautiful girl of the success-fantasy, even though he has just discovered the depths of her degradation. For Charley Anderson, money and success become inseparable from the possession of rich and aloof beautiful women, one whom he loses and the other whom he marries only to lose in another way. So the illusory equation of money with beauty and love, of success with the realization of sexual desire, that runs thematically through the dissimilar novels of Theodore Dreiser and F. Scott Fitzgerald, underlies Dos Passos' fiction. To the lonely young hero success holds out the glittering promise of losing himself, and so finding himself, in the soft arms of a beautiful woman. The relationship between the solitary search for identity and the promises of material success are summarized even in Dos Passos' reportorial writing, in a passage, for example, in *In All Countries*, which begins with the image of unidentified strangers walking New York streets.

> . . . somebody walking towards you . . . Who is he? What does he want? Where is he going? Who am I? What do I want? Where am I going? . . . and ten thousand young men in ten thousand hall bedrooms . . . sit on the edges of their sour beds and . . . want.
>
> Want maybe Madison Avenue and the smell of florists and newbought leather knickknacks and the plateglass shine and the brass, and Bacardi cocktails and speakeasy meals, the stiff white napkins and her leg in silk stocking against yours under the table and the fiveoclock bustle of furs and the warm room smelling of the perfume the girl wears and the tinkle of ice in the glasses and the bright black of the piano and smell of the dressingtable in her bedroom and the sidelong hand pulling down the shade. (But mostly they go to bed alone in the last stale swirl of some bunches of wornout drinks.) [33]

With a singular exception (in *Chosen Country*), Dos Passos' men are almost invariably drawn to women who confirm their success-image by fitting themselves into the glamorous urban picture. Many of the women, from Nancibel in *Streets of Night*, to Ellen Thatcher in *Manhattan Transfer*, and Eveline Hutchins, Eleanor Stoddard, and Margo Dowling in *U.S.A.* (as well as multitudinous minor women characters), pursue careers and seek success at the expense of personal love, marriage, and family. The failure of identity in the male results in large part from the women's coldness to him, her refusal to respond with love and assurance when he most needs them to define himself as a human being. Wenny, Jimmy Herf, and Glenn Spotswood plead with the woman they love for love in return, but Nancibel spurns Wenny because she is wrapped in her career, Ellen rejects Jimmy Herf only to accept the very successful George Baldwin, and Gladys fails Glenn because of an incapacity for love concealed beneath Party jargon. The women who give love are usually marked thereby for destruction: Daughter dies through recklessness born of shame; Mary French (in many ways the female counterpart to Glenn Spotswood) allows herself to be exploited and duped; and Georgia Washburn, warm-hearted, intelligent, generous, and unwisely submissive (how has she blundered into Dos Passos' fictional world?), is trapped in a maze of false relationships from which she finds no way out but suicide.

While the generic hero explores various social poses to express his anti-success orientation (and even in Dos Passos' latest novel *The Great Days*, the protagonist makes explicit the theme of success in failure), the thronging characters of *Manhattan Transfer* and *U.S.A.* dramatize the horrendous meaning of success. Perhaps few literary characters are flayed so unmercifully as the "successes" in *Manhattan Transfer*: James Merivale entranced by inflated and trite reveries of success at the very moment he is being duped by his sister's bigamous husband; Phineas P. Blackhead (ugly name) lying dead and spat on by his presumably faithful servant; Gus McNiel, corrupted by the temptations of power politics; and George Baldwin turned into a hollow man, embracing a brittle doll-woman as solace for his inner emptiness. In *U.S.A.*, Charley Anderson, Dick Savage, and Ward Moorehouse (whose name suggests materialistic grasping) seem caught in a Faustian bargain. They pay with their souls for their success, and at the end, though their souls are lost, their success is tenuous and under threat. The fact that J. W. had once wistfully associated success with the writing of sentimental love songs, that Charley Anderson had wanted the love of a decent woman, and that Dick Savage had dreamt of becoming a poet makes their ultimate fate more than ironical, tragic perhaps. In Jed Morris of *Most Likely to Succeed* (the title points the motif), the antipathetic success-figure merges with the Party-servant into the despicable image of a man traitor to his ideals and to the people who trust him. For Jed to refuse to make his betrayals would mean rejection by Hollywood and by the Party, neither of which possibility is tenable to someone of his meagre resources. He desperately needs his two masks, that of success which makes him seem important to other people, and that of the Party worker which makes him important to himself.

Success corrupts, but failure is corrosive. Neither the successes nor the failures achieve full stature as human beings. Indeed, none of the masks of social conformity, neither conformity to a positive pattern of success nor to a negative pattern of rebellion, resolves the search for identity. The peculiarly dehumanized quality of Dos Passos' characters, their flatness and helplessly drifting quality, is largely a result of their inability to find inner reality by assuming contemporary set codes of behavior.[34] The recurrent image that expresses their dehumanization is that of the puppet, the brittle doll, the marionette, the mummy. A catalogue of such images would be interminable, but aside from all the particular instances when the characters feel themselves turning into disjointed puppets, there is a general effect Dos Passos' characters give of being marionettes pulled by strings through compulsive gestures, of lacking the inner resiliency which is perhaps above all the distinctive human trait. Whatever social tensions are made responsible for this dehumanization [35] (and surely this is the "message" of Dos Passos' novels: that the pressures of war, materialistic society, or coercive political organizations—whether the Communist Party or, equally as bad to Dos Passos, the New Deal—devitalize the individual and distort his values until he is morally nothing more than a puppet), these social tensions are

brought to bear upon characters who are to begin with
marred and defective, lacking courage, insight, and
stamina as they are lacking also family love, stability, a
home, and a country. Success as it must be lived out in
a highly organized capitalistic society cannot satisfy
their deep personal longing. Failure which puts them
outside their society or keeps them in constant opposition to it leaves them more alone, more lost, and still
wandering, until finally they have no other direction
to take except that which leads back to the beginning
— to the mother, the father, and the chosen country.

After once more recapitulating the inner problems of
the generic hero in search of identity, *Chosen Country*
introduces for the first time an apparently tenable resolution. Unlike vagabondage, suicide, radicalism, or submission to military authority, this resolution places the
dissociated hero after his novitiate years of loneness and
wandering into a full context of personal and social relationships he has so far repelled or been unable to find.
It reconciles him with his father; it reunites him in his
wife with his mother; it conciliates him to his country;
it adjusts him to the success-goals of twentieth-century
America; and it affirms the certainty of his own reality
through a set of complex rationalizations concerning a
theory of history and his chosen profession, the law.

The recreation once again of the generic pattern in
Chosen Country seems almost obsessive. Jay Pignatelli
experiences the usual childhood circumstances of homelessness and wandering. He feels towards his father the
same overwhelming ambivalence of love and hate, although here, illegitimacy, finally brought into the open,
explains his emotional dislocation. He also focuses all
love upon the mother ("all his life he'd hate everything
but Petite Mère," p. 26). He reproaches himself for idle
adolescent dreaming and the sexual inhibition, which is
summarized in the early reiteration, "He never dared
cross the Rubicon." [36] He too clashes with army author-

ity, after frantic and extended efforts to enlist, and he suffers the same disillusionment with communism. Finally, he too experiences the confrontation of the generic hero's ultimate question: Who am I? What am I to do?

Perhaps the clue to this elaborate reproduction in *Chosen Country* of the hero's unchanging dilemmas lies in the novel that precedes it, *The Grand Design*. In many ways, *The Grand Design* seems a mutant among Dos Passos' work, unstamped by the generic features. But its very unique qualities indeed prepare for the final resolution in *Chosen Country*. *The Grand Design* introduces two unusually mature, organized, and self-possessed characters who point a new and hitherto unexplored direction in the search for identity. Milo Perkins and Paul Graves (characters to whom the author seems to give assent unadulterated by pity or embarrassment) are men of ideas and ideals. Both put themselves into public service at personal sacrifices in order to institute their ideas for the welfare of the country. Though both are so curiously flat and incomplete as the familiar Dos Passos characters, they avoid the usual stereotyped behavioristic gestures because they appear as primarily directive thinking people. Their ideas are hypostasized to the degree that problem-solving skill rather than wholeness and many-sidedness is their salient characteristic. In the desire to act as "custodians of the Republic" (in effect another way of achieving a public identity as replacement for a private self) they place their ideas at the service of the country, thus introducing a new mode for the generic hero—acceptance of one's country and devotion to the task of making it live up to its historic ideals. This mode lies at the extreme from vagabondage, which implies dissociation from one's country, and from revolution, which implies destruction of the country's foundations. The fundamental obsession with home remains in *The Grand Design*, but the relationship between hero and country has thus become inversed.

Ironically enough, now that the hero is at last willing

to work directly for his country, the ruling administration is unwilling to accept him. In *The Grand Design* Perkins and Graves are left thwarted in their well-intentioned and well-conceived schemes. But since their failure is attributed not to the deficiency of their ideas or their characters but to the selfish and confused machinations of the New Deal administration, the heavy burden of failure so long carried by the generic hero is at last lifted. The shift of the responsibility for failure from the man to the forces of power politics means for Dos Passos' protagonist that he need no longer recriminate himself for his ineffectuality: he has been blamelessly overwhelmed by a political clique against which he finds no redress. This clique is his enemy as well as the enemy of his country, the obstacle to his self-fulfillment and the fulfillment of America's founding dreams. Looking at personal and political events from this perspective, he can accept his country, sadly caught in the moil of politics, and, more important, he can accept himself. There is then a new target for his pent-up resentments and frustrations—Roosevelt, his satellites, the New Deal, the entire Democratic administration and its policies. His animosity against these frustrating elements can be no less than the hatred he has for so long borne against himself, and its expression can be no less vehement.

The Grand Design suggests also a new family role for the generic hero. While family life in *The Grand Design* is subordinate to politics, nevertheless Perkins and Graves are clearly drawn within a family circle. Glenn Spotswood had once envied Graves precisely because he had a wife and family, and now as the generic hero personified by Jay begins to coincide with his "double," his family relationship also must be solidified. *Chosen Country* emphasizes the family background by a structural device—the alternation of sections on family lineage with the narrative blocs. This structural pattern departs decidedly from that of the earlier novels, *Manhattan Transfer* and *U.S.A,* in which the characteristic method of fleeting disjointed impressions had been an implicit commentary on the discontinuity of experience.[37] In *Chosen Country*, the heavy structural units emphasize the presence and solidity of family background and continuity of a traditional line. The Prolegomenon introduces Jay's father as a colorfully distinctive personality and, more important, as a man with family background, profession, and patriotic pride, someone with a legacy of attachments and purposes to leave his son. Thus Jay is not as denuded a hero as Jimmy Herf, who has no father, or as the Camera Eye, whose father resembles Jay's, but is delineated more perfunctorily and unsympathetically. But Jay cannot accept his father without a struggle. To begin with, illegitimacy is a barrier he must gradually overcome. At first he acknowledges his father only parenthetically: "(of course Dandy was his father but he had never dared to call him that)" (p. 29). His idealization of his mother, and her idealization in turn of the father, intensifies his alienation. And his father's personality—the same self-dramatization and love of attention, and also the same virility, that characterize the Camera Eye father—arouses in the boy embarrassment tinged with envy. The sense of estrangement from the father therefore exists, but with this distinction, that there exists also a positive and still attractive father-image to which the boy can return. He *has* a father who is fully characterized as a person and as the embodiment of certain virtues and stable ideals sought by his son. Thus when Jay asserts his profession, it is that of his father. When he determines the country of his choice, it is the country chosen by his father: "My father was an American by choice; I feel the same way" (p. 389). When he chooses a wife, it is inevitably the same kind of woman chosen by his father: "Lulie's light-brown hair was up in back and plastered in little curls across her forehead that made him think of somebody (of course it was Petite Mère in her long lace sleeves)" (p. 454). (And so at last the hero has within grasp those symbolic leg-of-mutton sleeves that have haunted him since lonely childhood.)

The Prolegomenon devoted to Lulie's family is equally important in establishing a sense of lineage and tradition. By marrying Lulie, Jay becomes part of a family and a future progenitor; he achieves what most he wants: "You ungrateful bastard," he says to himself in this happiness, "haven't you wanted a family more than anything in the world?" (p. 466). As the modern counterpart of the lovely mother-image, Lulie is unique in Dos Passos' gallery of women since she is neither the frigid career-driven rejector of the man nor is she, like Mary French or Georgia Washburn, the victim of social sensibilities and submissiveness to men. As a fictional character, she is less striking than the women of *U.S.A.*, perhaps because her function in the novel makes her bland, and perhaps also because Dos Passos seems embarrassed in his attempt to make her interesting.

At the end of *Chosen Country*, Jay and Lulie face the future like a new Adam and Eve. Unlike previous Dos Passos novels, the book ends with the beginnings of things, the usual historical perspective thus having become reversed. For in *Manhattan Transfer* and *U.S.A.*, the underlying historical view-point was always retrospective, implying a comparison of the present with an idealized past. These earlier novels indicted present-day America for betraying its founding democratic ideals, which, the novels implied, were actually realized as social realities sometime in the past. The historical viewpoint in *Chosen Country* is prospective, looking towards a still malleable future in which the founding dreams can yet come true. America is visualized as young, too young to have yet achieved her unique democratic goals. The work of creating civilization out of wilderness still remains to be done, and the now-willing hero has found the means to an orderly evolution of social institutions in his chosen profession, the law. The burden of *Chosen Country* is then a decision between two alternative ways to social change, the way of the revolutionaries, anarchists, and communists, which can destroy America's foundations, and the way of the law, which can build upon the existing scaffolds of the Republic. "Isn't it conceivable," Jay asks, "that a man might practice law as a public service?" (p. 389). Like Milo Perkins and Paul Graves, Jay tackles a public chore; like all the generic heroes, he seeks self-fulfillment in a public role. If he suspects that this role conceals a capitulation to the idol of success (since it requires him to join a prosperous New York law firm), he reassures himself of his basic social disinterestedness by thoughts of his "projects." In his "spare time," he can "work on a new *Decline of the West* only more like Gibbon than like Spengler" (p. 422). Also he hopes "to take a couple of months off and do a little work on my *Influence of War on Twentieth Century Civilization*" (p. 459). These schemes sound admirable, if grandiose, and the man who can sandwich monumental tomes between his duties as tireless "custodian of the Republic" is a hero indeed.

Chosen Country ends with Jay's plans for the future: we can only guess his actual accomplishments. However, some adumbration may have been given us in *The Grand Design* through the defeat of Perkins and Graves by political opponents; and perhaps further light is thrown on his difficulties in Dos Passos' latest novel, *The Great Days*. Roland Lancaster, the protagonist of *The Great Days*, had also considered himself a custodian of the Republic, but he saw himself defamed as reactionary and fascist by the government he wished to help. Lancaster attributes his loss of prestige to the failure of his contemporaries to understand him or to see current events from his point of view. (No one seems to realize as clearly as he for example that Franklin Roosevelt is as culpable a war-criminal as Goering, and that the Nuremberg trials insofar as they do not try Roosevelt are a mockery of international justice.) Aside from releasing into open expression an accumulation of political hostilities, *The Great Days* is the implicit expression of the protagonist's cry for public recognition. Although Lancaster thinks he can accept failure as the meaningful essence of life ("That's what life's made up

of, really"),[38] he still desires to climb a second time up
the ladder of success which is symbolized in his thoughts
by the dizzying ladder he had climbed as a reporter.
Even in the sordid circumstances of his fall from public
grace, he still hopes that "Someday I might be needed"
(p. 312); and he sees himself as still serving the public
interest by the very act of his waiting. What he waits for
is some social catastrophe that will prove his diagnosis
of political events correct and that will necessitate his
recall to Washington in a crucial advisory position. What
he waits for also is renewed or belated recognition and
approval, without which he is merely an over-aged Vag,
trying to meet his problems with the old solutions of
woman's love, or failing that, travel and change ("in the
old days when things got bad he always used to cook up
a trip") (p. 293). The young woman, more disheveled
than usual, addicted to sneakers, daiquiris, and certain
eccentricities, is typically frigid and disturbed, the self-
centered, dehumanized, brittle doll who aggravates the
man's impotency. The upshot of Lancaster's lurid wan-
derings is a desire to return home. Only his country
holds what he most needs and desires — the purpose and
recognition it had given him in the great days to which
his thoughts inevitably return. Thus unlike *Chosen
Country* which looks to the future, *The Great Days*
divides into past and present. Half of the novel is Lancaster's spectacular recall of his reporting career (in
long passages where Dos Passos flagrantly plagiarizes his
own reports from *Tour of Duty*).[39] The other half traces
his dismal attempt to find love and vocation in Cuba.
In the end, the search is futile, because for Lancaster the
reality of his identity is dependent upon or indivisible
from his country's response to him. He can only wait
for the social crisis that will force the government to
recognize the validity of his views and his indispensabil-
ity as custodian of the Republic. The almost paranoiac
elements in Jay's dreams of his historic mission are here
intensified, necessarily so, since the need for identity
grows stronger as it is denied. The hero's growing sense

of political persecution reflects his growing frustration, his helplessness in grappling with neglect and public failure. He must see himself as the victim of a capricious and powerful antagonist, as the object of slander, the pawn of political chance—otherwise his defeat is too overwhelming for him to bear its responsibility. He focuses his attention outward and locates his enemy in a tyrannical leader and his self-seeking crew. He retains self-respect only by extolling failure, while at the same time he blames his failure upon inimical men and invidious times.

Thus the generic hero's response to the sociopolitical scene gradually changes nuance through the novels as he loses perspective and objectivity. While he may feel motivated by the same underlying human sympathies, he has become less and less capable of making valid social judgments because his judgments are becoming more and more involved in the psychological projection of personal problems upon political causes. Politics, however, cannot account for the fact that the generic hero had always felt inadequate, puny, and besieged by doubts. Nor can the course of political events obscure the persistence of the same pressing problem of self-identity. Out of inner necessity, perhaps the necessity for preservation,[40] the generic hero finds new targets for the hatred he had for so long directed against himself: the Army, the ruling capitalistic class, the Communist Party, and finally, the New Deal. That these hatreds imply social and moral judgments which call for the reader's consideration must be recognized. But it must also be recognized that these hatreds are always implicated in the characters' neurotic pattern of inner need and self-defeating conflict. The hero's inner compulsion to define himself through a social role in turn defines the novels. It gives them logical sequence, direction, and plot. It determines their characters and their method of characterization. It produces the distinct dissonant overtones which give emotional unity to all Dos Passos' novels. And it gives them also their pertinence and moving power, for this problem of achieving a whole and innerly motivated "real" identity is one of the characteristic and driving problems of our time.

John Dos Passos and the French

BEN STOLTZFUS

John Dos Passos, according to Thelma M. Smith and Ward L. Miner,[1] shares the distinction, along with Faulkner, of having most strongly influenced present-day French novelists. Sartre, during a moment of youthful exuberance, even wrote in the *Atlantic Monthly* in 1946 that Dos Passos was the world's greatest living writer:

> Dos Passos has revealed the falsity of the unity of action. He has shown that one might describe a collective event by juxtaposing twenty individual and unrelated stories. These revelations permitted us to conceive and write novels which are to the classic works of Flaubert and Zola what the non-Euclidian geometry is to the old geometry of Euclid. In other words, the influence of American novels has produced a *technical* revolution among us. They have placed in our hands new and supple instruments, which allow us to approach subjects which heretofore we had no means of treating: the unconscious; sociological events; the true relation of the individual to society, present or past.[2]

French critics like Coindreau, Magny, Pouillon, Brodin, and Astre (along with Sartre) give Dos Passos a literary eminence which American critics in general are

From *Comparative Literature*, 15 (Spring 1963), 146–63. Reprinted by permission of the author and the editor of *Comparative Literature*.

reluctant to admit. *Manhattan Transfer* and the *U.S.A.* trilogy have achieved a celebrity in France, at least among intellectuals, which they do not have in the United States.

Many modern French writers, as Sartre points out, have learned much from the "objective" technique of Hemingway, Faulkner, and Dos Passos. But novels like *Manhattan Transfer* and *U.S.A.*, while profoundly American in language and content are, technically and artistically speaking, in the French grain. Maupassant and Mérimée, long before Dos Passos, had written "objective" novels in which analysis, at least in the French sense of "analyse psychologique," was absent.[3] The symbolism and imagery of *Manhattan Transfer* also echo technical antecedents in the work of Flaubert, while the very dimensions of *U.S.A.* provide analogies with Balzac's *Comédie Humaine*, Zola's *Rougon-Macquart*,[4] Romain Rolland's *Jean Christophe*, and Roger Martin du Gard's *Les Thibault*.[5]

Dos Passos has also adapted art forms such as cubism, futurism, and "simultanéisme" (all of which were evolving in Paris around 1910) to the domain of the novel and to the aesthetic pattern of his work. Furthermore, *Manhattan Transfer* and *U.S.A.*, bear the unmistakable imprint of Blaise Cendrars, Apollinaire, and Delaunay, whose poetry and modernism were vital in the creative influences emanating from Paris just before World War I.[6] It is time, I think, in keeping with Sartre's article in the *Atlantic Monthly*, to place French influence and American counter-influence in their proper perspective.

With the exception of one or two poems by Sandburg, Masters, and the imagists, Dos Passos saw in American letters and art after the turn of the century nothing but parlor entertainment for high-school English classes.[7] He therefore turned to the poetry of Cendrars and Apollinaire, to futurism, to cubism, and to vorticism for salutary influence and inspiration. Paris at that time, writes Dos Passos, "was a center of unrest" spreading modernism in the arts in every direction. In 1909 futurists like Marinetti, Balla, and Carà were extolling the dynamism of modern life, the beauty of speed, and the harmony of aggressive movement. All things move and run, change rapidly, and it is this "vortex" of modern life that the artist should strive to represent. And so Dos Passos, like the futurists, began to render sound as a succession of waves: "At the corner of Third Avenue he stopped and stood shivering in the hot afternoon sunlight. . . . Jagged oblongs of harsh sound broke one after another as an elevated past [*sic*] over." [8] Color was for the futurists and became for Dos Passos a prismatic rhythm, iridescent and scintillating: "The light of the sunset flamed in the windows of factories on the Long Island side, bashed in the portholes of tugs, lay in swaths of curling yellow and orange over the swift brown green water. . . ." (p. 66). *Manhattan Transfer* is full of light, grit, noise, and speed. The vortex of the metropolis is presented in terms of sunlight, car lights, arc lights, neon lights, fire engines, taxis, the rumble of the elevated, and the sound of tugboat whistles. Motion and light destroy not only the materiality of brick and glass; they also negate significant human relations: "They didn't shake hands. The taxi kicked dust and a rasp of burnt gasoline in his face. He stood on the steps reluctant to go back into the noise and fume" (p. 231).

In his café in rue d'Amsterdam, Apollinaire was recording his "conversation-poems," while Cendrars, in *Paris-Midi*, was creating "telegram-poems." The forerunner of simultaneity is of course Whitman, but Dos Passos' "Newsreel" and "Camera Eye" of *U.S.A.* owe more to the collage of Cendrars' and Apollinaire's poetry than to the American bard. As early as 1900 Levet's *Cartes postales* had illustrated the aesthetic possibilities inherent in simultaneity, the discontinuous, and all manner of synchronized juxtapositions. Apollinaire adopted this technique for "Venu de Dieuze" in *Calligrammes*, in which he blended bits of song and snatches of dialogue with variations in type size. Cendrars even inserted a blurb from the Denver Chamber of Commerce in one of his poems, a technique Dos Passos was to borrow[9] to reinforce one of his main themes—the opposition between man and the industrialism of big business. The use of advertising in a poem illustrated how the moneyed slogans of the machine age—the intrusion of material reality into man's personal dream world—would do violence to the intimacy of his private domain. In "Zone" Apollinaire compared the flash of neon lights to the raucous cry of jungle parrots and thus blended the visual-impact blurbs of the advertising world with an aboriginal primitivism:

> *Les inscriptions des enseignes et des murailles*
> *Les plaques les avis à la façon des perroquets*
> *criaillent . . .*

Such juxtapositions paralleled the evolution of the movies, and the technique was to give startling if not dazzling results. Cendrars accentuated the rhythms of speed and the machine, while Apollinaire applied the lessons of cubism to poetry in order to communicate "the truth" of simultaneous experience. Thus a cubist tea cup or a collage poem allows us to see "reality" from top and bottom and front and back and inside and outside in the same way that Dos Passos' juxtaposed perspective of "Camera Eye," "Newsreel," the biographical sketches, and the fictional narrative of *U.S.A.* allows the reader a multidimensional view of a quarter century of American life. "Camera Eye" is the world seen through the eyes of the individual. This "I" contrasts forcefully with the historical perspective of "Newsreel" and produces the simultaneity of the historical as well as the personal point of view—an objective outer shell with the resultant reverberations within one man's private world.

In 1931 Dos Passos translated and illustrated Cendrars' *Panama or the Adventures of My Seven Uncles*. He saw in Cendrars one of the primary exponents of the artistic revolution, and he describes him as "a kind of medicineman trying to evoke the things that are our cruel and avenging gods. Turbines, triple-expansion engines, dynamite, high tension coils. Navigation, speed, flight, annihilation." [10] Like Cendrars in his *Prose du Transsibérien,* Dos Passos' characters are obsessed by speed and motion which, like a drug, have to be taken in ever increasing doses. [11] His characters are perpetually crossing the continent. Their ears are deafened by the grind of wheels and the roar of airplane motors. But, in spite of giant machines and the babel of city piled on city, his protagonists remain anxious people. This is why Dos Passos admires Cendrars: "We need sons of Homer going about the world beating into some sort of human rhythm the shrieking hullabaloo, making us less afraid." [12]

In *La Prose du Transsibérien* Cendrars used the color scheme of Delaunay, who illustrated the book, in order to achieve an additional dimension of simultaneity: "Et voici des affiches, du rouge, du vert multicolore comme mon passé bref, du jaune. . . ." The experiments of the futurists in color and light were continued by Delaunay, who proclaimed the primacy of pure color in pictorial construction. He believed that, when a primary color does not determine its complementary, it shatters in the atmosphere and produces simultaneously all the colors of the spectrum. A painting then looks like a kaleidoscope of fragmented rainbows. Color, he insisted, was capable of producing pure expression by means of simultaneous contrast. Like Picasso and Braque, he strove to combine different aspects of figures and objects in the same painting: "Nothing horizontal or vertical—light deforms everything, breaks everything up." A passage from *Manhattan Transfer* gives us a literary equivalent:

> . . . windows blurt light. Night crushes bright milk out of arclights, squeezes the sullen blocks until they drip red, yellow, green into streets resounding with

feet. All the asphalt oozes light. Light spurts from lettering on roof, mills dizzily among wheels, stains rolling tons of sky [P. 112].

In 1909 Delaunay produced the Saint-Séverin series, in 1910 the "Eiffel Tower," in which divergent planes are superimposed, the perspectives multiply and swell, and space acquires a new thickness and consistency; and in 1912 he painted "The Windows" and "The City of Paris." Apollinaire, who called Delaunay's technique "orphic," wrote a poem, "Les Fenêtres," influenced directly by Delaunay's painting bearing the same name:

> O Paris
> Du rouge au vert tout le jaune se meurt
> Paris Vancouver Hyères Maintenon New-York et
>   les Antilles
> La fenêtre s'ouvre comme une orange
> Le beau fruit de la lumière

Thus Dos Passos wrote novels with materials which, until then, had only been used in poetry and in painting. The refraction of light and the simultaneity of color gives *Manhattan Transfer* a pictorial dimension. An East Side street is created as a patterned succession of colors: "the sunstriped tunnel hung with skyblue and smokedsalmon and mustardyellow quilts" (p. 10). Dos Passos uses the technique of dramatizing color by giving it the quality of movement, so that colors "agitate," "flutter," and "slide together," as they do in futurism and in orphism. The beauty of Manhattan is captured in terms of color formations, sometimes brilliant and gaudy, sometimes muted and subdued. The technique of *U.S.A.* with its superimposed simultaneity of the historical and the personal, the general and the specific is a direct literary rendition of cubism.

Dos Passos wrote *U.S.A.* in the same condensed telegraphic style that Cendrars used in *L'Or* to tell the story of General Johann August Sutter and the incredible events of the California gold rush. In a chapter of *Orient Express* Dos Passos says that *L'Or*

> traces the swiftest leanest parabola of anything I've ever read, a narrative that cuts like a knife through the washy rubbish of most French writing of the present time. . . Cendrars has managed to capture the grandiose rhythms of America of seventy-five years ago, the myths of which our generation is just beginning to create. . . . In *L'Or* he's packed the tragic and turbulent absurdity of '49 into a skyrocket. It's over so soon you have to read it again for fear you have missed something [P. 162].

Instead of one swift parabola, Dos Passos arcs "skyrocket" again and again to describe the lives and the tragic and turbulent rhythms of the first part of the twentieth century. The lives of Joe Williams, Eveline Huchins, Richard Savage, J. Ward Moorehouse, Charley Anderson, and all the others mesh, blend, arc, and wobble as Dos Passos tries to re-create the dynamism and the tragedy of a vast nation. *U.S.A.* combines not only the narrative style of *L'Or* but the simultaneity of *Panama*, which describes the adventures of Cendrars' seven imaginary uncles. Cendrars takes the reader on a vast epic jaunt around the world: the first uncle is a butcher in Galveston, the second is a gold prospector in Alaska, the third is a Buddhist in Papeete, the fourth is General Robertson's valet in South Africa, the fifth is manager of a club-hotel in Chicago, the sixth is, like Dan Yack, an explorer in Patagonia, the seventh is an incarnation of Cendrars himself, who travels around the globe and stops only long enough to describe the French failure at Panama and the triumph of primitive and dense vegetation.

Dos Passos, in an attempt to capture the modernism and the dynamism of the metropolis, used the techniques of art and poetry and applied them to the novel. But artists were not the only ones at the turn of the century to focus their attention on the city. Durkheim,

Le Bon, and Tarde, three of the earliest and most
prominent French sociologists, had already written in
considerable detail about the behavior of groups and
the psychology of the crowd, while Auguste Comte had
spoken of a new spiritual force whose principal doctrine
was love and whose end was progress based on order.

Other similarities between Dos Passos and the French
stemmed from the forces shaping the artistic tastes of
France's most prominent nineteenth-century writers.
One of these molding forces was the emergence of the
city as a generic source of artistic experience. The orientation toward the city (rather than toward the people in
it) and toward the nation parallels Jules Romains'
unanimism, in which a city, or parts of a city, or Europe
are re-created and developed as the main protagonists.[13]
This attempt to describe and evoke the city as a collective sociological phenomenon is relatively recent. It
was not until the 1830s that a physical unit, such as a
church or a locomotive, assumed the role of hero or
heroine in lieu of a Moll Flanders, a Clarissa, or a
Manon. Thus, in Hugo's *Notre Dame de Paris*, the
cathedral is the real protagonist, while in Zola's novels
the street, the store, the factory, the mine, and the
theater live a collective existence in which individuals
are absorbed into the greater entity. Baudelaire is one
of the first poets of the big modern city. Not long after
the publication of the *Fleurs du Mal*, Verhaeren (in
Les Villes tentaculaires, 1895) sang of modern life, of
the work in the factories and the ports, and of the
dizzying pace of city life.[14] That same year Léon-Paul
Fargue began to write prose poems about "Mon Quar-
tier" and "Saint-Germain-des-Prés," in which he described the life of a city square or a city unit. Literary
reviews such as *La Nouvelle Revue Moderne* and *La
Vie* were beginning to use the city as a source of
inspiration, and in 1897 Claudel wrote a play entitled
La Ville.

In 1906 Jules Romains published *Le Bourg régénéré* (the first "synoptic" novel of its kind) in which,

for the first time, a town becomes the protagonist of a novel.[15] In 1911 he published *Mort de quelqu'un*, an "ecological" novel which, in addition to the simultaneous juxtapositions, evokes the psychic unity of an apartment house and the psychic bond between people in a train compartment. This "death of a nobody" created disparate nuclei of group experience. In 1911 Romains also published *Puissances de Paris* (an ecological and synoptic work), in which a street, a square, a theater is described as an organic whole possessing a life of its own. Paris gradually emerges as the main protagonist. In 1911 also appeared Georges Chennevière's long dramatic poem, *Le Printemps*, which, inspired from part 1, scene 3 of *Faust*, imbues Paris streets with a collective existence and a group soul. This new orientation to the city as a source of poetic inspiration, sprouting from the very sidewalks of Paris, was to be known as unanimism.

Unanimism, the term Romains coined in order to express the activity and the behavior of groups, began in 1905 and paralleled the evolution of cubism, orphism, and futurism. It was, in great measure, a literary application of sociological theory and was to express, as Romains conceived it, the evolving consciousness of the collective life of groups and the city. (Although both Dos Passos' work and Romains' work has been labeled "unanimiste," they deny cognizance of each other's novels.)

The most important American "synoptic" novel, comparable to Romains' *Le Bourg régénéré*, in which the total city is revealed as a personality in itself, is *Manhattan Transfer*. Dos Passos not only carried further the social criticism of Dreiser, but also explored the aesthetic and symbolic potentialities of urban material. *Manhattan Transfer* resembles Romains' early unanimistic novels, while *U.S.A.*, in its scope, amplitude, and social message, is comparable to *Les Hommes de bonne volonté*.

In contrast to unanimism, however, or perhaps because unanimism seems to combat those very elements which the American city novel was stressing, writers like Dreiser or Wolfe or Dos Passos frequently accentuated the theme of personal dissociation—the self-divided man. These writers were concerned with man's aloneness and alienation, and, rather than construct a quasireligious sociological system such as unanimism, they preferred to write about the collapse of the community, the breakdown of tradition, the ineffectuality of love and religion, and the conflict between the individual and the group. Thus, from the first "city novel" of the century, *Sister Carrie*, to such recent works as Nelson Algren's *The Man With the Golden Arm*, American city fiction has portrayed man searching for a total self in an urban society where personal integration or completeness does not seem possible.[16]

In the United States, in contrast to France, the literary emphasis has been upon the destructive elements in city life. *Streets of Night*, as opposed to *Le Bourg régénéré*, describes the social and spiritual isolation of individuals who, though they remain in physical proximity, find it impossible to communicate with each other. Wenny commits suicide and Nan has a dreadful sense of loneliness. *Streets of Night* represents, among other things, the inability of people to establish significant contact. The city gives them no sense of group solidarity. It fragments their lives and their existence. Fanshaw, the stereotyped proper-Bostonion intellectual, reflects on this absence of unity:

> Streets, he thought of, long streets of blind windows, dark, cold under arclights, and himself and Wenny and Nan walking arm in arm, hurrying from corner to corner. Can't seem to find that street, and on to the next corner between endless rows of blind windows converging in a perspective utterly black beyond the cold lividness of arclights. Must have lost our way in these streets.[17]

The reaction to the city is always in terms of the self, seldom, if ever, in terms of the group. The only allusion to the vaguest kind of group experience is the newspaper account of Wenny's suicide:

> In offices and stores and front parlors and lonely hall bedrooms sallow-jowled faces sucked the blood through the nasty smelling print of the extras. The streets swarmed and seethed with faces drinking Wenny's blood.[18]

But even here whatever group unity exists, as the unanimists would have it, is a negative one and only serves to reinforce Nan's isolation. Joe Williams' death and Daughter's airplane crash in *Nineteen Nineteen* are no more than a newspaper item or a topic of conversation.

Death for Dos Passos is not a unifying force. It is an event which, if anything, only accentuates man's sense of alienation. No one cares about the death of a stranger. Romains, on the other hand, in *Mort de quelqu'un,* uses the theme of death as a cohesive factor. Before his death, Jacques Godard, a retired mechanic, "exists" only in the minds of his parents. After his biological death, he continues a "spiritual" existence in the memory of people who lived in the same apartment house. This is ecological unity; the residents of this particular apartment house think, breathe, and dream the persistent image of Godard. Their thoughts and their activity focus on Godard who, though dead, has given the group a fleeting but nevertheless unified impetus:

> Le groupe ressemblait de plus en plus à l'homme qui avait été vivant sous ce plafond, entre ces meubles. Les mêmes pensées ressuscitaient, les mêmes mots et jusqu'à l'accent trainard de certaines syllabes. Mais le groupe mourut la minute après.[19]

A year after Godard's funeral, a young man who re-members the event thinks, not of the finality of death or, like Nan, of a terrible loneliness, but of death as a kind of mystic continuity in the collective unconscious, as a lasting participation in a group soul: "Pourtant, si je mourais tout de suite, je suis sûr que je ne disparaîtrais pas. J'entrerais de plain-pied dans une grande âme qui ne pent pas mourir.[20] *Mort de quelqu'un* is, in my opinion, the best unanimistic novel Romains wrote, and is infinitely better than *Streets of Night*. Dos Passos groped throughout his early novels for a form which was to climax the *U.S.A.* trilogy, but Romains seems to have found himself early and almost immediately. Thus *La Vie unanime*, *Les Copains*, and *Mort de quelqu'un*, in spite of their brevity, are more original than the massive twenty-seven volume *Hommes de bonne volonté*, which was to be the ultimate expression of unanimism, but which lacks organic unity in spite of Romains' preface to *Le 6 Octobre* (the first volume) anticipating its great cohesion.

Verdun, the sixteenth volume of *H.B.V.*, which is sometimes referred to as one of Romains' best, is no more successful artistically than *First Encounter*, though the conception is vastly different. Neither novel is as good as Barbusse's *Le Feu*, or Duhamel's *Vie des martyrs*, or Henry Malherbe's *La Flamme au poing*, or *Farewell to Arms*, for that matter. If *First Encounter* lacks unity and if its theme dangles like an appendix at the very end, *Verdun* suffers from a ponderous unity in its attempt to evoke the simultaneity of the battle on all fronts—military, social, political, economic, etc.— and achieves for the most part only a forced artificial unity. It has none of the poetry of Malraux's *L'Espoir* and is comparable in a way to Sartre's *Le Sursis*, which tries to re-create a vast European simultaneity but is too contrived and too heavy, and is interesting only when Sartre writes about individuals and their freedom.

Three Soldiers, as the subdivisions of the book indicate ("Making the Mould," "The Metal Cools," "Machines," "Rust," "The World Outside," "Under the Wheels"), evidently reflects an elaborate aesthetic plan that was to give it a machine-like anonymity. But this anonymity breaks down as John Andrews, the only character through whose sensibility the outside world assumes meaning, and the only one who verbalizes a moral attitude toward war, becomes Dos Passos' direct spokesman. In *Manhattan Transfer* Dos Passos succeeds in submerging his characters in anonymity; the best passages in the book are those in which he captures the pulse of Manhattan in analogues of speed, light, noise, and smell. *U.S.A.* is a virtuoso performance in that Dos Passos retains reader interest and artistic tension on all levels. But in *Three Soldiers* there is no sense of group unity. Andrews, Chrisfield, and Fuselli are not integrated into the whole. This is a novel of man's aloneness—of the individual versus the social machine, in this case the army organization. Dos Passos is pleading for the individual: the book is about the meaning of desertion.

In Romains' novels the theme is the enrichment of the individual through participation in the group. Yet in *Verdun* we have only the monolithic structure of simultaneity; Jallez, with Jerphanion, leads the reader from the first through the twenty-seventh volume of *H.B.V.*; but Jallez in *Verdun* is just another of the many people moving about. *Three Soldiers*, on the other hand, is a good novel because the original structure collapses and reveals John Andrews as the spokesman for the ordinary people who are tired of being trampled under the system and who hate "the miserable dullness of industrialized slaughter." [21] The last pages of the book achieve a lyricism, impact, and stylistic beauty which overshadow its initial framework. Dos Passos' emotional intensity no doubt owes much to Barbusse's *Le Feu*,[22] which is also a denunciation of war. As the subdivision "Rust" in *Three Soldiers* implies, men, like machines, oxidize. Dos Passos, like Barbusse, is against everything which crushes the weak, negates happiness, and suppresses human dignity. Andrews' desertion is therefore an assertion of the individual against the group, against the stultifying effect of the mass intelligence. For Andrews, human society will always be "organizations growing and stifling individuals." [23]

Dos Passos and Romains are thus antipodal in relating the individual to the group. Romains' didactic unanimism stresses the role of the leader as an agent of social progress. Dos Passos' didacticism, though no less fervent, stresses the negative aspects of group organization. Both authors, however, are looking for a solution to the alienation of the individual either from himself or in society. In *Le Bourg régénéré* a young postal employee arrives in a small dormant town which does not understand, as Romains phrases it, "why modern cities are so anxious and what prevents them from being happy." The young man decides to awaken the town by writing on the wall of a urinal: "Celui qui possède vit aux dépens de celui qui travaille; quiconque ne produit pas l'équivalent de ce qu'il consomme est un parasite social." The idea germinates slowly, but finally succeeds in undermining a complacent city organization. Dormant energies are aroused and decisions are made. The town vibrates with new rhythms, rouses itself from its torpor, and is as though reborn by a new consciousness of self. It has become in unanimistic terminology a "god." The postal clerk, like John Andrews for Dos Passos, is Romains' spokesman. He even speaks as though he might have written passages in the *Manuel de déification*:

> Il faut choisir et façonner les paroles que vous direz au groupe. Toute son âme future dépendra des paroles que vous leur aurez dites. Vous serez le magicien, la fée sur le berceau. Songez que vos paroles jetteront un sort.

As a novelist, Romains accentuates the essential bond between men rather than their distance,[24] and tries to capitalize on the nascent dynamism of twentieth-century mass behavior. In his poetry, we witness the force with which he molds group consciousness:

> *Foule! Ton âme entière est debout dans mon corps* . . .

Ne te défends pas, foule femelle,
C'est moi qui te veux, moi qui t'aurai!
Laisse tout mon souffle qui te crée
Passer comme le vent de la mer . . .

Les corps qui sont ici, la ville peut les prendre:
Ils garderont au front, comme une croix de cendre,
Le vestige du dieu que tu es maintenant.[25]

Unlike the unanimists Dos Passos does not seek the unity of a group or a street in terms of psychic cohesion. He makes no attempt to force the group into consciousness of self. Several lines from "Quai de la Tournelle" [26] reflect the purpose and scope of the early Dos Passos: "I grope through the streets of the night / culling out of the pool / of the spring-reeking, rain-reeking city / gestures and faces." Another poem, reminiscent of Verhaeren, describes the barges, the arcades, the women, the scents, the scenes, and the sounds of Paris: "Barges casually come from far towns / towards far town unhurrying bound." [27] Sometimes he captures something of the spirit of Baudelaire's "Crépuscule du matin."

In "Phases of the Moon" [28] the blending of nature with a city landscape resembles Chennevière's long dramatic poem, *Le Printemps*. Many of the poems in *Pushcart at the Curb* are city poems ranging from Paris to New York, to Castile, to Istanbul. There is variety here, but no group unity as envisaged by the unanimists. In *Puissances de Paris* Romains animates a street, or a square, or the inside of a theater by stressing the elastic and ephemeral grouping and dispersion of people. The sections entitled "Les Rues," "Les Places," "Les Squares," "Les Métamorphoses," "Les Ephémères," and "Les Vies intermittentes" communicate the dynamism of city life which Dos Passos achieves in *Manhattan Transfer*. But *Puissances de Paris* deifies the metropolis, and does not represent it as a menace or a threat to the individual. The individual has willingly been assimilated into the whole without any fragmentation of self:

> La Salle n'a pas une connaissance complète de son corps. Les auditoires des grands théâtres s'observent avec plaisir. Entre les moments de vie intérieure et d'exaltation, ils regardent leurs formes, se réjouissent de contenir des femmes belles et richement vêtues.[29]

The inside of a theater is not merely space limited by walls, but a living being. City consciousness is the composite of hundreds if not thousands of similar units. The role of the unanimist was to help the entire city to develop a concept of self so that one day it might pronounce a group Cartesian "I am." The seventh and final part of *Puissances de Paris* (Réflexions") stresses the deification of groups whose purpose it is to develop this higher consciousness. A similar process was at work in *Le Bourg régénéré* and in *Les Copains.* Nowhere in *Manhattan Transfer* is there any suggestion of such a tendency. A city street is not perceived as a whole but as a succession of "sunshades, summer dresses, straw hats" (p. 136); a subway is a series of "elbows, packages, shoulders, buttocks" (p. 148). The fact that people are perceived on the same level as objects suggests the impersonality of the city crowd as well as loneliness within the crowd. A unanimist would be able to participate in mystic communion with the "soul" of even an anonymous crowd.

Dos Passos shows Manhattan changing through the decades from an ideal modern metropolis to a disordered agglomeration of vice and corruption that, at the end of the novel, sets the mad tramp raving with a vision of urban doom. Bud's inability to make any warm human contacts, his persistent sense of aloneness, and his unmourned death are all essential factors in the larger pattern of impersonal relations that exist in the metropolis, where people are indifferent to and remain unmoved by his efforts to live or by his decision to die. Ellen's abortion is also an act of death and defeat. Her wish to bear Stan's child is destroyed in the frenetic but sterile activities that make up her life. The abortion becomes symbolic of an inner emptiness and loss of humanity. Modern city life robs woman of her womanhood, deprives man of his sense of purpose, and does away with the normal cycle of human life. In *Streets of Night* Wenny kills himself because there is "no place for love in the city of Boston" (p. 200).

Yet, in spite of their differences, *U.S.A.* and *Les Hommes de bonne volonté* present striking similarities. *U.S.A.* begins at the turn of this century and ends in 1927 with the Sacco-Vanzetti execution. *H.B.V.* begins on October 6, 1908 and ends on October 7, 1933. Both works cover approximately the same quarter century, and both try to capture the dynamic impetus of Western civilization—Dos Passos, the United States; Romains, Europe. *The 42nd Parallel* begins around 1900 and ends in 1917 when the United States enters World War I. *Nineteen Nineteen* is a novel of two decisive war years for the United States. The title of the final volume, *The Big Money*, is a symbol—a climactic title for the geographical, historical, social, and economic tendencies of a gigantic nation. Not only New York is depicted, but other major American cities as well.

H.B.V., twenty-seven volumes of approximately 8,000 pages compared to the trilogy's 1,500, has, within its ramifications, three big concentric circles. The first circle, Paris in 1908, expands in 1914 to include all of France, and by 1933 the third circle includes all of Europe. The circles radiate from Paris to englobe representative regions and cities in France: Nice, Digne, Tours, Périgord, Velay; then the cities of Europe: London, Berlin, Geneva, Odessa, etc.; and finally the nations of Europe: France, England, Germany, Switzerland, Russia. The important historical, political, and economic events of this epoch are seen through the eyes of the two main protagonists, Jallez and Jerphanion, who, unlike the protagonists of *U.S.A.* (with the exception perhaps of J. Ward Moorehouse), are with the reader from the beginning to the end.

But, in spite of the people who inhabit the pages of

U.S.A. and *H.B.V.*, both are primarily the record of an era. *U.S.A.* is the record of a socio-economic struggle of vast geographic dimensions, in which man's spiritual quest for beauty and justice and self-fulfillment is destroyed by the machine, by the big city, and by the "big money." The central theme of *H.B.V.*, though perhaps more obvious, as the title indicates, is at the same time less palpable. Romains treats the machine and modern industrialism as an inherent and indispensable aspect of city life. The factories, the railroads, and the speed of an accelerated tempo are not forces which threaten man. His protagonists have assimilated the noise and the pace of the new age. The sirens, the arc lights, and all the variegated aspects of the big metropolis are not symbols negating man. The very presense of the city not only affirms man's immediate greatness; it affirms as well, according to Romains, man's very tendency to assemble in ever larger and more efficient collective units.

War, however, emerges as Europe's main preoccupation between 1908 and 1933, and the "men of good will" (as its Biblical derivation implies) are those Europeans who, like Jaurès and thousands of others like him, are working or have worked towards peace on earth. There is a spiritual unity to *H.B.V.* which is an extension of Romains' earlier unanimism, just as Wenny's suicide in *Streets of Night* has its final echo in Charley Anderson's car-train crash in *The Big Money*. But, while the main protagonist of *U.S.A.* is America itself, in *H.B.V.* Europe does not emerge as a clear-cut entity. The real protagonist of *H.B.V.* is a spiritual force, that mysterious undercurrent which Romains described as "l'unanime." *H.B.V.* ends on the eve of Hitler's rise to power; and Hitler's demagoguery was, ironically enough, to use the same cohesive forces which Romains had already prescribed, to mold Germany into a lethal war machine. Thus Jerphanion's political failures and final abdication parallel, ironically, Dos Passos' "success-failure" epic, in which Jefferson's ideals and the American principles of freedom of opportunity for all find themselves contradicted by the actual socio-political events of history during the first quarter century. "Big-money," monopolies, and propaganda, within the context of the trilogy, are the very forces which run counter to the principles on which the United States was founded. One of the most forceful themes of the trilogy is the tragedy of a nation whose present values oppose the very idealism on which it was conceived.

Both *U.S.A.* and *H.B.V.* evoke the vast collective forces at work within a nation or group of nations. The authors have rendered the simultaneity of these forces in their own individual ways. Both Dos Passos and Romains attempted to blend history with fiction. The inherent danger in such a technique, as Malraux has pointed out, is that their books run the risk of being dated early; and this seems to have happened to both Dos Passos and Romains in the wake of their remarkable celebrity. "The Camera Eye" and "Newsreel," though examples of technical virtuosity and an ingenious device to capture the simultaneity of historical epoch, collective self, and the reverberations of events within an individual, have lost their immediacy and therefore their importance. The universality of human emotion has faded into almost forgotten historical events. And Romains' attempt to blend history and fiction has suffered a similar fate; in his attempt to give his "novel" historical perspective, he sacrificed an artistic dimension for the sake of historical detail which is not properly the domain of art. Cuisenier in his book, *Jules Romains et les Hommes de bonne volonté*, states that no historical study of the first quarter century of this era would be complete without reading *H.B.V.* But what does this have to do with literary value?

Dos Passos and Romains both tried to solve the problem of narrative simultaneity; and both authors were forced to abandon characters and the events surrounding their lives in order to begin the narration of new and different and perhaps simultaneous lives. There is no perfect device for the capture of historical simultaneity. Sartre's method, in *Le Sursis*, of switching places and events and people within the same sentence is at best a ponderous *tour de force*, not as satisfactory as Dos Passos' "Camera Eye" and "Newsreel." Romains seeks simultaneity by describing "twin" scenes. Thus both Jallez and Jerphanion undergo similar periods of depression, a kind of male menopause, during which Jallez goes to see the dying Sampeyre while Jerphanion is at Quinette's bedside before he too dies. Hawerkamp contemplates the countryside from his airplane, which Jallez is watching from the window of his train compartment, and so on and so on. Unlike Dos Passos, whose narrative technique is always "objective," Romains uses the interior monologue or an objective narrative as the occasion demands.

Both Dos Passos and Romains, to capture the essence of a collective dynamism, described those aspects which in their opinion illustrated the tendencies and strivings of their era. Dos Passos described the impact and impetus of big business, the restlessness of a nation moving towards an ever greater industrialization, and the conflicts of a country which, in his opinion, has done violence to the ideals of its founders. Romains described the milieux in which "good will" grows and in which it is sometimes stifled. The church, petroleum interests, political factions, the nobility, the world of crime, the police, the intellectuals, the Masons are all presented, and the reader makes the acquaintance of one French family after another as he is introduced to various facets of these collective existences. Throughout runs the theme of "good will" which, though it may not always be evident, as the author himself admits, at least reflects the efforts of a few men bound by a common ideal and working for a common cause. As a unanimistic novel, *H.B.V.* derives its unity from the premise and mystique of the universal soul. Those men of good will who strive towards some kind of union with man's collective psyche, even though the effort be that of an isolated individual, are part of man's élan towards a more harmonious social structure. The central theme of *H.B.V.* rests on the interrelationships between individuals and groups and between groups and individuals; hence the recurrent cycle in Romains' work—the effect of society on a particular character and vice versa in a kind of chain reaction by means of which any number of protagonists, as they interact with the group and as the group pressure begins to operate in return, develop insight into the behavior patterns of the collective psyche.

The novelist, within this context, has an historical mission. If he succeeds in this mission he will have accentuated and intensified man's relationship to an epoch. Both Dos Passos and Romains are in this sense moralists. Under the minutiae of their protagonists' lives, under the surface play of opinions, newspaper headlines, and bits of dialogue, lurk the deeper currents which, Dos Passos has said, affect the course of history itself.[30] Important books have the power to influence and to transform the thinking of people and thereby to reconstruct the very thinking of a community. Insofar as the novelist is capable of molding public opinion and insofar as he can give coherent form and direction to the chaotic events in life, he becomes an "architect of History." [31]

From Rabelais, whom Dos Passos considers the greatest of all French writers, to present-day authors, the moralist and the aesthete have created works of art reflecting their own particular vision of the world and their own inner necessity. If Dos Passos' writing lacks the verve and the humor of the Rabelais he admires so much, this is perhaps characteristic of our age. Nevertheless, Dos Passos has succeeded in combining an historical message with an aesthetic form which stems from the very dynamism and explosive simultaneity of the sprawling cities of the United States. The techniques and ideas that characterize his success—unanimism, futurism, cubism, and simultanéisme—were part of the literary explosion in Paris between 1900 and 1925 and are all in the French grain. The colors of the machine and the big city are refracted through the prism of the author's eye; the rainbow of man's fragmented world is splashed across a nation germinating with turmoil, activity, and the pound of wheels. The "windows" through which we see Dos Passos' world give us the picture of a vast social striving and opposition—of the contradiction of man's essential ideals by the power and speed of a frenetic machine age. Man's self is shattered in the process in the same way that light, when passing through a prism, is shattered. Dos Passos' cubistic novels give us the planes, the angles, the superimpositions, and the color perspectives of his protagonists' alienated selves within the vast rhythmic impulses of the continental *U.S.A.* In her preface to the 1949 French edition of *The 42nd Parallel*, Claude-Edmonde Magny universalizes the message of the book:

> The Trilogy is a terrible indictment against civilization which permits man to be alienated, dispossessed. . . . And so the "message" of the book goes beyond America; it concerns us all, and the introspective reader will no doubt tremble at finding in Eveline, Eleanor, Janey, Mac the specter or the caricature of what he secretly fears himself to be. . . . *The 42nd Parallel* is not limited to a single latitude—it is *la condition humaine.*

The Trilogies of Jean-Paul Sartre and John Dos Passos

It has been for sometime a commonplace of literary history that Jean-Paul Sartre's trilogy, *Les Chemins de la Liberté,* reveals a huge debt to John Dos Passos' trilogy, *U.S.A.*; yet no one has ever tried to determine precisely the nature or extent of this debt. Sartre himself tells us that "It was after reading a book by Dos Passos that I thought for the first time of weaving a novel out of various lives with characters who pass each other and who all contribute to the atmosphere of a historical period." [1] Sartre has gone so far as to say, "I regard Dos Passos as the greatest writer of our time." [2] One questions Sartre's literary values after such a statement. The praise becomes more understandable, however, when one realizes that Sartre is carried away with Dos Passos' ability to immerse a reader in a historical situation and to create a kind of existential reality. Sartre is also interested in Dos Passos' experimental technique which allows a sense of history at the same time as it does away with the omniscient point of view.

Sartre is certainly correct when he points out that Dos Passos' heroes are very much a part of history and keep pace with the turbulent and chaotic growth of America. One of the controlling motives in *U.S.A.* is the desire for quick money. The lives of many of the main characters even parallel the Horatio Alger formula. J. Ward

From *Iowa English Yearbook,* 9 (1964), 60–64. Reprinted by permission of the author and publisher.

Moorehouse rides the waves of ambition until he becomes the head of a leading advertising firm. Dick Savage outdistances his humble beginning and eventually becomes an executive in the Moorehouse firm. Eleanor Stoddard goes beyond her sordid childhood environment, becomes a successful interior decorator, and finally marries into Russian nobility. Charley Anderson leaves North Dakota to become eventually a wealthy airplane manufacturer. Margo Dowling runs away from Long Island poverty to become a wealthy movie star.

These are some of the people involved in the frenetic activity that accompanied postwar prosperity. Along with this mad scramble for wealth, rioting and fighting run through U.S.A. and engage Charley Anderson, Mac, and Joe Williams. The chaos of the times is reflected by the chaotic lives. A kind of abandon characterizes Dos Passos' unheroic men and women. Almost all the characters are promiscuous: Eleanor Stoddard and Eveline Hutchins sleep with Moorehouse, Margo Dowling with Charley Anderson, Anne Elizabeth Trent (Daughter) with Dick Savage. All the characters move away from their families and childhood surroundings and wander aimlessly through life, never seeming to mind their deracinated conditions. These lives never have any sense of completion. Even Dos Passos' "good people" lead rootless lives. Mac, Joe Williams, Benny Compton, and Mary French flounder about as badly as the others. The various characters in U.S.A. come and go and disappear. Their problems are rarely resolved in the manner of the traditional novel because they are the unresolved problems of an age.

In *Les Chemins de la Liberté* there is also a direct relationship between the historical and the individual situation. The historical situation contains all of the characters, and yet they remain autonomous and free to define themselves. The novels take place a year before World War II, at the time of the Munich conference, and during the French capitulation to Germany. Sartre saves his characters from becoming types by personalizing what would otherwise be a general state of mind. France is restless, fearful, anxious, yet unable to grasp the meaning of the situation or to act meaningfully in terms of it. Like the country as a whole, the freedom of the individual is often wasted because it is undirected and unengaged. Mathieu, for example, restlessly looks for the single act that will define him. Boris lives aimlessly because he greatly admires Mathieu and does not know what he wants to be. Lola demands the love of young Boris to prove that she is not growing old. Daniel desires to be punished because he is a homosexual, tries to kill his prize cats, then to castrate himself, and finally marries Marcelle as a form of self-punishment. He likes to see others suffer because he is a sufferer, and he longs for war. Gros-Louis, a shepherd, is too stupid to understand the meaning of war. Jacque, Mathieu's brother, never has to think because he accepts without question the values of the bourgeoisie. These wasted and pitiful lives are Sartre's objective correlative, his dramatic metaphor, of the political and social situation of France at this time.

The characters in the fiction of Sartre and Dos Passos are either a part of the historical moment or in some way embody that moment, and they do this without losing their autonomy. This is not to say that there is no difference between the novels of Sartre and Dos Passos. Their fiction does differ in one essential way— and that is in the manner in which they handle time. Dos Passos' characters exist in a well of time. At first everything is seen in a historical perspective, then follows a sudden shift from a very general to a specific time. A typical passage in *U.S.A.* reveals Dos Passos' method:

Winters the brick sidewalks were icy. . . . One winter they got in the habit of walking up the hill. . . . One afternoon she asked Pearl to come in and they played dolls together. . . . Summer evenings when the twilight was long after supper they played lions

and tigers with other kids from the neighborhood.
. . . About once a week Joe would get spanked. . . .
Once a drizzly Saturday night she stood against the
fence in the dark looking up at the lighted window.
She could hear Popper's voice and Joe's in argument.

Dos Passos here sets time in motion with such general
words as "winters," "summer evenings," and then
jumps into a more particular realization of time with
words like "one afternoon" and "once" serving as tran-
sitional links. The following fragment reveals the
method again:

July was hot that summer, in the office they worked
in a continual whir of electric fans, the men's collars
wilted and the girls kept themselves overplastered
with powder; only Mr. Dreyfus still looked cool and
crisply tailored as if he'd just stepped out of a band-
box. The last day of the month Janey was sitting a
minute at her desk when Jerry Burnham came in.[3]

Sartre's novels never lose a sense of duration as do
those of Dos Passos. Sartre adds the dimension of
freedom to his fiction by constructing a narrative future,
the realm of time in which the reader's will functions.
The character may remain consistent with the first image
he creates of himself, but he always has the opportunity
to transcend his initial nature. In *Les Chemins de la
Liberté* the moment continually weighs upon the reader.
Sartre often prefaces chapters with the hour of the
day in which the following action is to take place; he
continually makes the reader aware of the passing of
time by working the hour of day into the dialogue. *The
Age of Reason* takes place in 48 hours and 35 minutes,
and every minute can be accounted for. *The Reprieve*
starts at 4:30 P.M. Berlin time (3:30 P.M. London
time), Friday, September 23, and ends a few minutes
past 1:30 A.M. on Friday, September 30. Every ten
pages of the novel equals approximately one hour of
time. It is 4:30 on page one, 5:30 on page eleven, 8:10

on page 31, 4:00 A.M. on page 64, 6:00 A.M. on page 74, 7:00 A.M. on page 81, and so on.

Despite the difference in the handling of time, the final effect of *U.S.A.* is strangely enough the same as *Les Chemins de la Liberté*. As Sartre himself pointed out, Dos Passos' novels seem to take place in the present. The reason for this is that they sustain a horizontal structure, a quantitative time, in which one action or event is made to seem as important as the next. There are no real crises in *U.S.A.* One action also never seems to be the result of another. As Sartre puts it, "not for an instant does the order of causality betray itself in chronological order. There is no narrative, but rather the jerky unreeling of a rough and uneven memory. . . . As a result of this, past things retain a flavor of the present; they still remain, in their exile, what they once were, inexplicable tumults of color, sound, and passion. Each event is irreducible, a gleaming solitary *thing* that does not flow from anything else." [4]

In the collective novel the reader is the real source of this temporal unity. He also holds the various scenes together. Not only does the camera tend to move toward a common center and catch lives crossing and recrossing, but the various candid shots—the individual pictures—follow each other in such rapid succession that the novels of Sartre and Dos Passos are a prose form of the film technique. Claude-Edmonde Magny had pointed out in *L'Age du roman américain* that the technique of the camera eye and the newsreel are not limited merely to Dos Passos' interlinking sections, and Sartre himself seems to be aware of this. In *The Reprieve* Sartre sets the film in motion and employs quick narrative transitions to smash the life of one character into that of another. Such montage often produces a certain mood or emotional effect and the transition from one mood to another produces a third. In *U.S.A.* and *Les Chemins de la Liberté* characters are in such bad faith, so similar, that the transition from one to the other is fluid, and the reader becomes aware of a world gone rotten at the core. Thus instead of diffusing the effect, montage in these novels intensifies and reinforces the controlling mood. The tone of the novel "solidifies," so at the end of the novel the reader sees each character in terms of all the others, the bad faith of one magnifying the unauthenticity of the other. In *The Reprieve*, for example, Daladier is troubled about the French commitment to protect Czechoslovakia against Hitler. Sartre comments obliquely on his vacillation by juxtaposing Daladier's reflections against a picture of Philippe, the deserter, in the arms of a Negro prostitute: the pronoun "he," which opens the second paragraph, refers by implication to Daladier as well as Philippe:

> He [Daladier] stared at the dark flowers in the carpet and felt a little dizzy. Peace—war. I have done all I could to preserve peace. But he now wondered whether he didn't actually want to be swept away like a straw in this vast torrent, whether he didn't long for that tremendous holiday—war.
>
> He [Philippe] looked about him in bewilderment and exclaimed: "I haven't gone." She had opened the shutters and was now back beside the bed, leaning over him. He felt her warm body and inhaled her fishy odor.[5]

The plight and moral failure of one character is transferred to another until the reader is submerged in the evidence of a helpless and hopeless society.

Another narrative device Sartre seems to have borrowed from Dos Passos is that of shifting from outside to inside a character in order to secure transition from the world of things to the world of consciousness and from the individual to the collective consciousness. Sartre, himself, refers to the passage in *1919* in which Joe Williams is killed in a barroom brawl:

> Joe laid out a couple of frogs and was backing off towards the door, when he saw in the mirror that a

big guy in a blouse was bringing down a bottle on his head held with both hands. He tried to swing around but he didn't have time. The bottle crashed his skull and he was out.

"We are inside him," says Sartre, "until the shock of the bottle on his skull. Then immediately, we find ourselves outside with the chorus, part of the collective memory." [6] The passage in *The Reprieve* which describes the beating of Gros-Louis seems consciously to employ what Sartre describes as Dos Passos' method:

> "They are going to kill me," thought Gros-Louis, and fear froze him to the marrow, he seized Mario by the throat with his free hand and lifted him off the ground; but at the same moment his head was cloven to the chin, he let go of Mario and fell to his knees, blood pouring over his eyebrows. He tried to steady himself by grabbing Mario's coat, but Mario jumped backwards, and Gros-Louis saw him no more.

To say that there is an interior reality here overstates the quality of narration. There is an overwhelming sense of fact in the writing of both Sartre and Dos Passos. Each incident has the quality of a *thing*. And yet the facts are related to personal consciousness ("he saw in the mirror that. . . ." " 'They are going to kill me,' thought Gros-Louis. . . ."). And suddenly that consciousness disappears. The very identities of Joe and Gros-Louis become just another fact, another descriptive detail with the words "and he was out," "and Gros-Louis saw him no more." Characters disappear into the gelatinous realm of "things as they are," a realm Sartre described at length in his first novel, *La Nausée*. And as such, they can be judged. I think this is what Sartre means when he says, "we find ourselves outside with the chorus, part of the collective memory."

Sartre, of course, reads into Dos Passos' novels much more than can be justified textually. Sartre has a tendency not only to read literature but to judge it in terms of his existential ideas. That is why Sartre makes a great deal out of Dos Passos' ability to describe a character from without and then to personalize the facts. Such transition is important for Sartre because it takes into account his philosophical duality—*en soi* and *pour soi*—and admits both an objective and a subjective existence. In *U.S.A.* and *Les Chemins de la Liberté* the reader is allowed to participate in the two realms. The reader identifies himself with the various protagonists, becomes a part of the social consciousness, and engages himself in the freedom of the characters. Such a point of view forces the reader to participate in the novel as part of a chorus, a social conscience. He pieces together the fragmented images, views them in relation to the main social problem, and finally passes judgment on himself at the same time that he passes judgment on the characters. "If you name the behavior of an individual," Sartre has said, "you reveal it to him; he sees himself. And since you are at the same time naming it to all others he knows that he is *seen*." [7] Thus the final image in the mirror—and it is often an ugly one—is really that of the reader himself, and the final problem is one of identity. Sartre uses the technique of John Dos Passos to show man, sick of soul, trying to define himself at the crossroads of modern history.

John Dos Passos
Technique vs. Sensibility

MARSHALL MCLUHAN

Most elaborate of the many spoofs made by James Joyce was his obeisance to Dujardin as his "master" of the interior monologue. Only less elaborate have been the jokes played by Mr. Eliot, as in presenting to Harvard his copy of Jessie Weston with many pages uncut. To darken the counsel of those who choose to live in darkness has always been a form of light-bringing among the wits. But easily the most esoteric literary high-jinx of our time is the very formal debate, conducted far above the heads of Bloomsbury, between Wyndham Lewis and James Joyce. Lewis's "attack" on Joyce as a romantic time-snob, and Joyce's "counterattack" in *Finnegans Wake* are not just obscurantist trifling but a means of offering important insights of those readers who have acquired certain preliminary disciplines.

The reader of Dos Passos, however, is not required to have much more reading agility than the reader of the daily press. Nor does Dos Passos make many more serious demands than a good movie. And this is said not to belittle an excellent writer who has much to offer, but to draw attention to the extreme simplification to which Dos Passos has submitted the early work of James Joyce. *Three Soldiers* (1921), *Manhattan Trans-*

fer (1925) and *U.S.A.* (1930–36) would not exist in their present form but for the *Portrait of the Artist as a Young Man, Dubliners,* and *Ulysses.* It is as a slightly super-realist that Dos Passos has viewed and adapted the work of Joyce in his own work. And since his technical debt to Joyce is so considerable, one useful way of placing the achievement of Dos Passos is to notice what he took over and, especially, what he did not take.

As a young man in Chicago and at Harvard Dos Passos was much alive to the imagists, Sandburg, Fletcher, Pound, Amy Lowell and the French poet Cendrars. From them he learned much that has continuously affected his practice. Their romantic tapestries and static contemplation of the ornate panorama of existence have always held him in spite of his desire to be a romantic of action. The same conflict, between the man who needs to participate in the life of his time and the artist who wishes to render that life more luminous by self-effacement in his art, appears also in Whitman and in Hemingway. Hemingway's solution may prove to have been in some ways the most satisfactory insofar as he has succeeded occasionally in holding up the critical mirror to the impulse of romantic action, and not just to the action itself.

Dos Passos has been less sure than Hemingway of his artistic direction, though more confident in his politics. But everywhere from *One Man's Initiation—*1917 to the trilogy *U.S.A.* he has been conscious of the need for some sort of detachment and some sort of commitment. *Three Soldiers* is a portrait of the "artist" as G.I. in which, as in E. E. Cummings' *The Enormous Room,* the demand of the individual for some kind of intelligibility in a merely bureaucratic order is met by savage group-reprisal. That has remained the vision of Dos Passos.

For in recent decades the artist has come to be the only critical spectator of society. He demands and confers the heightened significance in ordinary existence which is hostile to any self-extinction in the collective consciousness. So that when the balance is lost between individual responsibility and mass solidarity, the artist automatically moves to the side of the individual. With equal inevitability, the less resourceful man, faced with the perplexities of planned social disorder, walks deeper into the collective sleep that makes that chaos bearable to him. The work of Dos Passos is almost wholly concerned with presenting this situation. His people are, typically, victims of a collective trance from which they do not struggle to escape. And if his work fails, it is to the extent that he clings to an alternative dream which has little power to retract the dreamers from their sleep, and even less power to alert the reader to a sense of tragic waste.

Born in 1896, John Dos Passos grew up in a milieu that had brought to a focus a number of discordant themes and motivations. The popularity of Darwin and Spencer had by then led to the profession of a doctrinaire individualism which got melodramatic treatment at the hands of a Frank Norris. Louis Sullivan and Frank Lloyd Wright were considerably affected by the spirit associated with the flamboyant extroversion and aggression of "frontier" Darwinism. Carl Sandburg's "Chicago" illustrates the curious blend of democratic lyricism and megalomaniac brutality that existed at that time. Robinson Jeffers has the gloomy distinction of representing today the then fashionable code of doctrinaire sadism which found a center in Chicago at the turn of the century.

Superficially it may appear odd that the cosmic humanitarianism of Whitman should have fostered such diverse expressions as the work of Sandburg and Jeffers. But as Sidney Lanier pointed out long ago, Whitman himself was a Byronic dandy turned inside out. Reared on the picturesque art of Scott with its preoccupation with the folk and their crafts, nurtured equally on the heroic panoramas of Byron with his vistas of world history, Whitman found no difficulty in transferring this aristocratic art to the democratic scene. Had not the aristocratic Chateaubriand earlier acquired in America the palette and the scenes which were to attract to him the discipleship first of Lord Byron and later of Stendhal and Flaubert? And the Jeffersonian dream of democracy was of a leveling-up rather than a leveling-down process. An aristocratic dream after all.

Co-existing with the fashionable Darwinism of mid-West tycoons was the grass-roots populism which found an academic spokesman in the formidable Thorstein Veblen. Veblen is ably presented in *The Big Money*, the last of the *U.S.A.* trilogy, as are Henry Ford and Sam Insull. Taken together, Veblen, Ford, and Insull are strikingly representative of the unresolved attitudes and conflicts of the milieu in which Dos Passos grew up. Nor does Dos Passos attempt any reconciliation of these conflicts. While his sympathies are entirely with the agrarian Veblen and the grass-roots, his art is committed to rendering the entire scene. And it is attention to the art of Dos Passos that the critic finds most rewarding. For Dos Passos is not a thinker who has imposed a conceptual system on his material. Rather, he accepted the most familiar traditions and attitudes as part of the material which his art brings into the range of the reader's vision. It is by the range of his vision and the intensity of his focus that he must receive criticism.

As a boy in Chicago, Dos Passos was devoted to Gibbon's *Decline and Fall of the Roman Empire*. Artistically, Gibbon's late use of baroque perspectivism, the linear handling of history as a dwindling avenue, concurred with the eighteenth-century discovery of the picturesque, or the principle of discontinuity as a means of enriching artistic effect. So that the later discovery of contemporary imagism and impressionism by Dos Passos, and his enthusiasm for the cinematic velocity of images in the French poet Cendrars, corresponded pretty much with the original revolution in eighteenth-century taste and perception which carried letters from the style of Gibbon to Sterne.

Looking first at the technical means which he employs

as a writer, there is the basic imagistic skill in sharpening perception and defining a state of mind with which *Manhattan Transfer* opens:

> Three gulls wheel above the broken boxes, orange-rinds, spoiled cabbage heads that heave between the splintered plank walls, the green waves spume under the round bow as the ferry, skidding on the tide, crashes, gulps the broken water, slides, settles slowly into the slip.

Many passages of this wry lyricism counterpoint the episodes of the book. The episodes and characters are also features of a landscape to which these lyric chapter overtures give point and tone. The point is readily seized and the tone extends over a very narrow range of emotions: pathos, anger, disgust. But Dos Passos employs the impressionist landscape monotonously because he has never chosen to refract or analyze its components to zone a wide range of emotions. Open any page of Pound's *Cantos* and the same impressionist landscapes will be found to be presenting a variety of carefully-discriminated mental states. Pound does not accept the landscape as a homogeneous lump of matter. Even satire is managed by Dos Passos in a direct, lyric mode though the technique seems to be impersonal:

> He's darn clever and has a lot of personality and all that sort of thing, but all he does is drink and raise Cain . . . I guess all he needs is to go to work and get a sense of values.

or:

> The terrible thing about having New York go stale on you is that there's nowhere else. It's the top of the world. All we can do is go round and round in a squirrel cage.

Manhattan Transfer is full of such planned incongruities which achieve a weak pathos when they could

more successfully have effected a robust guffaw. The
author is sensitive to the ugliness and misery as things
he can see. But he is never prepared to explore the
interior landscape which is the wasteland of the human
heart:

> Ellen stayed a long time looking in the mirror,
> dabbing a little superfluous powder off her face,
> trying to make up her mind. She kept winding up a
> hypothetical dollself and setting it in various po-
> sitions. Tiny gestures ensued, acted out on various
> model stages. Suddenly she turned away . . . "Oh,
> George I'm starved, simply starved . . . we've got to
> be sensible. God knows we've messed things up in
> the past both of us. . . . Let's drink to the crime
> wave."

The effect is comparable to that of *The Great Gatsby*,
which sustains this Hansel and Gretel sort of wistful
despair to create a child-pastoral world. Out of the same
situations Hemingway at his best—as in the first page of
A *Farewell to Arms*—can obtain moments of tragic
intensity—landscapes of muted terror which give dignity
to human suffering.

But Dos Passos too often seems to imply that the
suffering is sordid and unnecessary or that some modifi-
cation of the environment might free his characters from
the doll-mechanism that is their private and collective
trap. Seeing nothing inevitable or meaningful in human
suffering, he confronts it neither in its comic, intelligible mode, nor in a tragic way. It angers and annoys
him as something extraneous.

The difference from Joyce is instructive. For in
Ulysses the same discontinuous city landscape is also
presented by imagistic devices. The episodes are
musically arranged to sound concordantly. But Joyce
manipulates a continuous parallel at each moment between naturalism and symbolism to render a total spectrum of outer and inner worlds. The past is present
not in order to debunk Dublin but to make Dublin
representative of the human condition. The sharply-

focussed moment of natural perception in Joyce floods the situation with analogical awareness of the actual dimensions of human hope and despair. In *Ulysses* a brief glimpse of a lapidary at work serves to open up ageless mysteries in the relations of men and in the mysterious qualities of voiceless objects. The most ordinary gesture linked to some immemorial dramatic mask or situation sets reverberating the whole world of the book and flashes intelligibility into long opaque areas of our own experience.

To match Joyce's epiphanies Dos Passos brings only American know-how. And, indeed, there seems to be no corner of the continent with whose speech and cooking he is not familiar. There is no trade or profession which he does not seem to know from the inside. Joyce contemplates things for the being that is theirs. Dos Passos shows how they work or behave.

Earlier, Joyce had opened the *Portrait* with an overture representative of the stages of human apprehension, which with Aristotle he held to be a shadow of the artistic process itself, so that the development of the artist concurs with the retracing of the process of poetic experience. By a technique of cubist or overlayering perspectives both of these processes are rendered present to the reader in an instant of inclusive consciousness. Hence the "portrait" claim of the title. The very setting side-by-side of these two operations is typical, therefore, of the level and extent of symbolic implication in Joyce. (The "Oxen of the Sun" section of *Ulysses* fused both these processes with both the human biological and civilized processes, as well as with the parts and totality of the book itself, and yet has been read as a series of parodies of English prose styles.)

The difference between this kind of art and that of Dos Passos is that between one of univocal, psychological and one of properly analogical effect. Joyce constantly has his attention on the analogy of being while Dos Passos is registering a personal reaction to society.

It is not a serious criticism of Dos Passos to say that

he is not James Joyce. But Joyce is his art master and the critic is obliged to note that Dos Passos has read Joyce not as a greater Flaubert, Rimbaud or Mallarmé, but as it were through the eyes of Whitman and Sandburg, as a greater Zola or Romains. This is negative definition which does not bring into question the competence of Dos Passos or belittle the quality of positive delight he affords. His *U.S.A.* is quite justly established as a classic which brought into a focus for the first time a range of facts and interests that no American had ever been able to master. But it is in the main an ethical and political synthesis that he provides, with the interest intentionally at one level—the only level that interests Dos Passos.

Manhattan Transfer, which corresponds roughly to Joyce's *Dubliners,* cuts a cross-section through a set of adult lives in New York. But the city is not envisaged as providing anything more than a phantasmagoric back-drop for their frustrations and defeats. The city is felt as alien, meaningless. Joyce, on the other hand, accepts the city as an extension of human functions, as having a human shape and eliciting the full range of human response which man cannot achieve in any other situation. Within this analogy Joyce's individuals explore their experience in the modes of action and passion, male and female. The stories are grouped according to the expanding awareness of childhood, adolescence, maturity and middle age. Man, the wanderer within the labyrinthine ways at once of his psyche and of the world, provides an inexhaustible matter for contemplation. Dos Passos seems to have missed this aspect of *Dubliners.* But in *U.S.A.,* while extending his back-drop from the city to the nation, he did make the attempt to relate the expanding scene to the development of one mind from childhood to maturity. That is the function of "Camera Eye." "Newsreel" projects the changing environment which acts upon the various characters and corresponds to riffling the back issues of *Life* magazine.

But *Ulysses,* with which *U.S.A.* invites comparison, shows a very different conception of history in providing a continuous parallel between ancient and modern. The tensions set up in this way permit Joyce to control the huge accretions of historic power and suggestion in the human past by means of the low current of immediate incident. The technological analog of this process occurs in the present use of the electronic valve in heavy-power circuits. So that Joyce does not have to step up the intensity of the episode or scene so long as he maintains its function in the total circuit. Deprived of this symbolic "feed-back" process implicit in the historic sense, and which is manipulated alike by Joyce, Pound, and Eliot, Dos Passos is left with little more current or intensity than that generated by his immediate episodes.

Since criticism, if it is to be anything more than a review of the "content" of works of art, must take cognizance of the technical means by which an artist achieves his effects, it is relevant to consider some of the stages by which the kind of art found in *U.S.A.* came into existence. If there is anything to be explained about such a work it can best be done by noting the extraordinary preoccupation with landscape in eighteenth-century art. For it was the discovery of the artistic possibilities of discontinuity that gave their form to the novels of Scott as well as to the poems of Byron and Whitman.

Whitman, a great reader of Scott in his youth, later took pains to bring into his poetry as much of the contemporary technology as he could manage. Whitman's poems are also camera-eye landscapes in which human tasks are prominent. In his numerous portraits which he strove to bring into line with the techniques of the impressionists' painting, he wove the man's work into his posture and gestures. His aim was to present the actual, and he took pride that in his *Leaves of Grass* "everything is literally photographed." As for the larger lines of his work, it is plain that he uses everywhere a cinematic montage of "still" shots.

It is not only in the details but in the spirit of much of his work that Whitman resembles Dos Passos. And it is hard to see how anyone who set himself to rendering the diverse existence of multitudes of people could dispense with the technique of discontinuous landscapes. In fact, until the technique of discontinuous juxtaposition was brought into play it was not even possible to entertain such an ambition. "Remember," he said of the *Leaves* to Dr. Bucke, "the book arose out of my life in Brooklyn and New York from 1838 to 1853, absorbing a million people, for fifteen years, with an intimacy, an eagerness, an abandon, probably never equalled." Taken in connection with his technical inventiveness, this enables us to see why the French were from the start so much more interested in Whitman than either his countrymen or the English. Hopkins, struggling with similar technical problems at a more serious level, remarked, however, that he had more in common with Whitman than with anybody else of his time.

From this point of view it is plain, also, why Tolstoy and Hugo could take Scott and Byron with the same artistic seriousness with which Dostoevsky regarded Dickens. Dickens was probably the first to apply the picturesque to discoveries in technique, to the entire life of an industrial metropolis. And the brilliance of his technical development of this matter provided D. W. Griffiths with his cinematic principles seventy years later.

However, it was in Flaubert's *Sentimental Education* that the acceptance of the city as the central myth or creation of man first leads to the mastery of that huge material by means of the technique of discontinuous landscape. Moreover, Flaubert makes a continuous parallel between the fatuity of Frederic Moreau's "education" and the deepening sordor and banality of nineteenth-century Paris.

It is slightly otherwise in *U.S.A.*, where the development of political consciousness of the "Camera Eye" persona is not so much parallel with as in contrast to the unfolding landscape of the nation. And this again is close to the way in which the development of Stephen Dedalus in the *Portrait* as a self-dedicated human being runs counter to the mechanisms of the Dublin scene. The author's political and social sense unfolds without comment in the "Camera Eye" sections, with "Newsreel" providing the immediate environmental pressures which are felt in different ways by everybody in the book. Both of these devices are successfully controlled to provide those limited effects which he intends. But the insights which lead to these effects are of a familiar and widely accepted kind.

That, again, in no way invalidates the insights but it does explain the monotony and obviousness which creeps into so many pages. The reader of Dos Passos meets with excellent observation but none of the unending suggestiveness and discovery of the *Sentimental Education* or *Ulysses*. For there is neither historical nor analogical perception in the *U.S.A.*, and so it fails to effect any connections with the rest of human society, past or present. There is a continuous stream of American consciousness and an awareness that there are unAmerican elements in the world. But as much as in any political orator there is the assumption that iniquity inside or outside the U.S.A. is always a failure to be true to the Jeffersonian dream. The point here is that this kind of single-level awareness is not possible to anybody seriously manipulating the multiple keyboards of Joyce's art.

Dickens as a newspaper reporter had hit upon many of his characteristic effects in the course of his daily work. Later, when he turned to the serial publication of his stories, he was compelled to do some of that "writing backwards" which, as Edgar Poe saw, is the principle underlying the detective story and the symbolist poem alike. For in both instances the effect to be attained is the point at which the writer begins. The work finally constructed is a formula for the effect which is both the beginning and the end of the work.

It is interesting to note how Browning moved toward a fusion of these interests in the *Ring and the Book,* turning a police romance into a cross-section of an inclusive human consciousness by the technique of the reconstruction of a crime. Artistically he is more complex than Dos Passos in the use he makes of the dramatic process of retracing or reconstruction. For that retracing reveals many of the labyrinthine recesses of the human heart which the merely panoramic impressionism of Dos Passos cannot even attempt to do. And it is also this profound drama of retracing the stages of an experience which enables the popular detective story to sound varied depths of the greatest human themes in the hands of Graham Greene. In the art of Eliot (as in *The Cocktail Party*) it permits the sleuth and the guardian of souls to meet in the figure of Harcourt-Riley, as in Browning's Pope.

The failure of Dos Passos' insights to keep pace with the complex techniques at his disposal is what leaves the reader with the sense of looseness and excessive bulk in *U.S.A.* In the equally bulky *Finnegans Wake,* on the other hand, which exploits all the existing techniques of vision and presentation in a consummate orchestration of the arts and sciences, there is not one slack phrase or scene. *U.S.A.,* by comparison, is like a Stephen Foster medley played with one finger on a five keyboard instrument. There is that sort of discrepancy between the equipment and the ensuing concert; but it is not likely to disturb those readers who have only a slight acquaintance with Joyce.

Manhattan Transfer and the *U.S.A.* trilogy are not novels in the usual sense of a selection of characters who influence and define one another by interaction. The novel in that sense was a by-product of biological science and as such persists today only among book-club practitioners. The novel as it has been concerned with the problems of "character" and environment seems to have emerged as a pastime of the new middle classes who were eager to see themselves and their problems in action. Remove from these novels the problems of money and the arts of social distinction and climbing and little remains. From that point of view Flaubert's *Madame Bovary* was the deliberate reduction of the middle-class novel to absurdity. And Sinclair Lewis's *Babbitt* is, as Ford Madox Ford pointed out, the American *Madame Bovary*. But the *Sentimental Education* is a great step beyond this, and taken with *Bouvard and Pecuchet*, provided the framework for the symbolic epic of the commonplace which is *Ulysses*. The middle classes found romance and glamour in the commonplace, but they were not prepared for the profound existentialist metaphysic of the commonplace which Joyce revealed.

In such a perspective as this the collective landscapes of *U.S.A.* represent only a modest effort at managing the huge panorama of triviality and frustration which is the urban milieu of industrial man.

But the fact that a technological environment not only induces most people into various stages of automatism but makes the family unit socially non-effective, has certainly got something to do with the collective landscapes of *U.S.A.* Its structure is poetic in having its unity not in an idea but a vision; and it is cubist in presenting multiple simultaneous perspectives like a cycle of medieval mystery plays. It could readily be maintained that this method not only permits comprehensiveness of a kind indispensable to the modern artist, but makes for the intelligible rather than the concupiscible in art. The kind of pleasure that Dos Passos provides in comparison with Hemingway is that of detached intellectual intuition rather than that of sympathetic merging with the narrative and characters.

The current conception of art as vicarious experience, on the other hand, seems mainly to support the attitude of behavioristic merging with the lives of the characters portrayed. And since this tendency is geared commercially with the demands of an untrained reader mass, it is irresistible. It helps to explain why a Dos Passos is considered high-brow although he offers no more strain

on the attention than a detective story. It is because of
the kind rather than the degree of effort he invites that
he is deprecated as high-brow by readers who accept
the cubist landscapes of the newspaper, and the musical
equivalent in jazz, without perturbation.

Although Dos Passos may be held to have failed to
provide any adequate intellectual insight or emotion for
the vast landscape of his trilogy, his themes and attitudes are always interesting, especially in the numerous
biographies of such folk heroes as Edison and the Wright
brothers, Debs, and La Follette, Steinmetz and Isadora
Duncan, Ford and Burbank. These sections are often
masterly in their economy and point. The frustration of
hopes and intentions in these public figures provides
the main clue to the social criticism which underlies
the presentation of dozens of nonentities. For it is
usually pointed up that the great are as helplessly en-
snared in merely behavioristic patterns irrelevant to
their own welfare as the crowd of nobodies who admire
them.

The frustration and distortion of life common to the
celebrated and the obscure is, in Dos Passos, to be
attributed to "the system." No diagnosis as crude as this
emerges directly. But over and over again in the contrast
between humble humanity and the gormandizing power-
gluttony of the stupidly arrogant few, there is implied
the preference for a world of simple, unpretentious folk
united in their common tasks and experience. It has
often been noted that there is never love between the
characters of Dos Passos. But there is the pathos of those
made incapable of love by their too successful adjust-
ment to a loveless system. Genuine pathos is the pre-
dominant and persistent note in Dos Passos, and must be
considered as his personal response to the total landscape. Yet it is a pathos free from self-pity because he
has objectified it in his analysis of the political and
economic situation.

The homelessness of his people is, along with their
individual and collective incapacity for self-criticism or

detachment, the most obvious feature about them. And home is the positive though unstated and undefined dream of Dos Passos. In wandering from the Jeffersonian ideal of a farmer-craftsman economy in the direction of Hamiltonian centralism, power, and bigness, Dos Passos sees the main plight of his world. Hamilton set up the false beacon that brought shipwreck. But out of that shipwreck, which he depicts, for example, as the success of Henry Ford's enterprise, we can recover the dream and create a reality worthy of it. That is an unfailing note. For those who are critically aware he prescribes the duty of selfless dedication to the improvement of the common civilization. And in three uninteresting, short novels since *U.S.A.* he has explored the problem of discovering a self worth giving to such a cause. The current need would seem to be for a historic sense which can resolve the Hamilton-Jefferson dichotomy.

There is, perhaps, little point in dwelling on these aspects of Dos Passos, in which without new insight he reflects the ordinary attitude of the great majority. Yet, there is great social hope in the fact that this common intellectual ground is so large and so admirably chosen. But it is outside the province of criticism, which is concerned with the means employed and effects obtained by an artist. By the time the critic comes to the point of confronting Dos Passos the Jeffersonian radical, he has moved into a territory shared by Frank Capra.

And Dos Passos may have lost his stride as an artist through the very success of those social causes which were the militant theme of *U.S.A.* To have a cause to defend against a blind or indifferent world seemed to give tone and snap to the artist in him who has since been overlaid by the reporter. But if this is the case, nobody would be happier than Dos Passos to have lost his artistry on such excellent terms.

Dos Passos and Painting

GEORGE KNOX

Perhaps no American novelist since Henry James studied painting more seriously during the years of technical experimentation than Dos Passos. He was not only a passionate spectator but a worker in the art. From his Harvard years onward he was exploring his potentials for perception and expression, gradually finding himself in the world of art as well as in the welter of raw experience during World War I, and during the years of political unrest that followed. His sensitive young heroes are projections, in part, of a personal search for meaningful relations between life and "art" in times of shock and disorder. His literary apprenticeship culminated in *Manhattan Transfer,* and by the early thirties he had what he needed, the skills of art, autobiography, poetry, fiction, and drama. Moreover, he was intensely interested in politics and history. He reached the apotheosis of formal sophistication in *U.S.A.,* although as explorer of the roots of American civilization he was to extend modulations of his earlier works into *District of Columbia, Midcentury,* and purely historical works which reach ever deeper into our past.

Since the painterly qualities of his work have been totally neglected, I have set for this essay a brief survey of influences and parallels in *One Man's Initiation—1917* (1920); *Three Soldiers* (1921); *Rosinante to the Road*

From *Texas Studies in Literature and Language,* 6 (1964), 22–38. Reprinted by permission of the author and the editor of *Texas Studies in Literature and Language.*

Again (1922); *A Pushcart at the Curb* (1922); *Streets of Night* (1923); *Manhattan Transfer* (1925); and *U.S.A.* (1930–36).[1] I will direct the reader's attention to uses of color and changing modes of painterly composition, ranging roughly from impressionism to cubism. Only the briefest mention will be made of some works, and space limit forbids discussion of his paintings—for example, his illustrations of *Orient Express* (1927), and those executed for his own translations of Blaise Cendrar's *Panama* (1931), of paintings shown at the National Arts Club and at the Pierre Matisse Gallery. His latest showing was "Figuig, Sahara, 1927," a watercolor contributed to the United Nations Art Club Exhibit, April and May, 1960. Dos Passos also painted dustjackets for plays written by members of the New Playwrights Theatre, a repertory group writing and producing in New York from 1926 through 1929, and was responsible for most of the stage design and set construction. It should be mentioned that many of their plays were expressionistic and their sets constructivist. Most of his paintings have been given to friends, although he retains some in his possession.

In tracing changes in painterly techniques and effects I hope to add to the appreciation of his range and virtuosity. I admit the dangers of a restricted view, for Dos Passos was aware of the major streams in the nineteenth-century novel, and like many writers of his generation, was a follower of Gustave Flaubert. He has written me of the impact of *The Temptation of St. Anthony*, *Madame Bovary*, and *The Sentimental Education* on his own prose style. Both Flaubert's "realism" and his impressionism, particularly the latter, impressed the young American novelist. His interest in atmospheric effects, he says, was first aroused by a study of the Barbizon painters. In passing, he studied the realism of Courbet, the romantic landscapes of Corot, certain realistic effects in Rousseau. He soon became specifically concerned with Manet and Monet, before turning to various post-Impressionist modes.

One notices in the early fiction his expertise in controlling light, shadows, and delicacy of color relations. He worked from a fairly concrete color-object realism (probably under the influence of Courbet) toward an ever more abstract "realism" which culminated in Grosz-like depictions of city life, plastic color effects of certain Expressionists, and cubist portraiture in the mode of Braque and Picasso. However, as a fictionist, he could not strictly adhere to the pronouncements or techniques of painters. He has always been intuitional and individualistic, reacting against rigidifications of style and thought. Further, Dos Passos was one who created as much of the total climate of impressionism (and other "isms") as he simulated. Some of the formulations of Kandinsky and Denis seem to offer close parallels with his own thinking and practice. He, like them, was striking out against an overscientific copying of reality as though it had some absolute photographic fixity, while yet remaining close to referential material.

Much of his early painterly quality is nineteenth-century in spirit, perhaps deriving from Baudelaire and and developing through Delaunay.[2] According to Delaunay, some of whose paintings remind us strongly of passages in *Manhattan Transfer*, art should free itself from the object and from descriptive and literary implications. Expression and form, rhythms and harmonies of color, and plastic independence of light were desiderata. We may also think of Delaunay's precinematic *rythme tourbillant* of his colored disks as we read *Manhattan Transfer*. But first I must show how he worked toward these goals, going back to his impressionistic capturing of the "air" and tone of places (countrysides, landscape segments, small towns and sections of cities, usually perceived *en passant*). He was also striving to catch the rhythms and energies of "nature" (sun, water, trees) and steadily isolating psychological equivalents (remembered configurations, moods, images) of the retinal world. The war stories, although "immediate" in an actional sense, in the movement and flow of events convey mostly a pathos of recall. They are tonal dramas in color and mood, developed through juxtapositions, requiring establishment of a sensor or temperament through which a "subject" is filtered and transmuted.

Often his young isolates are "looking dreamingly out through half-closed eyes," as they observe the world:

> Martin Howe sat at a table on the sidewalk under the brown awning of a restaurant. Opposite in the last topaz-clear rays of the sun, the foliage of the Jardin du Luxembourg shone bright green above deep alleys of bluish shadow. From the pavements in front of the mauve-coloured house rose little kiosks with advertisements in bright orange and vermillion and blue. In the middle of the triangle formed by the streets and the garden was a round pool of jade water. Martin leaned back in his chair looking dreamily out through half-closed eyes, breathing deep now and then of the musty scent of Paris, that mingled with the melting freshness of the wild strawberries. (*OMI*, p. 23)

One perhaps thinks of Monet or Pissarro, but Dos Passos' range is so great one is uneasy about tagging him. He depicts harbor scenes filled with purple light, winking lights, moving shapes, spilled reflections. Aerial textures are very important. Movement composition is subtle.

> It was noon. A pallid little sun like a toy balloon hung low in the reddish-grey sky. The train had stopped on a siding in the middle of a russet plain. Yellow poplars, faint as mist, rose slender against the sky along a black shining stream that swirled beside the track. In the distance a steeple and a few red roofs were etched faintly in the greyness. (*TS*, p. 70).

Faint rains, light mists, opalescent fogs, and patches of black lace-work against reddish-grey skies are recurring elements in his scenes.

> They were going into the suburbs of a town. Rows and clusters of little brick and stucco houses were appearing along the roads. It began to rain from a sky

full of lights of amber and lilac color. The slate roofs and the pinkish-grey streets of the town shone cheerfully in the rain. The little patches of garden were all vivid emerald-green. Then they were looking at rows and rows of red chimney pots over wet slate roofs that reflected the bright sky. In the distance rose the purple-grey spire of a church and the irregular forms of old buildings. They passed through a station. (*TS*, pp. 134–35)

Often, as the observer is in motion, these scenes are broken into fragments, gyrations, blendings, and fusions. But on the whole the reader finds little distortion of objects in the early fiction. One does notice a gradual interaction of figure and setting, the two elements becoming reciprocal components—as when John Andrews walks through the drifting fog in the streets of Paris, muffled and contained by it, passing through the halos of the lamps, the psychological and the phenomenological dimensions quite complementary.

Looking down rows of trees, avenues, and alleys, we perceive light and objects being transmitted in patinas, luminosities, and glows. In a cinematic fashion, scenes pass through a series of refinements. Also, we notice a gradual sophistication of "scene" through action and dialogue. His art is dramatized:

They climbed into a taxi, and lurched fast through streets where, in the misty sunlight, grey-green and grey-violet mingled with blues and pale lights as the colors mingle in a pigeon's breast feathers. They passed the leafless gardens of the Tuileries on one side, and the great inner Courts of the Louvre, with their purple mansard roofs and their high chimneys on the other, and saw for a second the river, dull jade green, and the plane trees splotched with brown and cream color along the quais, before they were lost in the narrow brownish-grey streets of the old quarters.

"This is Paris; that was Cosmopolis," said Henslowe.

"I'm not particular, just at present," cried Andrews gaily.

The square in front of the Odéon was a splash of white and the colonnade a blur of darkness as the cab swerved round the corner and along the edge of the Luxembourg, where, through the black iron fence, many brown and reddish colors in the intricate patterns of leafless twigs opened here and there on statues and balustrades and vistas of misty distances. The cab stopped with a jerk.

"This is the Place des Médicis," said Henslowe.

At the end of a slanting street looking very flat, through the haze, was the dome of the Panthéon. In the middle of the square between the yellow trams and the green low busses, was a quiet pool, where the shadow of horizontals of the house fronts was reflected. (*TS*, p. 304)

Perhaps one senses something of the naive American on a guided tour, or the amateur photographer exposing film for his home movies. But one should not miss the essential irony which Dos Passos directs against his innocent and sensation-hungry spectators.

Moreover, he was trying to move *through* a surface realism, from mere subject matter, to form.[3] His "forms" became increasingly excited, tense and restless, approaching Van Gogh-like kinesis and agitation. This growing tendency toward tortured forms would culminate eventually in visions of metropolitan violence, frenetic fantasies, feverish merging lines, and excited handling of color consonant with postwar moods. Dos Passos became acquainted with the line drawings and paintings of George Grosz during World War I. Grosz skirted or joined a number of movements. In one role he called himself "Propagandada." He was on the edge of expressionism, cubism, and surrealism. He writes in his autobiography that childhood memories of panorama art, with scenes of holocaust, violence, and catastrophe, exactly fitted the sense of impending disaster in modern Germany. This kind of "folk art" perhaps conditioned him to feel and think about the grotesque horrors which were to come and which he would brutally satirize. At any rate, the sense that some sinister force lurks under the most commonplace of everyday life scenes is to be found among many of the Expressionists.

The movement in Dos Passos' fiction was, then, from simple realism of color composition to Monet-like impressionism, to explosions of force, cacophony, and finally a handling of cubistic techniques suitable to depicting the confused planes and psychic dimensions of metroplex life. Although color as we encounter it in the early work almost disappears in *Manhattan Transfer*, the color *sense* remains. It is as though he, like Grosz, oscillated between the dramatism of pure line depiction and color, with subdued shadings in between. Here we may make a tentative comparison, also, with the increasing use of black among the Expressionists, black and white with dashes of red, as in Munch and Kirchner. He was certainly aware of Jugendstil (Art Nouveau) techniques and of wood-block printing. He gradually uses colors to enhance distorted perspectives and to accentuate the sense of spaces and masses moving in diverse directions.

As Grosz started from the graceful tracing of entwining Jugendstil lines but moved into the harsher geometry of his satirical cartoons, so did Dos Passos abandon the Art Nouveau preciosity of his Pre-Raphaelite poetry and take up the jagged rhythms and agitated lines of *Manhattan Transfer*. In the early fiction we are preoccupied almost entirely with experiments in chromatic transformations, in the handling of changing and flickering play of atmospheric effects, an art of abridgment and control of luminous vibrations. At times he uses pure and intense colors when articulating his pictures, revealing the influence of Delaunay and the Munich painters. In fact, Delaunay's series of the ambulatory of St. Séverin seems to have affected several of Dos Passos' illustrations for *Orient Express*. Around

1910–11, Delaunay began a number of abstract views of the city, as seen through his open windows. "There is little depth or perspective, but luminous color overflows all limitations of space. His friend Apollinaire coined the term 'Orphism' for these highly abstract works, which inspired his poem 'Les Fenêtres'." [4]

Much of the scenery of *Manhattan Transfer* and *U.S.A.* resembles this through-the-window world. But he had worked at depicting up-reaching masses and interacting color planes before. The following passage was written at least three years prior to *Manhattan Transfer*:

Against the grey and ochre-streaked theatre of the Cigarrales were piled masses of buttressed wall that caught the orange sunset light on many tall plane surfaces rising into crenellations and square towers and domes and slate-capped spires above a little of yellowish tile roofs that fell away in terraces from the highest points and sloped outside the walls toward the river and the piers from which sprang the enormous arch of the bridge. The shadows were blue-green and violet. A pale cobalt haze of supper-fires hung over the quarters near the river. (RTRA, pp. 236–37)

Innumerable passages in the early works suggest a proto-cubism, even a proto-expressionism, as he groped for a more legible design and satisfying textural idiom. His romanticism became articulate first in a Monet-like impressionism. He became fluent later in Fauvist colors. The experiments with color and symbol and light reached formal resolution in *U.S.A.*

In the Camera Eye, Newsreels, and the Biographies transmutations of all his earlier effects occur. The Camera Eye passages, in which we trace the authorial sensibility, run the gamut of painterly elements in miniscule. The whole work exemplifies the kind of open, abstract views in which one plane overlaps and intersects another. In the Biographies an undeniable cubist ordering of materials is evident. Like Die Brücke painters, Dos Passos learned how to use pure colors as structural elements. His prose can be conceived as simulating Delaunay's cubism, when Dos Passos dissolves the city into motifs, into color planes in the shapes of squares, triangles, rhomboids, and trapezoids which interpenetrate to convey kaleidoscopic and spectral effects. Although the early fiction abounds in Pointillist and Divisionist handling of color, Dos Passos was never taken in by psycho-optical enthusiasms to the extent that his work became phenomenology, a collocation of perceptual motifs. Light as a formal element never usurped overall structural, plastic, or thematic integrity. The simulation of painterly techniques was a means, a part of his search through new forms, for he was above all a draftsman. Light and color, per se, did not satisfy his need for a comprehensive, synthetic medium.

In *One Man's Initiation* and *Three Soldiers*, a constant concern with a "field of vision" centers our reactions in the perceptions and moods of his sensitive young heroes. He elaborately juxtaposes colors, beauty and sordidness, elation and depression. Pound was to carry the technique of juxtaposition and superimposition to its ultimate in *The Cantos*. Dos Passos' early establishment of mechanical angles and positions of vantage seem rather amateurish, at least when taken out of context—as when his protagonist "raised his tumbler and looked at the candle through the pale yellow champagne. On the wall behind him, his arm and hand and the tumbler were shadowed huge in dusky lavender blue." (*OMI*, pp. 113–14) A symbolist viewpoint is latent here, however. It merely needs extension. Landscapes are animated, even anthropomorphized, but most of the color revelry is sheer virtuosity and indulgence in a new-found world: "The light all about was lemon yellow. The walls of the village behind them were fervid primrose color splotched with shadows of sheer cobalt. Above the houses uncurled green spirals of woodsmoke." (*RTRA*, p. 72)

He sustains a constant flow of vistas and concatenation of caught moments conditioned by light: "Thin wreaths of white mist still lingered in the trees and over the little garden plots. The sun had not yet risen, but ranks of clouds in the pale blue sky overhead were brilliant with crimson and gold." (*TS*, p. 185) And: "In the sky an escadrille of French planes had appeared and the three German specks had vanished, followed by a trail of little puffs of shrapnel. The indigo dome of the afternoon sky was full of a distant snoring of motors." (*OMI*, p. 61) He enshrouds his little scenes within the flow of his narrative, and these scenic moments in turn often depend on the impression of a larger solar envelope, the splash of light on objects through the magically changing French atmosphere.

Ever after the fleeting instant, as befits the precarious but intense thirst for experience his young men feel, he explores the brilliant surface of the world in all its synaesthetic possibilities.

However, much of it is brought home to the studio and seems obviously abstracted. Most of the poetry in *Pushcart at the Curb* (1922) is, like the fiction, "scenic," built up of arrested moments and bodied forth in perspectivist ingenuity. We notice a kind of *cloisonnisme*—neat stanzaic integrity, outlines superscribed on a few calligraphic details. The mood is *fin de siècle*. He tends to saturate his "canvas" with colors:

> Dark on the blue light of the stream
> the barges lie anchored under the moon.
>
> On icegreen seas of sunset
> the moon skims like a curved white sail
> bellied by the evening wind
> and bound for some glittering harbor
> that blue hills circle
> among the purple archipelagos of cloud.
>
> ("Phases of the Moon," Poem X, p. 206)

Pushcart presents picture after picture, portrait upon portrait, all built upon simple attitudes and easily defined moods. For example, a stanza from Poem I of "Winter in Castile":

> A long grey street with balconies.
> Above the gingercolored grocer's shop
> trail pink geraniums
> and further up a striped mattress
> hangs from a window
> and the little wooden cage
> of a goldfinch.
>   (P. 14)

Mood painting is the *raison d'être* of "Quai de la Tournelle," Poem IX:

> Looking out at the vast grey violet dusk
> A pale boy sits in a window, a book
> Wide open on his knees, and fears
> With cold choked fear the thronging lives
> That lurk in the shadows and fill the dusk
> With menacing steps.
> Far away the gaslamp glows dull gold
> A vague tulip in the misty night . . .
>   (*La Rue du Temps Passé*, p. 154)

Such poetry merely fixes or concretizes various moods in painterly fashion. Much of it carries the tone of Japanese and Chinese poetry in translation. For instance, Poem XI of "Quai de la Tournelle," entitled "A L'ombre des Jeunes Filles en Fleurs," p. 158:

> And now when I think of you
> I see you on your piano-stool
> finger the ineffectual bright keys
> and even in the pinkish parlor glow
> your eyes sea-grey are very wide
> as if they carried the reflection
> of mocking black pinebranches
> and unclimbed red-purple mountains
>   mist tattered
> under a violet-gleaming evening.

Often we find descriptions of objects moping in flowing lines, as plants vining, tendrils reaching, and this is reminiscent of Art Nouveau sinuosity. A certain preciosity and near-sentimentality pervades these landscapes. They are saved from sentimentality, however, by the detachment and impersonality of the author. Perhaps the "purest" scenic evocation is Poem X of "Quai de la Tournelle," p. 155. Each "picture" is followed by a refrain, on which the poem began, leading by incremental force into the next: "O douce Sainte Geneviève/ ramene moi à ta ville, Paris."

> In the smoke of morning the bridges
> are dusted with orangy sunshine.
>
> Bending their black smokestacks far back
> muddling themselves in their spiralling smoke
> the tugboats pass under the bridges
> and behind them
> stately
> gliding smooth like clouds
> with barges
> with blunt prows spurning the water gently
> gently rebuffing the opulent wavelets
> of opal and topaz and sapphire,
> barges casually come from far towns
> towards far towns unhurrying bound.

Each succeeding stanza fills out the scene, although little in the nature of psychological progression develops. This in effect recapitulates the structure of the first two novels. And so we are aware that Dos Passos' early impressionist experiments dwelt on surfaces and "touched" the subject. He also enclosed his subject in *cernes*. Gradually he was to penetrate surfaces, pierce the veils of a sensational world and embody the truer reality of forms with the modern psyche. Synaesthetic effects were extended into symbolic significance in the landscapes of *Manhattan Transfer* and *U.S.A.* In the early work the outer world, as recorded, is the never-quite-transformed component of consciousness. In the later it is the consciousness.

Although the early colorism is dominantly tonic and chromatic, it is used to create ironies: "Where the face had been was a spongy mass of purple and yellow and red, half of which stuck to the russet leaves when the body rolled over. Large flies with bright shiny green bodies circled about it. In a brown clay-grimed hand was a revolver." (TS, p. 157) Or: "A girl in a faded frock of some purplish material that showed the strong curves of her shoulders and breasts slouched into the room, her hands in the pocket of a dark blue apron against which her rounded forearms showed golden brown. Her face had the same golden tan under a mass of dark blonde hair. She smiled when she saw the two soldiers, drawing her thin lips away from her ugly yellow teeth." (TS, p. 148) Thus, he could exploit unromantic subjects with aesthetic effect, and with a shade of eroticism, like Toulouse-Lautrec, Degas in his bathing series, and Expressionists such as Egon Schiele (e.g., *Girl in Green Stockings*, 1914).

Moving from *plein air*, from the Fauvist revelry in color, and from the mood portraits, he arrived at the nervous syndromes of the city. We take a moment in the life of Cecily Baldwin as representative: " 'Oh I'm the most miserable woman,' she groaned and got to her feet. Her head ached as it were bound with hot wire. She went to the window and leaned out into the sunlight. Across Park Avenue the flameblue sky was barred with the red girder cage of a new building. Steam riveters rattled incessantly; now and then a donkey engine whistled and there was a jingle of chains and a fresh girder soared crosswise in the air. Men in blue overalls moved about the scaffolding. Beyond to the northwest a shining head of clouds soared blooming compactly like a cauliflower. Oh if it would only rain." (MT, p. 185)

Traces of this symbolism (Cecily is barred and caged and burning in spiritual drouth.) appeared in *Streets of Night*, evolving from the war fiction. In *Three Soldiers* the mechanism of war is overtly indicated in the section titles: "Parts," "Making the Mould," "The Metal Cools," "Machines," "Rust," "The World Outside," and "Under the Wheels." One thinks of Fernand Leger, who conjoined traditional perspectives with disarrangements and distortions in globes, cubes, and cylinders. Many passages in *U.S.A.* depict people in mechanical images. In *Manhattan Transfer* Dos Passos achieves his first sophistication in this vocabulary, as in the chapter headings: "Ferryslip," "Tracks," "Steamroller," "Fire Engine," "Rollercoaster," "Nickelodeon," "Revolving Doors," and "Skyscraper." Dos Passos subordinated color to this machine idiom, partly as a means of detaching himself from his characters and establishing the city as protagonist. People were objects. A mechanical metaphor helped envision a continuum of apparently discontinuous moments, or of continuous and sequential events apparently disjunct, as in futuristic paintings.

To show the evolution of this mode, we should go back to *One Man's Initiation,* his first novel. Perhaps we are reminded somewhat of Van Gogh's *Dance Hall at Arles,* or some of Toulouse-Lautrec, or of various Expressionist canvases:

> Their round table with its white cloth and its bottles of wine and its piles of ravished artichoke leaves was the centre of a noisy, fantastic world. Ever since the orgy of the hors d'oeuvres things had been evolving into grotesqueness, faces, whites of eyes, twisted red of lips, crow-like forms of waiters, colours of hats and uniforms, all involved and jumbled in the melee of talk and clink and clatter." (*OMI,* p. 64)

Then we jump ahead to a passage from *Manhattan Transfer,* quite surrealistic:

> Elbows joggling, faces set, gollywog eyes, fat men and thin women, thin women and fat men rotated densely about them. He was crumbling plaster with something that rattled achingly in his chest, she was an

intricate machine of sawtooth steel whitebright blue-bright copperbright in his arms. When they stopped her breast and the side of her body and her thigh came against him. He was suddenly full of blood steaming with sweat like a runaway horse. A breeze through an open door hustled the tobaccosmoke and the clotted pink air of the restaurant." (*MT*, p. 228)

But the transmogrification is even more startling in the opening of "Steamroller":

Dusk gently smooths crispangled streets. Dark presses tight the steaming asphalt city, crushes the fretwork of windows and lettered signs and chimneys and watertanks and ventilators and fire-escapes and moldings and patterns and corrugations and eyes and hands and neckties into blue chunks, into black enormous blocks. Under the rolling heavier heavier pressure windows blurt light. Night crushes bright milk out of arclights, squeezes the sullen blocks until they drip red, yellow, green into streets resounding with feet. All the asphalt oozes light. Light spurts from lettering on roofs, mills dizzily among wheels, stains rolling tons of sky." (*MT*, p. 112)

One will be reminded of many Expressionist or Futurist paintings. Delaunay we have mentioned. Blocks and planes of color and light, the fusion of spectral effects, may well call to mind Carra's *Funeral of the Anarchist Galli* (1910–11), the catastrophic and cataclysmic violence of Meidner's *Burning City* (1913), or the wild apocalyptic qualities of Grosz's *Funeral of the Poet Panizza* (1917–18), although no one of these exactly fits.

At any rate, we no longer see with Martin's bemused gaze, into the idyllic countrysides of France, into the misty vistas of Paris, through the last topaz-clear rays into the foliage of the Jardin du Luxembourg, in the style of Monet, Pissaro, or Renoir. No longer do we ride through a pleasant French village, looking up at fluffy mauve-tinted clouds drifting across the sky. The poetic odyssey of *Pushcart* and *Rosinante* is ended. New York's postwar confusion has supplanted the pathos of Paris. The moods of Munch, Kirchner, Nolde, and Grosz have replaced the Impressionist delicacies. Color is broken, surfaces distorted, rhythms syncopated and sprung. In the drawings and paintings of George Grosz we find a major influence. Dos Passos wrote introductory remarks to collections of his works.[5]

In addition to depicting terrors, cruelties, and all manner of nightmare, Grosz satirized subtly and used a kind of abstractionist sectioning that Dos Passos may have simulated in *Manhattan Transfer* and *U.S.A.* I cannot analyze pertinent examples at any length, but will refer particularly to his 1923 collection entitled *Ecce Homo*, and such drawings as No. 51, *Eva*, 1918; No. 24, *Der Bessessene Forstadtjunkt*, 1918; No. 6, *Marseille*, 1919; No. 73, *Vorstadt*, 1917; No. 18, *Buergliche Welt*, 1920; No. 40, *Der Hülsenbeck am Ende*, 1920; and No. 68, *Querschnitt*, 1920. Dos Passos has written me that he remembers the latter particularly. Perspectives are distorted, as lines cross and recross in superimposed scenes. There is no apparent attempt to relate figures who appear disjunctly in crazy perspectives. Interiors and exteriors intermingle. And yet, in spite of the jumble, one always detects some principle of coherence or composition, a feeling or mood of distress, violence, or chaos which unites the disparate facets.

Often, as in *Eva* and *Querschnitt*, a female nude occupies a central position. The woman is undeniably a prostitute. The amalgamations of sordid and lurid details cumulatively create revulsion, yet the design subsumes and objectifies the feeling. Grosz cuts, in panoramic, cycloramic, and dioramic manner, through every section of metropolitan life. Dos Passos felt that Grosz had discovered a radically new vocabulary, a revolutionary mode of expression. As with Dos Passos' novels of the city, we do not feel concern for these people. We see them only at some fortuitous moment. Shifting our attention we pass on to others, plunging into new moments. Grosz had evolved his geometry from *Jugendstil*, and Dos Passos worked out his own world of intersecting and interweaving lines of destiny in the modern mode of discontinuity.

Just as the story of actions is told in isolated and apparently unconnected episodes, so the meaning of the characters' existences is inherent in their failure to achieve proper fulfillment in any dynamic way. The discontinuity and superimposition of life-fragments parallels the disjuncture and transparency in psychic life. The author as super-camera-eye looks through any segment of the city and records it in a Grosz-like polyvisional sectioning. This method consciously, and necessarily, accepts the unfinished sketch, the *inachevé*. The deliberate oscillation of appearances in the flow of narrative is mirrored in the Biographies. The piling up of the Camera Eye, the Biographies, the Newsreel, and newspaper headlines is a complementary collocation, like a piling of Grosz drawings—sometimes Dadaistic, sometimes surrealistic, sometimes in collage effect. In the Biographies we discover various Cubist experiments in balance, contrast, and shifting of proportions.

The sketches of prominent Americans who emerge from the milieu of the trilogy are both poems and portraits. They remind one also of the movie short, or documentary film ("March of Time") style of portrayal. Brief as they are, a fluid quality prevails, as Dos Passos conveys a sense of background and foreground simultaneously. The personality of the subject takes shape within a larger course of events and becomes a distinct shape gradually and additively by superimposition of data in the manner of planes and surfaces. As the Newsreel passages are made up of headlines, stock-market reports, fragments of songs, advertising slogans, banal public statements, so, by analogy, the people of the Biographies are built up, or "composed," of multifaceted fragments, shards of milieu, motes (and *mots*) caught from the air.

The persons portrayed are themselves "angles of vision" in the flux of the trilogy—Roosevelt, Bryan, Wilson, the Wright brothers, Isadora Duncan, Rudolph Valentino, Edison, Big Bill Haywood, and many others —providing us with perspectives. They represent slants, tones, coloring, attitudes in the culture. The portraits themselves are divided into areas as factors and data are juxtaposed, superposed, or joggled to fit the "idea" of the subject. Correspondences, contrasts, and incongruities are erected into a structure which becomes that person as "expressed." Partial impressions are merged, overlapping and overlaying each other. The subject per se is not transfixed, but a momentary collusion, or collision, of impressions is composed.

This type of composition is adjusted to the mood and psychological patterns of lives in *U.S.A.* This speed with which stimuli assail us from the modern city world is the crucial analogy of these Biographies. Fragments from a character and his world loom, flit by, and leave vibrations in our consciousness. This results in an accumulation of pieces in layers, an assimilation of fragments. As in the Cubist portrait, we receive a swift flow of optic stimuli which cut across the boundaries of conventional placement and definition. Although synthesized of broken planes and particles, the Biographies are correlated as fields of force. The persons who "posed" for them are detritus of the times, compressed and attenuated, stratified as personality areas and a contrasting of axes. They emerge plastically for a moment then fade into the overall flux. The total panoramic scene contains them as motions, tones, ideas, and transmitters of energy who mesh or clash with others who have their peculiar vectorial qualities. The Biographies, by analogy, exemplify what Kahnweiler said of Picasso,[6] that he made it possible to "represent" the form of objects and their position in space instead of attempting to imitate them through illusionistic means, by showing a thing from several sides, and from above and below. One could profitably pursue parallels in technique with cinematic montage, painterly collage, and literary découpage and truncation—all commonplace artistic practices.

The sketch of Paxton Hibben, "A Hoosier Quixote," from 1919, although not the most complex, will illustrate most of my points. It is compounded of observations by the omniscient author; fragments of biographical data; direct italicized quotations from *Who's Who*; and impressionistic flashes as seen by Hibben himself at various moments in his life. For example:

At Princeton he was the young collegian, editor of the *Tiger,* drank a lot, didn't deny that he ran around after girls, made a brilliant scholastic record, and was a thorn in the flesh of the godly. The natural course for a bright young man of his class and position was to study law, but Hibben wanted

to travel and romance à la Byron and de Musset, wellgroomed adventures in foreign lands,

so

as his family was one of the best in Indiana and friendly with Senator Beveridge he was gotten a post in the diplomatic service:

3rd sec and 2nd sec American Embassy, St. Petersburg and Mexico City 1905–6, sec Legation and Chargé d'affairs, Bogotá, Colombia, 1908–9; The Hague and Luxemburg 1909–12, Santiago de Chile 1912 (retired).

Pushkin for de Musset; St. Petersburg was a young dude's romance:

goldencrusted spires under a platinum sky,

the icegray Neva flowing swift and deep under bridges that jingled with sleighbells;

riding home from the Islands with the Grand Duke's mistress, the most beautiful most amorous singer of Neapolitan streetsongs;

staking a pile of rubles in a tall room glittering with chandeliers, monocles, diamonds dripped on white shoulders;

white snow, white tablecloths, white sheets,

Kakhetian wine, vodka fresh as newmown hay, Astrakhan caviar, sturgeon, Finnish salmon, Lapland ptarmigan, and the most beautiful women in the world;

but it was 1905, Hibben left the Embassy one night and saw a flare of red against the trampled snow of the Nevsky

and red flags,

blood frozen in the ruts. . . .

And so it builds up, plane upon plane, viewpoint upon viewpoint. Also, in this way it ends, the stream of consciousness of the subject, the authorial interpolations merging with the persona, the public sentiments, and finally the extract from *Who's Who*:

In Moscow there was order,

in Moscow there was work,

in Moscow there was hope;

the *Marseillaise* of 1905, *Onward Christian Soldiers* of 1912, the sullen passiveness of American Indians, of infantrymen waiting death at the front was part of the tremendous roar of the Marxian *Internationale*.

Hibben believed in the new world.

Back in America

somebody got hold of a photograph of Captain Paxton Hibben laying a wreath on Jack Reed's grave; they tried to throw him out of the O.R.C.;

at Princeton at the twentieth reunion of his college class his classmates started to lynch him; they were drunk and perhaps it was just a collegeboy prank twenty years too late but they had a noose around his neck,

lynch the goddam red,

no more place in America for change, no more place for the old gags; social justice, progressivism, revolt against oppression, democracy; put the reds on the skids,

no money for them,

no jobs for them.

Mem Authors League of America, Soc of Colonial
Wars, Vets Foreign Wars, Am Legion, fellow Royal
and Am Geog Socs. Decorated chevalier Order of St.
Stanislas (Russian), Officer Order of the Redeemer
(Greek), Order of the Sacred Treasure (Japan).
Clubs Princeton, Newspaper, Civic (New York)
Author: Constantine and the Greek People 1920,
The Famine in Russia 1922, Henry Ward Beecher an
American Portrait 1927.
d. 1929.

There is more to it than this, but we can see how the
figure is "represented" by a series of motifs, shifting to
indicate angles of vision a spectator-reader must take.
Thus we derive *une impression multidimensionelle* but
must do our own synchronization of perspectives. In
terms of the movie short, the collision of "shots" creates
a dynamic dramatic quality. The subject is always the
historical person and the person as a symbol. Part of his
consciousness is conveyed in authorial voice, but this
merges with the psychic life of the persona, and the
effect is *dédoublement* of existential experience.

This technique is more elaborately developed in
other portraits. In the 1919 sketch of Isadora Duncan
("Art and Isadora") we see an interesting multiplanar
experiment, for in effect the portrait is a projection of
the person's own conception of role. Everything Isadora
did was art, the author repeats, and even her death had
a stagey dramatism about it, a choreography, "tragic" as
it was. Rudolph Valentino's portrait illustrates a mirror-
ing-within-mirrors aspect of these cubist depictions. The
actor lived under a fictitious name, had his being in a
press-agents' world, died wretchedly from peritonitis
(details of the autopsy given), and after a fantastic funeral "arrived" in Hollywood on some back page of the
New York *Times*, already on his way to oblivion. An
even more complex memorial ends 1919, "The Body of
an American," the portrait of the Unknown Soldier. The
Unknown Soldier is anonymous everyman, a series of

phony tributes, newspaper rhetoric, a voice that inter-
mittently intrudes to ask how he can find his way back
to his outfit, and a "real" body buried in Arlington.

The last of such portraits is an ironic *tour de force*:
"The Death of James Dean . . . Long Lament for an
Alter Ego," [7] another Hollywood "life."

Demonic, but lovable under it all.

The sinister adolescent is box office. Long before
his first picture is released James Dean is besieged by
Hollywood agents, promoters, feature writers, photog-
raphers.

He is serious about self-expression. "Acting is the
most logical way for people's neuroses to express
themselves." As soon as he's in the money he buys
himself a good camera and photographs himself in
melancholy moods,

sad and resentful and sorry, so soon to die,

but lovable under it all. Sharp lights and shadows,
his head in a noose, a kitchen knife shot for a dagger.
He talks a lot about wanting to sculpt.

He's crazy about racing cars. Speed's how to die.
He makes up his own mobiles. He's planning to be a
bullfighter: "Death in the Afternoon."

"Cool," echo the teen-agers. "Everything he said
was cool."

In Hollywood he goes on playing the part he plays
on the screen. "A wary suspicious loner," one director
calls him. Another is more forgiving: "Just a boy on
the rise."

"Rebel Without a Cause."

The teen-agers saw themselves in James Dean.
Everything he said was cool.

In this as in others Dos Passos begins from a definite
and clearly defined background from which he works
toward the front by a scheme of facets and motifs. He
also, like the Cubist, incorporates "real" objects into his
paintings. Braque initiated this technique, and I do not
doubt that Dos Passos' introduction of headlines, adver-

tisements, and other flotsam simulates the painterly innovation.

The repetitions which characterize the portraits indicate a process of "becoming" in the least possible space and time. We see the parts as instants in emergence. Even the spacing of lines forces a creative activity upon the reader, and every literal line is a painterly line of force (opinion, prejudice, hearsay, mood) building toward a total "image." The tag-ends of reality, like the pieces of cloth, scraps of newspaper, and labels on bottles in the Cubist painting, are extraneous but help the viewer to "see" the essential meaning. Ezra Pound developed similar techniques in *The Cantos*. Many of Dos Passos' contemporaries could be rewardingly studied for the utilization of artistic techniques. Gertrude Stein, William Faulkner, Ezra Pound, and James Joyce, e. e. cummings, come immediately to mind. This is an area of historical scholarship and exegesis not adequately explored. In this brief essay I hope the passages from Dos Passos' poetry and fiction have served the function that illustrations do in the art historian's analysis of a painter's work. Dos Passos certainly contributed as much as he derived from the climate of Impressionism and Cubism, and I have implied no lack of originality by entertaining the possibilities of "influence."

Notes

Introduction BELKIND

1. James T. Farrell, "How Should We Rate Dos Passos?" *New Republic*, April 28, 1958, pp. 17–18.

2. James T. Farrell, "Dos Passos and the Critics," *The American Mercury*, 47 (August 1939), pp. 489–94; Arthur Mizener, The Gullivers of John Dos Passos," *Saturday Review of Literature*, June 30, 1951, pp. 6–7, 34–35.

3. John H. Wrenn, *John Dos Passos* (New Haven: Twayne, 1961); John D. Brantley, *The Fiction of John Dos Passos* (The Hague: Mouton, 1968).

4. Granville Hicks, *The Great Tradition* (New York: Macmillan, 1935), pp. 287–91. See also Hicks's "Dos Passos' Gifts," *New Republic*, June 24, 1931, pp. 157–58.

5. "John Dos Passos: The Poet and the World," in *Think Back on Us*, ed. Malcolm Cowley (Carbondale and Edwardsville: Southern Illinois University Press, 1967), pp. 212–19. Cowley's article first appeared in the *New Republic*, April 27, 1932, pp. 303–5.

6. Lionel Trilling, "The America of John Dos Passos," *Partisan Review*, 4 (April 1938), 26–32.

7. Alfred Kazin, *On Native Grounds* (New York: Reynal-Hitchcock, 1942), pp. 341–59. See Kazin's recent appraisal of Dos Passos and U.S.A., "John Dos Passos: Inventor in Isolation," *Saturday Review*, March 15, 1969, pp. 16–19, 44–45.

8. Malcolm Cowley, "A Natural History of Naturalism," in *Critiques and Essays on Modern Fiction, 1920–1951*, ed. John W. Aldridge (New York: Ronald Press, 1952), pp. 370–87.

9. Philip Rahv, "Notes on the Decline of Naturalism," in Aldridge, *Critiques*, pp. 415–23. See also Richard Chase's

analysis of Norris' "naturalistic romances" in *The American Novel and its Tradition* (Garden City: Anchor paper, 1957), pp. 185–204.

10. Henry Steele Commager, *The American Mind* (New Haven: Yale University Press, 1950, 1959), pp. 270–71.

11. Charles C. Walcutt, *American Literary Naturalism, A Divided Stream* (Minneapolis: University of Minnesota Press, 1956), pp. 280–89.

12. See also Delmore Schwartz, "John Dos Passos and the Whole Truth," *Southern Review*, 4 (October 1938), 351–67. Schwartz effectively describes the stylistic divisions in *U.S.A.*, but overlooks the ironic tone of the narratives in his reduction of them to dead-level naturalism (to him, an accurate reflection of reality).

13. See also Michael Millgate, *American Social Fiction: James to Cozzens* (New York: Barnes and Noble, 1964), pp. 128–41. Agreeing essentially with the interpretation of Trilling, Millgate says: "Dos Passos' attack on the power and corruption of business is essentially based on moral indignation. So, for that matter, is his whole presentation of American society in *U.S.A.* His rationale may have been economic and political, but his impetus . . . was moral and emotional. . . . This, though his limitation as a sociologist, is his strength as a novelist" (pp. 134–35).

14. Marshall McLuhan, "John Dos Passos: Technique vs. Sensibility," in *Fifty Years of the American Novel — 1900 to 1950*, ed. Harold C. Gardiner (New York: Scribners, 1951), p. 155.

15. John Lydenberg, "Dos Passos's *U.S.A.*: The Words of the Hollow Men," in *Essays on Determination in American Literature*, ed. Sidney J. Krause (Kent, Ohio: Kent State University Press, 1964), pp. 97–107. See also Lydenberg's "Dos Passos and the Ruined Words," *Pacific Spectator*, 8 (1951), 16–23.

16. Joseph Warren Beach, *American Fiction: 1920–1940* (New York: Macmillan, 1941), pp. 25–66.

17. Blanche H. Gelfant, "John Dos Passos: The Synoptic Novel," in *The American City Novel* (Norman: University of Oklahoma Press, 1954), pp. 133–74.

18. Edmund Wilson, "Dos Passos and the Social Revolution," in *Shores of Light* (New York: Farrar and Strauss, 1952), p. 432.

19. Kazin, *On Native Grounds*, p. 274.

20. McLuhan, "Technique vs. Sensibility," p. 158.

21. Henry Longan Stuart, "John Dos Passos Notes the Tragic Trivia of New York," *New York Times Book Review*, November 29, 1925, p. 5.

22. George Snell, *Shapers of American Fiction* (New York: Dutton, 1947), p. 253.

23. Jean-Paul Sartre, "John Dos Passos and *1919*," in *Literary Essays*, trans. Annette Michelson (New York: Philosophical Library, 1957), pp. 88–96.

24. Wayne Booth, *The Rhetoric of Fiction* (Chicago: University of Chicago Press, 1961), p. 57.

25. Gilbert Highet, *The Anatomy of Satire* (Princeton: Princeton University Press, 1962), p. 190.

26. See, for example, the review of Coningsby Dawson, "Insulting the Army," *New York Times Book Review*, October 2, 1921, p. 1. Henry Seidel Canby, who wrote an important and highly favorable review of the novel, feared that it would not be discussed as literature, but "regarded as propaganda against war and its implications supported or refuted as if they were arguments, whereas the precise character of the creative skill involved is really much more important." See the *New York Evening Post*, October 8, 1921, p. 67.

27. John Chamberlain, "Dos Passos Satirizes America 'On the Make,'" *New York Times Book Review*, March 2, 1930, p. 5.

28. Horace Gregory, "Dos Passos Completes His Modern Trilogy: Eloquent and Incisive Satire Displayed in Scenario Style," *New York Herald-Tribune Book Review*, August 9, 1936, pp. 1–2.

29. Max Lerner, "The America of John Dos Passos," *Nation*, August 15, 1936, pp. 187–88.

30. See Farrell, "Dos Passos and the Critics." In his defense of the novel, Farrell declared that few critics had judged it "on purely literary grounds." Some, he said, withheld their "impression of the character and meaning of the book"; others dismissed it because they "would have none of its political judgments"; and still others made irrelevant attempts "to psychologize the 'disillusionment' of John Dos Passos without explaining why 'disillusionment' makes a novel bad." See also Daniel Aaron, *Writers on the Left* (New York: Harcourt, Brace, and World, 1961), pp. 343–45.

31. Maxwell Geismar, *American Moderns: From Rebellion to Conformity* (New York: Hill and Wang, 1958), pp. 66, 73. See also Geismar's perceptive study, "John Dos Passos: Conversion of a Hero," in *Writers in Crisis* (Boston: Houghton-Mifflin, 1942), pp. 87–139.

32. Geismar, *American Moderns*, pp. 78–79. See also Malcolm Cowley, "Washington Wasn't Like That," *New Republic*, January 17, 1949, pp. 23–24; and the argument between Cowley and John Chamberlain about Dos Passos as either declining novelist or continuing "great social reporter" in *New Republic*, February 28, 1949, pp. 21–23.

33. John Dos Passos, "Looking Back on *U.S.A.*," *New York Times*, October 25, 1959, section 2, p. 5. It is not clear from Dos Passos's statement if he was aware of these distortions at the time of writing his earlier novels or recognized them only after a later change in his historical and political perspective.

34. John Dos Passos, "Grosz Comes to America," *Esquire*, 6 (September 1936), 131. This article also appeared as the introduction "Satire as a Way of Seeing," in *Interregnum*, ed. Caresse Crosby (New York: Black Sun Press, 1937), a volume of George Grosz's drawings, and was later reprinted in *Occasions and Protests* (Chicago: Regnery, 1964), a collection of Dos Passos' essays. It should be studied with care, as it contains many ideas that bear upon Dos Passos' own intentions.

35. *American Academy of Arts and Letters and National Institute of Arts and Letters, Proceedings*, Second Series, No. 8 (New York, 1958), pp. 192–93.

36. See, for example, John Dos Passos, "The Desperate Experiment," *Book Week*, September 15, 1963, p. 3, and Joseph Hearned and Neil Goodwin, eds., *Art and the Craftsman: The Best of the Yale Literary Magazine 1836–1961* (New Haven, 1961), p. 207.

37. Charles F. Madden, *Talks with Authors* (Carbondale and Edwardsville: Southern Illinois University Press, 1968), pp. 10–11.

38. Mizener, "The Gullivers of Dos Passos."

39. In his book, *John Dos Passos* (New Haven, 1961), John H. Wrenn discusses Dos Passos as a kind of satirist *manqué* who lacks the degree of levity and detachment necessary to the true satirist. Wrenn describes the basic "method" of *U.S.A.* as that of tragedy which includes both naturalism and satire. However, Wrenn overlooks the fact

that satire may be more grim than humorous, that the satirist *is* involved, but feigns detachment (as does Dos Passos
in the narratives of *U.S.A.*), and that many episodes of
U.S.A. contain a good deal of both farcical humor and
humorous irony, e.g., those involving Mac, Doc Bingham,
and Margo Dowling. True, tragic overtones exist in Dos
Passos' depiction of the decline and fall of U.S.A. and this
country's failure to realize its ideal democratic possibilities;
and some of the martyred figures of the biographies (Veblen,
Reed, Bourne, Debs, and others) are tragically portrayed.
But the prevailing tone of *U.S.A.* is the bitter irony of dark,
tragical satire directed against "the system" which has
martyred these idealists, and, more specifically, against those
allegedly corrupt and imperialistic businessmen, journalists,
and politicians (Carnegie, Morgan, Insull, Ford, Hearst,
Wilson, and Roosevelt) most representative of the system.
(See Wrenn, pp. 99–107, 161–66.)

40. Blanche H. Gelfant, "The Search for Identity in the
Novels of John Dos Passos," *PMLA*, 76 (March 1961), 133–
49.

41. Farrell, "Dos Passos and the Critics."

42. George Orwell, "Politics vs. Literature: An Examination of *Gulliver's Travels*," in *Discussions of Jonathan Swift*,
ed. John Traugott (Berkeley: University of California Press,
1962), pp. 89–91.

43. Granville Hicks, "The Politics of John Dos Passos,"
Antioch Review 10 (March 1950), 85–98.

44. David Sanders, "The 'Anarchism' of John Dos Passos,"
South Atlantic Quarterly, 60 (Winter 1961), 44–45.

45. Chester E. Eisinger, "John Dos Passos and the Need
for Rejection," in *Fiction of the Forties* (Chicago: University of Chicago Press, 1963), pp. 119–25.

46. Alvin B. Kernan, *Modern Satire* (New York: Harcourt, Brace, and World, 1962), p. 172.

47. Edmund Wilson, *Shores of Light*, p. 433.

48. Martin Kallich, "John Dos Passos: Liberty and the
Father-Image," *Antioch Review*, 10 (March 1950), 100–105.

49. Gelfant, "The Search for Identity."

50. Claude-Edmonde Magny, *L'age du roman americain*
(Paris: Editions du Seuil, 1948), pp. 117–58. Chapter 1 also
contains many interesting analogies between literature and
film, and alludes several times to Dos Passos' cinematic
technique.

51. Georges-Albert Astre, *Thèmes et structures dans l'oeuvre de John Dos Passos* (Paris: Minard, 1956), pp. 166–72, passim.

52. See also E. D. Lowry, "The Lively Art of *Manhattan Transfer*," *PMLA*, 84 (October 1969), 1628–38. Lowry's interesting article relates *Manhattan Transfer* to the "modern movement" in the visual arts and presents some perceptive analogies between literary and cinematic montage. See also Edmund Wilson, "Dos Passos and the Social Revolution" and Knox and Stahl, *Dos Passos and "the Revolting Playwrights"* (Uppsala, Sweden: Uppsala University Press, 1964).

53. Ben Stoltzfus, "John Dos Passos and the French," *Comparative Literature*, 15 (Spring 1963), 146–63.

54. Richard Lehan, "The Trilogies of Jean-Paul Sartre and John Dos Passos," *Iowa English Yearbook*, 9 (1964), 60–64.

55. Astre, "Thèmes et structures," p. 39; also Dos Passos, "The Desperate Experiment," p. 3.

56. McLuhan, "Technique vs. Sensibility," pp. 151–64.

57. George Knox, "Dos Passos and Painting," *Texas Studies in Literature and Language*, 6 (1964), 22–38.

58. Dos Passos, "Satire as a Way of Seeing."

Collectivism and Abstract Composition   BEACH

1. Early in the story, but not at the very beginning, there is a reference to the signing of the Greater New York Bill by Governor Morton, 1895–96; and toward the end a reference to the reform movement against Mayor Hylan. In the course of the narrative, the time is indicated by references to such notable events as the taking of Port Arthur, the Stanford White murder, Sarajevo, the Liberty Loan drive, and the post-War deportation of communists by the Department of Justice.

2. Mr. Beach, I believe, is referring to Lewis' review in *The Saturday Review of Literature*, December 5, 1925, p. 361. Lewis called *Manhattan Transfer* "a novel of the very first importance . . . the vast and blazing dawn we have awaited." The novel, he said, "may be the foundation of a whole new school of novel-writing" and Dos Passos "the father of humanized and living fiction. . . . not merely for America but for the world!" Preferring "the breathless reality of *Manhattan Transfer* to the laboratory-reports of *Ulysses*," Lewis commented that Dos Passos's technique utilized an "experimental psychology and style" associated with Ger-

trude Stein, Marcel Proust, and Joyce; but whereas the others were "confoundedly dull," "Dos Passos is *interesting!*" The novel's technique was "indeed, the technique of the movie, in its flashes, its cut-backs, its speed." [Editor's note]

Dos Passos's U.S.A.   LYDENBERG

1. Page references documenting the quotations from *U.S.A.* are to the Modern Library edition (1937); those for *First Encounter* (originally published as *One Man's Initiation*) are to the New York, 1945, edition.

The "Anarchism" of John Dos Passos   SANDERS

1. See, e.g., Maxwell Geismar, "A Cycle of Fiction," in *Literary History of the United States,* ed. Spiller et al. (New York, 1952), pp. 1304–06, or in his recent *American Moderns* (New York, 1958), pp. 64–90. See the same view, however sympathetically offered, in John Aldridge, *After the Lost Generation* (New York, 1951), pp. 59–81.

2. Anarchist political organization—local or cellular—obviously contributes more to Dos Passos's position than does the anarchist tradition of violence. Similarly the anarchic qualities of Spanish regional and local loyalties—the concept of *patria chica*—are more influential than specific anarchist movements in Spain. See Gerald Brenan, *The Spanish Labyrinth* (London, 1943), pp. 131–202, for a concise summary of anarchism in Spain.

3. *Esquire,* January and February, 1937. Again, see Brenan, Preface, and observe also how the concept of *patria chica* affects Hispanophile Ernest Hemingway in *Death in the Afternoon,* 264–66.

4. *New Masses,* 1 (August, 1926), 10–12. Reprinted as *Facing the Chair: The Story of the Americanization of Two Foreignborn Workmen* (Boston: Sacco-Vanzetti Defense Committee, 1927) and in *In All Countries* (New York, 1934).

5. Isidor Schneider, "Greatness," *New Masses,* August 11, 1936, pp. 40–41; Samuel Sillen, "The Misadventures of John Dos Passos," *New Masses,* July 4, 1939, p. 21.

John Dos Passos: *Liberty and the Father-Image*

KALLICH

1. For example, see *Rosinante to the Road Again* (New York: Doran, 1922), pp. 18, 102, 134, 137, 139, 230–31, 244–45. Incidentally, these references have been suppressed; they

do not appear in the text that Dos Passos prepared for *Journeys Between Wars* (New York: Harcourt, Brace, 1938).

2. With respect to this conflict between ideals and money, freedom and the father, Herf is clearly Dos Passos's projection. A comparison of Camera Eye (46) with parts of *Manhattan Transfer* will make this statement incontrovertible. See in *Manhattan Transfer* (New York: Harper, 1925), pp. 176, 303, 353, 365–66, 383–84; in these pages Herf's conflicts can be traced and compared with Dos Passos'.

3. In early 1934, for example, Dos Passos' contributions to the *New Masses* cease and a few months later in the essay submitted to the first Writers' Congress (but submitted too late to be read and discussed), "The Writer as Technician," Dos Passos publicly announced his retreat.

The Search for Identity in the Novels of John Dos Passos   GELFANT

1. Marcel Proust, "The Past Recaptured," *Remembrance of Things Past* (New York: Random House, 1934), 2: 1031 ff.

2. John Dos Passos, *The Big Money*, (New York: Modern Library, 1937), p. 197. All subsequent references to the books of the *U.S.A.* trilogy are to this edition.

3. *The 42nd Parallel*, p. 224.

4. Modern psychology has placed great stress upon the psychological importance of a secure home and a childhood sense of belonging for the development of a strong sense of identity. The inverse relationship between homelessness and the lack of a sense of identity has recently been re-explored in an interesting study by Helen Merrell Lynd, *On Shame and the Search for Identity* (New York: Harcourt, Brace & Company, 1958). See particularly pp. 43 ff.

5. John Dos Passos, *Chosen Country* (Boston: Houghton Mifflin, 1951), p. 30.

6. John Dos Passos, *Manhattan Transfer* (New York: Harper & Brothers, 1925), p. 67.

7. Note the other revealing titles: *Manhattan Transfer, U.S.A., District of Columbia,* and among the nonfiction, *State of the Nation.*

8. *The 42nd Parallel*, p. 173.

9. John Dos Passos, *Streets of Night* (New York: George H. Doran, 1923), p. 75. Compare with *Manhattan Transfer*, p. 79.

10. John Dos Passos, *Adventures of a Young Man* in *District of Columbia* (Boston: Houghton Mifflin, 1952), p. 26. Published originally in 1939. All subsequent references are to the combined edition of 1952.

11. See *Chosen Country*, pp. 31 ff. and *Manhattan Transfer*, pp. 78 ff.

12. *1919*, pp. 9 ff.

13. John Dos Passos, *Most Likely to Succeed* (New York: Prentice-Hall, 1954), pp. 54, 150.

14. *The 42nd Parallel*, p. 369.

15. *1919*, p. 72.

16. *The 42nd Parallel*, p. 177.

17. *Streets of Night*, compare pp. 140 f. with p. 198.

18. Martin Kallich, "John Dos Passos: Liberty and the Father-Image," *Antioch Review*, 10 (Spring 1950), 99–106.

19. See Charles Bernardin, "The Development of John Dos Passos" (Ph.D. diss. University of Wisconsin, 1949, which infers from its biographical data that Dos Passos loved and admired his father.

20. *The Big Money*, p. 462.

21. *The 42nd Parallel*, p. 108.

22. Ibid., p. 81.

23. See *Streets of Night*, pp. 39, 65, and 220.

24. The apposition between bourgeois intellectual and workingman, as defined by Marx and taken over by the intellectual, is pivotal to the radical picture of society. Self-vilification by the intellectual runs through Dos Passos' novels, as it does through his early critical writings. The reasons why the American intellectual was attracted to the worker and why he was willing to debase himself and exalt the worker in his stead are neatly summarized by Arthur Schlesinger, Jr., in his book, *The Vital Center: The Politics of Freedom* (Boston: Houghton Mifflin, 1949), as he points out how the "worship of the proletariat becomes a perfect fulfillment for the frustration of the progressive" (p. 46).

25. Michael Gold, "A Barbaric Poem of New York," *New Masses*, 1 (August 1926), 25–26.

26. The interplay between the uniquely personal and the social motives that lies behind a decisive social commitment is traced by Arthur Koestler in his autobiographical *Arrow in the Blue* (New York: Macmillan, 1952), pp. 99–100. The recognition that personal, perhaps even neurotic, reasons force the decision does not invalidate the worthwhileness of the social cause.

27. Compare *Manhattan Transfer*, pp. 345 f.; *Streets of Night*, p. 124; and *Adventures of a Young Man*, p. 133.

28. John Dos Passos, *First Encounter* (New York: Philosophical Library, 1945). Published originally in 1920 as *One Man's Initiation*—1917. " 'Have we the courage, have we the energy, have we the power? . . .' " Martin queries, and the answer is, " 'No . . . we are merely intellectuals. We cling to a mummified world. But they have the power and the nerve. . . . The stupid average working-people'." p. 155.

29. John Dos Passos, *Three Soldiers* (New York: The Modern Library, 1932), p. 221. Published originally in 1921.

30. This fictional pattern is based upon his own experiences and those of many subsequently famous contemporaries who volunteered for service (for example, Robert Hillyer, F. Scott Fitzgerald, Ernest Hemingway, Edmund Wilson, Malcolm Cowley, Archibald MacLeish, E. E. Cummings). The incident in which the hero is censured for writing home critical or pacifistic letters (Dick Savage and Jay Pignatelli) is based upon his own experience. John Andrews's internment is based upon the experience of E. E. Cummings, who describes this situation in *The Enormous Room*.

31. *Manhattan Transfer*, p. 120.

32. See Camera Eye (44) in *The Big Money*, pp. 29–31.

33. John Dos Passos, *In All Countries* (New York: Harcourt, Brace, 1934), p. 11.

34. For a social and aesthetic explanation of his dehumanized quality, see Blanche H. Gelfant, *The American City Novel* (Norman: Univ. of Oklahoma Press, 1954), pp. 159–66.

35. The relationship of social tensions to personal dissociation is a salient point in my chapter on Dos Passos in *The American City Novel*, pp. 133–74.

36. *Chosen Country*, see p. 38 and in passing, chapter 1, called "The Little River Rubicon."

37. See Gelfant, *The American City Novel*, pp. 159–62.

38. John Dos Passos, *The Great Days* (New York: Sagamore, 1958), p. 311.

39. Lancaster's island-hopping in the Pacific (pp. 111–56) follows and condenses Dos Passos' report of his tour of the Pacific in *Tour of Duty* (Boston: Houghton Mifflin, 1946), Parts 1 and 2. The section on post-war Europe and the

Nuremberg Trials in *The Great Days*, pp. 213–34, also follows the itinerary, and repeats verbatim certain passages, in *Tour of Duty*, Part 3.

40. Suicidal thoughts occur to several of the generic heroes. Roland Lancaster almost gives in to his suicidal impulse. Wenny in *Streets of Night* of course does kill himself.

John Dos Passos and the French   STOLTZFUS

1. Thelma M. Smith and Ward L. Miner, *Translantic Migration: The Contemporary American Novel in France* (Durham, N.C., 1955), p. 27.

2. Jean-Paul Sartre, "American Novelists in French Eyes," *Atlantic Monthly*, 178 (August 1946), 117; *Literary Essays* (New York, 1957), p. 96.

3. French critics see in Dos Passos' "Behaviorism" an almost perfect goal of the "objective" novel. At one time Sartre considered this "objective" technique as the only way in which the author could reveal the workings of his protagonists' subconscious. Dos Passos has exteriorized the inner emptiness of man in terms of conversations, events, and narrative style. Thus the beautifully written death scene of the blind Charley Anderson anticipates the writing of Nathalie Sarraute. Charley Anderson's endless monologue, in which he is afraid to stop talking, reflects the inner void, the vast desert in which he has been living, the absence of an inner core whose nothingness can only be concealed by his desperate attempt to avert death and the inexorable flow of time.

4. "Read a good deal of Zola—the form of his novels often interested me more than the content. Read Balzac off and on from a very early age." Letter to the author from John Dos Passos, Jan. 22, 1961.

5. Critics have also referred to similarities in Dos Passos's and Jules Romains's work. While similarities exist, influences, in this case, are more difficult to trace and establish. *Manhattan Transfer* (Coindreau's translation was published in Paris in 1928) and *The 42nd Parallel* were both published several years before the first volume (*Le 6 Octobre*) of Romains's *Hommes de bonne volonté* appeared in 1932. It is not unlikely that *Manhattan Transfer* had some influence on Romains, in spite of the fact that H.B.V. is a logical sequel to Romains's own and earlier unanimism. In his preface to *Le 6 Octobre* Romains shows that he is not unaware of the

literary activity of certain American writers whom he does not name; but he feels that these writers were influenced by *Mort de quelqu'un* which, in 1932 had been in translation for almost twenty years (it was first published in French in 1910 and in English in 1914). Dos Passos was thoroughly familiar with avant-garde French writers, and it is improbable that Romains's notoriety, equalled in 1919 only by that of the late Apollinaire, would have escaped his attention.

6. "Cendrars I read with enthusiasm during that period [1919]." Letter from John Dos Passos, Jan. 22, 1961.

7. Translator's foreword, Cendrars, *Panama or the Adventures of My Seven Uncles* (New York and London, 1931).

8. Dos Passos, *Manhattan Transfer* (New York, 1925), p. 158.

9. "I [Dos Passos] felt that everything should go in [the novel]—popular songs, political aspirations and prejudices, ideals, delusions, clippings out of old newspapers." Quoted from a radio program produced by the Literary Society of the University of Massachusetts under a grant from the National Association of Educational Broadcasters. Participants included John Dos Passos, Maurice Coindreau, and Harry Levin.

10. John Dos Passos, *Orient Express* (New York, 1927), p. 165.

11. Ibid., p. 181.

12. Ibid., p. 167.

13. "I met Romains sometime in the thirties. It was after the *U.S.A.* books were well under way that I read some of his novels. He never mentioned *Manhattan Transfer*." Letter from Dos Passos, Jan. 22, 1961.

14. "[I] was much impressed by Verhaeren during the period of college and just after. Might well be an influence there." Ibid.

15. According to Mrs. Gelfant (*The American City Novel*, p. 11), three forms of the city novel have emerged as a genre in the United States: "the 'portrait' study which reveals the city through a single character, usually a country youth first discovering the city as a place and manner of life; the 'synoptic' study, a novel without a hero, which reveals the total city immediately as a personality in itself; and the 'ecological' study, which focuses upon one small spatial unit such as a neighborhood or city block and explores in detail the manner of life identified with this place."

16. Gelfant, *The American City Novel*, p. 23.
17. John Dos Passos, *Streets of Night* (New York, 1923),
p. 110.
18. Ibid., p. 213–14.
19. Jules Romains, *Mort de quelqu'un* (Paris, 1933), p. 34.
20. Ibid., p. 214.
21. Dos Passos, *Three Soldiers* (New York, 1932), p. 290.
22. In a recent letter to the author, Dos Passos says that
"*Le Feu* must have influenced me more than a little. I read
it, I think, while I was in the ambulance service in 1917.
Three Soldiers was started in early 1919." *Le Feu* (Paris,
1917) is a series of scenes and tableaux tracing the life of the
French soldier at the front, under fire, on leave, in waiting,
and of "les trente millions d'esclaves jetés les uns sur les
autres par le crime et l'erreur. . . ."
23. *Three Soldiers*, p. 458.
24. "Romains résume ainsi: 'Dos Passos compte sur les
éléments eux-mêmes pour se combiner, sans qu'il intervienne.'
Or Romains, tout en acceptant la dispersion, la confusion
primitive entreprend d'en dégager un ordre et, à travers 'ces
efforts zigzagants, ces touffes de désordre, ce pullulement non
orienté,' de démêler un sens, une direction." Letter to the
author from André Cuisenier, Feb. 24, 1961.
25. Romains, "Ode à la foule qui est ici," *Odes et prières*.
26. John Dos Passos, *A Pushcart at the Curb* (New York,
1922), p. 147.
27. Dos Passos, "O douce Sainte Geneviève," *Pushcart
at the Curb*, p. 155.
28. Ibid., p. 202.
29. Romains, "La Salle adulte," *Puissances de Paris* (Paris,
1919), p. 92.
30. Dos Passos, "The Writer as a Technician," *American
Writer's Congress* (New York, 1935), p. 832.
31. Dos Passos, Introduction, *Three Soldiers*, p. viii.

The Trilogies of Jean-Paul Sartre and John Dos
Passos LEHAN

1. Jean-Paul Sartre, "American Novelists in French Eyes,"
The Atlantic Monthly, 178 (August 1946), p. 115. Sartre
would have had little difficulty finding Dos Passos' novels in
translation. *The 42nd Parallel* was first translated by N. Gut-
erman and published in Paris by Bernard Gosset in 1933;
1919 was first translated by Maurice Remon and published

in Paris by Editions Sociales Internationales in 1937; *The Big Money* (*La grosse Galette*) was first translated by Charles de Richter and published in Paris by Gallimard in 1946.

2. Jean-Paul Sartre, "John Dos Passos and 1919," *Situations* I (Paris: Librairie Gallimard, 1947); *Literary and Philosophical Essays*, trans. Annette Michelson (London: Rider & Rider, 1955), p. 96.

3. John Dos Passos, *The 42nd Parallel* (New York: Modern Library, 1937), pp. 134–37, 157.

4. Sartre, *Literary and Philosophical Essays*, p. 90.

5. Sartre, *Le Sursis* (Paris: Librairie Gallimard, 1945); *The Reprieve*, trans. Eric Sutton (New York: Alfred A. Knopf, 1951), p. 303.

6. Sartre, *Literary and Philosophical Essays*, p. 96.

Dos Passos and Painting   KNOX

1. References in parentheses, after title abbreviations, follow pagination of first editions, except for *Three Soldiers*, which is more generally available in the Modern Library Edition (New York, 1932). For fairly complete bibliographical information refer to Jack Potter's *A Bibliography of John Dos Passos* (Chicago, 1950).

2. See "Sur la Lumière," translated by Paul Klee as "Über das Licht," in *Der Sturm*, 3 (1913), 272–73. See also Selz, *German Expressionist Painting* (Berkeley, 1957), p. 211.

3. Cf. Kandinsky, *Concerning the Spiritual in Art* (New York, 1947).

4. Selz, *German Expressionist Painting*, p. 211.

5. See Dos Passos's introductory comments to *Interregnum* (New York, 1936), and to *George Grosz* (London, 1948).

6. Kahnweiler, *The Rise of Cubism*, trans. Henry Aronson (New York, 1949), p. 11.

7. *Esquire*, 25 (October 1958), 121–23.

Selective Bibliography of Critical and Scholarly Work on Dos Passos

Books

Astre, Georges-Albert. *Thèmes et structures dans l'oeuvre de John Dos Passos*, 2 vols. Paris: Minard, 1956, 1958.

Brantley, John D. *The Fiction of John Dos Passos*. The Hague: Mouton, 1968. Studies in American Literature, vol. 16.

Davis, Robert Gorham. *John Dos Passos*. Minneapolis: University of Minnesota Press, 1962. (Pamphlet)

Knox, George A. and Herbert M. Stahl. *Dos Passos and "The Revolting Playwrights."* Uppsala, Sweden: Uppsala University Press, 1964.

Wrenn, John H. *John Dos Passos*. New Haven: Twayne, 1961.

Essays

Aaron, Daniel. "The Adventures of John Dos Passos." In *Writers on the Left*, pp. 343–53. New York: Harcourt, Brace, 1961.

Aldridge, John W. "Dos Passos: The Energy of Despair." In *After the Lost Generation*, pp. 59–81. New York: McGraw, 1951.

Beach, Joseph Warren. *American Fiction: 1920–1940*, pp. 25–66. New York: Macmillan, 1941; New York: Russell and Russell (paperback), 1960.

————. *The Twentieth-Century Novel: Studies in Technique*, pp. 437–48, 501–11. New York: Appleton-Century, 1932.

Borenstein, Walter. "The Failure of Nerve: The Impact of Pío Baroja's Spain on John Dos Passos." In *Nine Essays in Modern Literature*, ed. Donald E. Stanford, pp. 63–87. Baton Rouge: Louisiana State University Press, 1965.

Cowley, Malcolm. "John Dos Passos: The Poet and the

World," *New Republic,* 70, (April 27, 1932), 303–05; and 88 (September 9, 1936), 34. Reprinted in *Literary Opinion in America,* ed. M. D. Zabel, pp. 485–93. New York: Harper and Row, 1962. Also in *Think Back on Us,* ed. Malcolm Cowley, pp. 212–19, 298–301. Carbondale and Edwardsville: Southern Illinois University Press, 1967.

————. "A Natural History of American Naturalism," *Kenyon Review* 9 (Summer 1947). Reprinted in *Critiques and Essays on Modern Fiction, 1920–1951,* ed. John W. Aldridge, pp. 370–87. New York: Ronald Press, 1952.

Frohock, W. M. "John Dos Passos: Of Time and Frustration." *Southwest Review,* 33 (1948), 71–80. Reprinted in *The Novel of Violence in America,* pp. 23–51. Dallas: Southern Methodist University Press, 1957.

Geismar, Maxwell. "John Dos Passos: Conversion of a Hero." In *Writers in Crisis,* pp. 87–139. Boston: Houghton-Mifflin, 1942.

Gelfant, Blanche H. "John Dos Passos: The Synoptic Novel." In *The American City Novel,* pp. 133–74. Norman: University of Oklahoma Press, 1954.

Gurko, Leo. "John Dos Passos' 'U.S.A.': A 1930's Spectacular." In *Proletarian Writers of the Thirties,* ed. David Madden, pp. 46–63. Carbondale and Edwardsville: Southern Illinois University Press, 1968.

Hicks, Granville. *The Great Tradition,* pp. 287–91. New York: Biblo and Tannen, 1967. (Reprint of New York: Macmillan, 1935 ed.)

Kazin, Alfred. *On Native Grounds,* pp. 341–59. New York: Reynal-Hitchcock, 1942. Rpt. New York: Anchor Press, 1956. Pp. 265–82.

Lydenberg, John. "Dos Passos's *U.S.A.*: The Words of the Hollow Men." In *Essays on Determinism in America Literature,* ed. Sidney J. Krause, pp. 97–107. Kent, Ohio: Kent State University Press, 1964.

Lynn, Kenneth S. Introduction to *World in a Glass*: A View *of our Century Selected from the Novels of John Dos Passos,* pp. v–xv. Boston: Houghton-Mifflin, 1966.

Magny, Claude-Edmonde. *L'age du roman americain,* pp. 117–58. Paris: Editions du Seuil, 1948.

McLuhan, Herbert Marshall. "John Dos Passos: Technique Vs. Sensibility." In *Fifty Years of the American Novel—1900–1950,* ed. Harold C. Gardiner, pp. 151–64. New York: Scribners, 1951. Reprinted in *Modern American Fic-*

tion, ed. A. W. Litz, pp. 138–49. New York: Oxford University Press, 1963.

Millgate, Michael. "John Dos Passos." In *American Social Fiction: James to Cozzens,* pp. 128–41. New York: Barnes and Noble, 1964; Edinburgh: Oliver and Boyd, 1964.

Miner, Ward L. and Thelma M. Smith. *Transatlantic Migration: The Contemporary American Novel in France,* pp. 87–98, 217–21. Durham: Duke University Press, 1955.

Mizener, Arthur. "The Big Money." In *Twelve Great American Novels,* pp. 87–103. New York: New American Library, 1967.

Rideout, Walter B. *The Radical Novel in the United States: 1900–1954,* pp. 154–63. Cambridge: Harvard University Press, 1956.

Sartre, Jean-Paul. "John Dos Passos and 1919." In *Literary Essays,* trans. Annette Michelson, pp. 88–96. New York: Philosophical Library, 1957.

Walcutt, Charles, C. "Later Trends in Form: Steinbeck, Hemingway, Dos Passos." In *American Literary Naturalism, A Divided Stream,* pp. 280–89. Minneapolis: University of Minnesota Press, 1956.

Articles

Aaron, Daniel. "The Riddle of Dos Passos." *Harpers,* March 1962), pp. 55–60.

Beach, Joseph Warren. "Dos Passos: 1947." *Sewanee Review,* 55 (Summer 1947), 406–18.

Bernardin, Charles W. "Dos Passos' Harvard Years." *New England Quarterly,* 27 (March 1954), 3–26.

Chametzky, Jules. "Reflections on U.S.A. as Novel and Play." *Massachusetts Review,* 1 (February 1960), 391–99.

Chase, Richard. "The Chronicles of Dos Passos." *Commentary,* 31 (May 1961), 395–400.

Gelfant, Blanche H. "The Search for Identity in the Novels of John Dos Passos." *PMLA,* 76 (March 1961), 133–49.

Hicks, Granville. "Dos Passos' Gifts." *New Republic,* 67 (June 24, 1931). 157–58.

Kallich, Martin. "John Dos Passos: Liberty and the Father Image." *Antioch Review,* 10 (March 1950), 100–105.

Kazin, Alfred. "John Dos Passos: Inventor in Isolation." *Saturday Review,* March 15, 1969, pp. 16–19, 44–45.

Knox, George. "Dos Passos and Painting." *Texas Studies in Literature and Language,* 6 (1964), 22–38.

————. "Voice in the *U.S.A.* Biographies." *Texas Studies in Literature and Language,* 4 (1962), 109–16.

Landsberg, Melvin. "John R. Dos Passos: His influence on the Novelist's Early Political Development." *American Quarterly,* 16 (Fall 1964), 473–85.

Leavis, F. R. "A Serious Artist." *Scrutiny,* 1 (September 1932), 173–79.

Lehan, Richard. "The Trilogies of Jean-Paul Sartre and John Dos Passos." *Iowa English Yearbook,* 9 (1964), 60–64.

Lowry, E. D. "The Lively Art of *Manhattan Transfer*." *PMLA,* 84 (October 1969), 1628–38.

Lydenberg, John. "Dos Passos and the Ruined Words." *Pacific Spectator,* 8 (1951), 16–23.

Mizener, Arthur. "The Gullivers of John Dos Passos." *Saturday Review of Literature,* June 30, 1951, 6–7, 34–35.

Sanders, David. "The 'Anarchism' of John Passos," *South Atlantic Quarterly,* 60 (Winter 1961), 44–45.

————. " 'Lies' and the System: Enduring Themes from Dos Passos' Early Novels." *South Atlantic Quarterly,* 65 (1966), 215–28.

Schwartz, Delmore. "John Dos Passos and the Whole Truth." *Southern Review,* 4 (October 1938), 351–67.

Smith, James S. "The Novelist of Discomfort: A Reconsideration of John Dos Passos." *College English,* 19 (May 1958), 332–38.

Stoltzfus, Ben. "John Dos Passos and the French." *Comparative Literature,* 15 (Spring 1963), 146–63.

Trilling, Lionel. "The America of John Dos Passos," *Partisan Review,* 4 (April 1938), 26–32.

Reviews

Canby, Henry Seidel. "*Three Soldiers*." *New York Evening Post Book Review,* October 8, 1921, p. 67.

Chamberlain, John. "John Dos Passos." *Saturday Review of Literature,* June 3, 1939, pp. 3–4, 15–16. (*Adventures of a Young Man*)

Cowley, Malcolm. "Disillusionment." *New Republic,* June 14, 1939, p. 163. (*Adventures of a Young Man*)

————. "The End of a Trilogy." *New Republic,* August 12, 1936, pp. 23–24. (*U.S.A.*)

————. "Success that Somehow Led to Failure." *New York Times Book Review,* April 13, 1958, pp. 5, 45. (*The Great Days*)

DeVoto, Bernard. "John Dos Passos: Anatomist of our

Times," *Saturday Review of Literature*, August 8, 1936, pp. 3–4, 12–13. (*U.S.A.*)

Farrell, James T. "Dos Passos and the Critics." *The American Mercury*, 47 (August 1939), 489–94. (*Adventures of a Young Man*)

Geismar, Maxwell. "The Failure of Nerve" and "Finale." In *American Moderns: From Rebellion to Conformity*, pp. 76–90. New York: Hill and Wang, 1958. (*The Grand Design* and *The Great Days*)

Hicks, Granville. "Dos Passos—The Fruits of Disillusionment." *New Republic*, September 27, 1954, pp. 17–18. (*Most Likely to Succeed*)

Jones, Howard Mumford. "Sound Truck Caesar." *Saturday Review of Literature*, March 6, 1943, pp. 7–8. (*Number One*)

Josephson, Matthew. "A Marxist Epic." *Saturday Review of Literature*, March 19, 1932, p. 600. (*1919*)

Lerner, Max. "The America of John Dos Passos." *Nation*, August 15, 1936, pp. 187–88. (*The Big Money*)

Lewis, Sinclair. "Manhattan at Last!" *Saturday Review of Literature*, Dec. 5, 1925, p. 361 (*Manhattan Transfer*)

Moore, Harry T. "*Midcentury*." *New York Times Book Review*, February 26, 1961, pp. 1, 51.

Whipple, T. K. "Dos Passos and the U.S.A.," *Nation*, February 19, 1938, pp. 210–12. (*U.S.A.*)

Wilson, Edmund. "Dahlberg, Dos Passos, and Wilder." *New Republic*, March 26, 1930, pp. 157–58. Reprinted in *Shores of Light*, pp. 446–50. New York: Farrar and Strauss, 1952. (*The 42nd Parallel*)

Bibliographies

Gibson, Martin. "A Dos Passos Checklist." *Book Collector's Journal*, 1 (April 1936), 7; (May 1936), 9.

Kallich, Martin. "A Bibliography of John Dos Passos." *Bulletin of Bibliography*, 19 (May–August 1949), 231–35.

Potter, Jack. *A Bibliography of John Dos Passos*. Chicago: Normandie Press, 1950.

Reinhart, Virginia S. "John Dos Passos Bibliography: 1950–1966." *Twentieth-Century Literature*, 13 (1967), 167–78.

White, William. "John Dos Passos and his Reviewers." *Bulletin of Bibliography*, 20 (May–August 1950), 45–47.
———. "More Dos Passos: Bibliographical Addenda." *Papers of the Bibliographical Society of America*, 45 (1951), 156–58.

Index

284

DATE DUE

	PRINTED IN U.S.A.